Making
Human Beings
HUMAN

The SAGE Program on Applied Developmental Science

Consulting Editor
Richard M. Lerner

The field of Applied Developmental Science has advanced the use of cutting-edge developmental systems models of human development, fostered strength-based approaches to understanding and promoting positive development across the life span, and served as a frame for collaborations among researchers and practitioners, including policymakers, seeking to enhance the life chances of diverse young people, their families, and communities. The **SAGE Program on Applied Developmental Science** both integrates and extends this scholarship by publishing innovative and cutting-edge contributions.

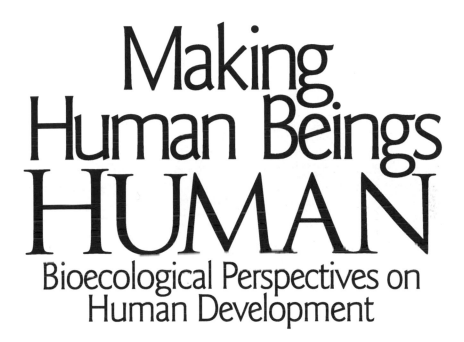

Making
Human Beings
HUMAN
Bioecological Perspectives on
Human Development

Urie Bronfenbrenner, Editor
Cornell University

SAGE Publications
Thousand Oaks ▪ London ▪ New Delhi

For information:

Sage Publications, Inc.
2455 Teller Road
Thousand Oaks, California 91320
E-mail: order@sagepub.com

Sage Publications Ltd.
1 Oliver's Yard
55 City Road
London EC1Y 1SP
United Kingdom

Sage Publications India Pvt. Ltd.
B-42, Panchsheel Enclave
Post Box 4109
New Delhi 110 017 India

Printed in the United States of America

Library of Congress Cataloging-in-Publication Data

Making human beings human : bioecological perspectives on human development / edited by Urie Bronfenbrenner.
    p. cm.
Includes bibliographical references and index.
   ISBN 0-7619-2711-5 (cloth) — ISBN 0-7619-2712-3 (pbk.)
1. Developmental psychology. 2. Environmental psychology.
3. Nature and nurture. I. Bronfenbrenner, Urie, 1917-
BF713.M332 2004
155.9—dc22

2004003255

04   05   06   07   08   10   9   8   7   6   5   4   3   2   1

Acquiring Editor:	Jim Brace-Thompson
Editorial Assistant:	Karen Ehrmann
Production Editor:	Sanford Robinson
Typesetter:	C&M Digitals (P) Ltd.
Copy Editor:	Elisabeth Magnus
Indexer:	Kathleen Paparchontis
Cover Designer:	Ravi Balasuriya

Contents

Acknowledgments

This retrospective and integrative book could not have been compiled without the use of materials written with or by others. I am particularly indebted to Robert and Beverly Cairns, and Stephen Ceci, as well as the many other coauthors, colleagues, teachers, mentors, and students whose work and ideas have influenced and inspired me for more than six decades.

I also wish to thank Kate Bronfenbrenner, Liese Bronfenbrenner, Kristen Hamilton, Clare Holmes, Gerri Jones, Holly Mistlebaum, Beth Soll, and Chong Wang, without whose dedicated assistance as constructive critics, library consultants, typists, computer technicians, and proofreaders the manuscript could never have been completed on schedule. I am especially indebted in this regard to the editing skills of Gerri Jones based on her familiarity with the evolution of the bioecological model.

I am grateful to Richard M. Lerner for writing the Foreword and to Stephen F. Hamilton and Stephen J. Ceci for writing the Afterword to this book. I appreciate also the editorial advice of several anonymous reviewers. I thank as well Jim Brace-Thompson, my editor at Sage Publications, Karen Ehrmann, the editorial assistant, and their colleagues for their editorial and technical contributions throughout the preparation and production of this book.

*To my dear wife, Liese, without whose mind and heart
this book could never have been written.*

Foreword

Urie Bronfenbrenner: Career Contributions of the Consummate Developmental Scientist

Richard M. Lerner

Tufts University

The contemporary scientific study of human development is characterized by a commitment to the understanding of the dynamic relationships between the developing individual and the integrated, multilevel ecology of human development. This approach to developmental science is marked by a theoretical focus on temporally (historically) embedded person-context relational processes; by the embracing of models of dynamic change across the ecological system; and by relational, change- sensitive methods predicated on the idea that individuals influence the people and institutions of their ecology as much as they are influenced by them (Bronfenbrenner, 2001; Bronfenbrenner & Morris, 1998; Damon & Lerner, 1998; Lerner, 2002).

The plasticity (potential for systematic change) associated with the engagement of the active individual with his or her active context legitimates an optimistic approach to the possibility that applications of developmental science may improve the course and contexts of human life. From this perspective, the basic processes of human development may be instantiated and refined through their application to policies and programs designed to promote healthy human development (Bronfenbrenner, 1974; Lerner, 2002).

All of these ideas that define the cutting edge of contemporary developmental science owe their origin, persuasive articulation, and refinement to the singularly creative, theoretically elegant, empirically rigorous, and humane and democratic scholarly contributions of Urie Bronfenbrenner. For more than 60 years, Urie Bronfenbrenner has been both the standard of excellence and the professional conscience of the field of human development, a field that—because of the scope and synthetic power of his vision— has become productively multidisciplinary and multiprofessional. Today, scholarship in human development is as likely to integratively combine history, social policy, medicine, economics, political science, home economics (family and consumer sciences), education, child care, community youth development, nursing, and law as it is to integrate psychology, sociology, and biology. This broad coalition of scientists and practitioners, working together to advance understanding of, and capacities to enhance, human development across the life span, finds its intellectual and societal legitimization in the career contributions of Urie Bronfenbrenner.

The Scope of Bronfenbrenner's Scientific and Societal Vision

Developmental science in the first half of the twentieth century was largely a descriptive field, either cataloguing presumptively maturational changes or depicting the covariation between controlled stimulation and the responses of what Bronfenbrenner (1977) characterized as artificial "experimental" conditions. Bronfenbrenner argued that "[m]uch of contemporary developmental psychology is the science of the strange behavior of children in strange situations with strange adults for the briefest possible periods of time." Accordingly, he asserted that only "experiments created as real are real in their consequences" and stressed that research should begin to focus on how children develop in settings representative of their actual world (i.e., in ecologically valid settings). For instance, instead of studying children only in the laboratory, one should study them in their homes, schools, and playgrounds.

In addition, and heralding what was to become an increasing emphasis on developmental processes and on the explanation of such changes, Bronfenbrenner (1963), in a review of the history of developmental science, noted that from the 1930s to the early 1960s there had been a continuing shift from studies involving the mere collection of data toward research concerned with abstract processes and constructs. Accordingly, in depicting the status of the field in 1963, Bronfenbrenner stated that "first and foremost, the gathering of data for data's sake seems to have lost favor. The major concern in today's developmental research is clearly with inferred processes and constructs" (p. 257).

Bronfenbrenner's emphasis on the process of development was prophetic. The ensuing 40 years of developmental science bore witness to the emphasis on theory that he envisioned. In a review a decade after his 1963 publication, Looft (1972) found a continuation of the trends noted by Bronfenbrenner. Looft's review, like Bronfenbrenner's, was based on an analysis of major handbooks of developmental psychology published from the 1930s through the time of the review. Each handbook represented a reflection of the current content, emphasis, and concerns of the field. Looft found that in the first handbook (Murchison, 1931) developmental psychology was largely descriptive. Consistent with our analysis and with Bronfenbrenner's conclusions, Looft saw workers devoting their time essentially to the collection of norms. However, a shift toward more general integrative concerns was seen by 1946, and this trend continued through 1963 (Bronfenbrenner, 1963) to 1972 (Looft, 1972). Indeed, as a case in point, we may note that the editor of the 1970 edition of the *Handbook of Child Psychology*, Paul H. Mussen, pointed out that "the major contemporary empirical and theoretical emphases in the field of developmental psychology . . . seem to be on *explanations* of the psychological changes that occur, the mechanisms and processes accounting for growth and development" (p. vii).

In commenting on Mussen's 1970 edition, William Damon, the editor-in-chief of the 1998 edition of the *Handbook of Child Psychology*, underscored the consistency between the history of the field and Bronfenbrenner's (1963) articulation 35 years earlier of the importance of theory:

> As for theory, Mussen's *Handbook* was thoroughly permeated with it. Much of the theorizing was organized around the approaches that, in 1970, were known as the "three grand systems": (a) Piaget's cognitive-developmentalism, (b) psychoanalysis, and (c) learning theory. Piaget was given the most extensive treatment. He reappeared in the *Manual*, this time authoring a comprehensive (and some say, definitive) statement of his entire theory, which now bore little resemblance to his 1931/1933 sortings of children's intriguing verbal expressions. In addition, chapters by John Flavell, by David Berlyne, by Martin Hoffman, and by William Kessen, Marshall Haith, and Philip Salapatek all gave major treatments to one or another aspect of Piaget's body of work. Other approaches were represented as well. Herbert and Ann Pick explicated Gibsonian theory in a chapter on sensation and perception, Jonas Langer wrote a chapter on Werner's organismic theory, David McNeill wrote a Chomskian account of language development, and Robert LeVine wrote an early version of what was soon to become "culture theory." (p. xv)

In short, Bronfenbrenner's early vision of the importance of theory was realized in the 1970 edition of the *Handbook* and, as well, in subsequent editions (Damon, 1998).

Bronfenbrenner's Transformational Scholarship

Bronfenbrenner not only bore witness to the increasing emphasis on theories of developmental process but has himself been the foremost theoretician of human development over the past half-century. Indeed, although there have been other great contributors to human development theory in this era—(Jean Piaget, Erik H. Erikson, Paul B. Baltes, David Magnusson, Glen H. Elder Jr., and Gilbert Gottlieb, to identify some of the obviously major members of this elite group—Urie Bronfenbrenner stands as first among his peers. His ideas have been the ones that have stood the test of time to represent the fundamental concepts used in all of the developmental systems theories that constitute the cutting-edge models of human development (Damon & Lerner, 1998). And his singular role in this history has been to lead the way in specifying the necessary linkage between theory and application, between research and practice.

For instance, in 1974 Bronfenbrenner argued that engagement with social policy not only enhances developmental research but also augments understanding of key theoretical issues pertinent to the nature of person-context relations:

> In discussions of the relation between science and social policy, the first axiom, at least among social scientists, is that social policy should be based on science. The proposition not only has logic on its side, but what is more important, it recognizes our proper and primary importance in the scheme of things. The policymakers should look to us, not only for truth, but for wisdom as well. In short, social policy needs science.
>
> My thesis in this paper is the converse proposition, that, particularly in our field, science needs social policy—needs it not to guide our organizational activities, but to provide us with two elements essential for any scientific endeavor—vitality and validity. (p. 1)

Bronfenbrenner contended that "the pursuit of [social policy] questions is essential for the further development of knowledge and theory on the process of human development" (p. 2) because "issues of social policy [serve] as points of departure for the identification of significant theoretical and scientific questions concerning the development of the human organism as a function of interaction with its enduring environment—both actual and potential" (p. 4).

Bronfenbrenner's view of the power of the theory-application linkage, predicated on the plasticity of the human development system that his theory would so eloquently and creatively depict, was indeed transformative for the field of human development. Bronfenbrenner moved the field from being an area of scholarship that described what "is" in human development to a science that, through its collaborations with policy makers, practitioners, and other social change agents, envisioned what "could be" about human development. His theory and the research that he and his students and colleagues conducted within its frame moved the field of human development beyond description and explanation. His vision included optimization—the enhancement of the life course—and the production, through the person's relations within the developmental system, of positive and healthy development. His ideas focused the field on what was, and what could be, the best of being human.

Bronfenbrenner's theoretical vision is embodied in his bioecological theory of human development. From the 1970s up to the present, this theory has evolved to provide fuller and more powerful understanding of the importance of the dynamic and multitiered ecology of human development.

The Bioecology of Human Development

In his 1977 article "Toward an Experimental Ecology of Human Development" and then in his classic 1979 book *The Ecology of Human Development*, considered by all scholars of human development a watershed contribution to the understanding of human ontogeny, Bronfenbrenner explained the importance for human development of interrelated ecological levels, conceived of as nested systems. He described the *microsystem* as the setting within which the individual is behaving at a given moment in his or her life. It is "the complex of relations between the developing person and environment in an immediate setting containing the person" (Bronfenbrenner, 1977, p. 515). In turn, the *mesosystem* is the set of microsystems constituting the individual's developmental niche within a given period of development: it is "the interrelations among major settings containing the developing person at a particular point in his or her life" (p. 515).

In addition, the *exosystem* is composed of contexts that, while not directly involving the developing person (e.g., the workplace of a child's parent), have an influence on the person's behavior and development (e.g., as may occur when the parent has had a stressful day at work and as a result is less able to provide quality caregiving to the child). Bronfenbrenner defined this system as "an extension of the mesosystem embracing . . . specific social structures, both formal and informal, that do not themselves contain the developing person but impinge upon or encompass the immediate settings in which the person is found, and thereby delimit, influence, or even determine what goes on there" (p. 515).

Finally, the *macrosystem* is the superordinate level of the ecology of human development; it is the level involving culture, macroinstitutions (such as the federal government), and public policy. The macrosystem influences the nature of interaction within all other levels of the ecology of human development.

Bronfenbrenner's (1977, 1979) formulation had a broad impact on the field of human development, promoting considerable interest through the 1980s in the effects of the ecological system on the life course of individuals. Yet by the end of that decade and into the 1990s, Bronfenbrenner indicated that he was not pleased by the nature of his contribution to either theory, research, or policy applications pertinent to enhancing the ecology of a child's life to promote his or her positive development. For instance, in 1989 Bronfenbrenner observed:

> Existing developmental studies subscribing to an ecological model have provided far more knowledge about the nature of developmentally relevant environments, near and far, than about the characteristics of developing individuals, then and now. . . . The criticism I just made also applies to my own writings. . . . Nowhere in the 1979 monograph, nor elsewhere until today, does one find a parallel set of structures for conceptualizing the characteristics of the developing person. (p. 188)

Bronfenbrenner believes, as do other theorists drawn to developmental systems notions of human development (e.g., Baltes, 1997; Baltes, Lindenberger, & Staudinger, 1998; Brandtstädter, 1998; Elder, 1998; Gottlieb, 1997; Magnusson, 1999a, 1999b; Sameroff, 1983; Thelen & Smith, 1998), that *all* the levels of organization involved in human life are linked integratively in the constitution of the course of individual ontogeny. While his 1979 book made an enormous contribution to such a conception of human development by giving scholars conceptual tools to understand and study the differentiated but integrated levels of the context of human development, Bronfenbrenner recognized that his theory would be incomplete until he included in it the levels of individual structure and function (biology, psychology, and behavior) fused dynamically with the ecological systems he described.

Accordingly, Bronfenbrenner and his colleagues (e.g., Bronfenbrenner, 2001; Bronfenbrenner & Ceci, 1993, 1994; Bronfenbrenner & Crouter, 1983; Bronfenbrenner & Morris, 1998) have for more than a decade worked to integrate the other levels of the developmental system, starting from biology, psychology, and behavior, into the model of human development he was formulating. The span of the levels he has sought to synthesize in his model—from biology through the broadest level of the ecology of human development—accounts for the label *bioecological* that he has attached to the model. In short, then, Bronfenbrenner has sought for more than a decade to bring the features of the developing person into the ecological system he has elaborated (Bronfenbrenner, 2001; Bronfenbrenner & Morris, 1998).

The Process-Person-Context-Time (or PPCT) Model

By Bronfenbrenner's (1977) description, the model that has emerged from this scholarship has four interrelated components: (a) the developmental *process*, involving the fused and dynamic relation of the individual and the context; (b) the *person*, with his or her individual repertoire of biological, cognitive, emotional, and behavioral characteristics; (c) the *context* of human development, conceptualized as the nested levels, or systems, of the ecology of human development he has depicted (Bronfenbrenner, 1977, 1979); and (d) *time*, conceptualized as involving the multiple dimensions of temporality—for example, ontogenetic time, family time, and historical time—constituting the chronosystem that moderates change across the life course (e.g., Elder, 1998).

Together, these four components of Bronfenbrenner's formulation of bioecological theory constitute a *process-person-context-time* (or *PPCT*) model for conceptualizing the integrated developmental system and for designing research to study the course of human development. Bronfenbrenner believes that just as all the components of the model must be included in any adequate conceptual specification of the dynamic, human development system, so too must research investigate the role of all of them to provide data adequate for understanding human development.

According to Bronfenbrenner and Morris (1998), the first component of the model, process,

> encompasses particular forms of interaction between organism and environment, called proximal processes, that operate over time and are posited as the primary mechanisms producing human development. However, the power of such processes to influence development is presumed, and shown, to vary substantially as a function of the characteristics of the developing Person, of the immediate and more remote environmental Contexts, and the Time periods, in which the proximal processes take place. (p. 994)

Of the three remaining defining properties of the model—person, context, and time—Bronfenbrenner and Morris (1998) indicated that they gave priority in their scholarship to defining the biopsychosocial characteristics of the person (p. 994) since, as noted by Bronfenbrenner in 1989, his earlier formulations of the model (e.g., Bronfenbrenner, 1979) had left a gap with regard to this key feature of the theory.

> Three types of Person characteristics are distinguished as most influential in shaping the course of future development through their capacity to affect the direction and power of proximal processes through the life course. The first are dispositions that can set proximal processes in motion in a particular developmental domain and continue to sustain their operation. Next are bio-ecological resources of ability, experience, knowledge, and skill required for the effective functioning of proximal processes at a given stage of development. Finally, there are demand characteristics that invite or discourage reactions from the social environment of a kind that can foster or disrupt the operation of proximal processes. The differentiation of these three forms leads to their combination in patterns of Person structure that can further account for differences in the direction and power of resultant proximal processes and their developmental effects. (Bronfenbrenner & Morris, 1998, p. 995)

Consistent with the integrative character of development systems theory, Bronfenbrenner and Morris pointed out that when the person component of the bioecological model is expanded in this way the result is a richer understanding of the context—the ecological system—with which the developing person is fused:

> These new formulations of qualities of the person that shape his or her future development have had the unanticipated effect of further differentiating, expanding, and integrating the original 1979 conceptualization of the environment in terms of nested systems ranging from micro to macro. . . . For example, the three types of Person characteristics outlined above are also incorporated into the definition of the microsystem as characteristics of parents, relatives, close friends, teachers, mentors, coworkers, spouses, or others who participate in the life of the developing person on a fairly regular basis over extended periods of time. (p. 995)

Indeed, Bronfenbrenner redefined the character of the microsystem to link it centrally to what is described as the "center of gravity" (Bronfenbrenner & Morris, 1998, p. 1013)—the biopsychosocial person—within the theory as it has now been elaborated. That is, although Bronfenbrenner still saw the ecology of human development as "the ecological environment . . . conceived as a set of nested structures, each inside the other like a set of Russian dolls" that he had described earlier (Bronfenbrenner, 1979, p. 3), he magnified his conception of the innermost, microsystem structure within this ecology by incorporating the activities, relationships, and roles of the developing person into this system. In 1994, he defined a microsystem as

> a pattern of activities, social roles, and interpersonal relations experienced by the developing person in a given face-to-face setting with particular physical, social, and symbolic features that invite, permit, or inhibit engagement in sustained, progressively more complex interaction with, and activity in, the immediate environment. (p. 1645)

What may be particularly significant to Bronfenbrenner in this expanded definition of the microsystem is the inclusion of the person's interactions not only with other people in this level of the ecology but also with the world of symbols and language (the semiotic system)—a component of ecological relationships that action theorists also believe is especially important in understanding the formulation of intentions, goals, and actions (cf. Brandtstädter, 1998, 1999).

> Even more broadly, concepts and criteria are introduced that differentiate between those features of the environment that foster versus interfere with the development of proximal processes. Particularly significant in the latter sphere is the growing hecticness, instability, and chaos in the principal settings in which human competence and character are shaped—in the family, child-care arrangements, schools, peer groups, and neighborhoods. (p. 995)

The emphasis on a redefined and expanded concept of the microsystem leads to the last defining property of the current formulation of his theory of human development. According to Bronfenbrenner and Morris (1998, p. 995),

> the fourth and final defining property of the bioecological model and the one that moves it farthest beyond its predecessor [is] the dimension of Time. The 1979 volume scarcely mentions the term, whereas in the current formulation, it has a prominent place at three successive levels—micro-, meso-, and macro-. Microtime refers to continuity versus discontinuity within ongoing episodes of proximal process. Mesotime is the periodicity of these episodes across broader time intervals, such as days and weeks. Finally, Macrotime focuses on the changing expectations and events in the larger society, both within and across generations, as they affect, and are affected by, processes and outcomes of human development over the life course.

Propositions of the Bioecological Model

Bronfenbrenner's bioecological model is in at least two senses a living system (Ford & Lerner, 1992). First, the theory itself depicts the dynamic, developmental relations between an active individual and his or her complex, integrated, and changing ecology. In addition, the theory is itself developing (e.g., as in Bronfenbrenner, 2001), as Bronfenbrenner seeks to make its features more precise so that it can be a more operational guide for PPCT-relevant research about the dynamic character of the human developmental process.

Thus the bioecological model has developed to include several propositions. These sets of ideas promote a dynamic, person-context relational view of the process of human development. As explained by Bronfenbrenner and Morris (1998), a key proposition of the bioecological model states:

> Especially in its early phases, but also throughout the life course, human development takes place through processes of progressively more complex reciprocal interaction between an active, evolving biopsychosocial human organism and the persons, objects, and symbols in its immediate external environment. To be effective, the interaction must occur on a fairly regular basis over extended periods of time. Such enduring forms of interaction in the immediate environment are referred to as proximal processes. Examples of enduring patterns of proximal process are found in feeding or comforting a baby, playing with a young child, child-child activities, group or solitary play, reading, learning new skills, athletic activities, problem solving, caring for others in distress, making plans, performing complex tasks, and acquiring new knowledge and know-how. (p. 996)

A second proposition of bioecological theory states:

> The form, power, content, and direction of the proximal processes effecting development vary systematically as a joint function of the characteristics of the developing person; the environment—both immediate and more remote—in which the processes are taking place; the nature of the developmental outcomes under consideration; and the social continuities and changes occurring over time through the life course and the historical period during which the person has lived. (Bronfenbrenner & Morris, 1998, p. 996)

Both these propositions emphasize a theme found in other instances of developmental systems theory (Lerner, 2002)—that within the bioecological system the individual, in dynamic relation to his or her temporally embedded, multilevel ecology, is an active agent in his or her own development. Indeed, Bronfenbrenner and Morris (1998, p. 996) ask their readers to note that

> characteristics of the person actually appear twice in the bioecological model—first as one of the four elements influencing the "form, power, content, and

direction of the proximal process," and then again as "developmental outcomes"; that is, qualities of the developing person that emerge at a later point in time as the result of the joint, interactive, mutually reinforcing effects of the four principal antecedent components of the model. In sum, in the bio-ecological model, the characteristics of the person function both as an indirect producer and as a product of development.

In sum, the individual's contribution to the process of development is made by a synthesis, an integration, between the active person and his or her active context.

Within bioecological theory, as in other developmental systems models, relations between the active individual and the active context constitute the basic process of human development. Indeed, Bronfenbrenner (2001, p. 6965) provides additional propositions that underscore the relational character of human development. According to one proposition,

> Over the life course, human development takes place throughout life through processes of progressively more complex reciprocal interaction between an active evolving biopsychological human organism and the persons, objects, and symbols in its immediate external environment. To be effective, the interaction must occur on a fairly regular basis over extended periods of time. Such enduring forms of interaction in the immediate environment are referred to as proximal processes. (p. 6965)

In sum, the relations between an active individual and his or her active and multilevel ecology constitute the driving force of human development. These relations are also the focus of Bronfenbrenner's vision for enhancing the course of human life. The adaptive regulation of person-context relations—exchanges between the person and his or her ecology that function to benefit both—should, from the perspective of the bioecological model, be the focus of human development scholarship and of efforts to improve the course of human life at the levels of both individuals and their social world. Indeed, the plasticity of these relations, and thus the ability to maximize the possibility for adaptive developmental regulations, defines the essence of being human within Bronfenbrenner's system.

Whether writing the *Two Worlds of Childhood* (1970), in which he sought to enhance scientific and cultural understanding of human development in the United States and his native Russia (he was born in Moscow in 1917 and emigrated to the United States at the age of six); working as one of the founders of Head Start; striving to influence scientific or public policies through presentations, papers, and publications; or enlightening others, one by one or in small groups, through his always engaging and incisive conversational style, Urie Bronfenbrenner has championed the idea that we can—as scholars and as citizens—act to "make humans human" by improving the dynamics of the relations between individuals and their designed and natural ecologies. At the same time, he has been the moral compass for the field of human development. His voice has been clear and unwavering, for example in *The State of Americans: This Generation and the Next* (Bronfenbrenner et al., 1996), in alerting scholars and policy makers to the existence of macrosystem threats to humanity and, nevertheless, reminding them of our capacity to remain humane, just, and democratic. Indeed, the events of September 11, 2002, motivated Professor Bronfenbrenner to prepare this book, to once again marshal his keen and uniquely creative intellect to explain that individually and collectively we have the capacity to promote the best of human development.

The Plan of This Book

This book is divided into two sections, "On the Nature of Bioecological Theory and Research" and "Using the Ecology of Human Development to Enhance the Human Condition." Section I, "On the Nature of Bioecological Theory and Research," presents edited versions of key papers published by Professor Bronfenbrenner over his more than 60-year scholarly career that reflect the bases and development of his bioecological theory. These entries manifest his continuing conviction that rigorous research aimed at elucidating the interdependencies across the bioecological system can advance both theory about and applications pertinent to the role of children, families, and communities in promoting positive human development. The articles in Section I begin with Professor Bronfenbrenner's most recent writing on the bioecology of human development. In Article 1, he revisits his earlier concerns about the model's shortcomings as a basis for a scientific discipline of study. In response to his previous self-generated concerns, he describes an updated conceptualization of the bioecology of human development and its defining properties. In most of his writings on the bioecology of human development, he draws heavily on one or two studies to show the promise of the full model; in this case, it is the study by Small and Luster (1990) about Wisconsin youth at risk. He shows how the full bioecological model (person ↔ process ↔ context ↔ time) can be applied to reveal processes with both beneficial and baleful consequences. Readers are shown how parental monitoring, for example, can work for or against a child's best interests, depending on systematic variations in the components of the model.

In Article 2, Robert Cairns and Beverly Cairns discuss Professor Bronfenbrenner's publications over a span of more than 50 years. Their goal is to account for the key ideas used in contemporary developmental science to understand the contributions of the social ecology to human development. Cairns and Cairns place his work in the context of the more than century-long appeal for the use of an integrated developmental science to understand social ontogeny. They trace the development of the modern understanding of the role of the social ecology that derives from the publication in 1943 and 1944 of his dissertation data in the journal *Sociometry*. Cairns and Cairns explain that the ideas he presented about the integrated character of social development remained an emphasis in his writings and have become a focus in developmental science. These ideas evolved in the context of the elaboration of new research methods and data analysis techniques, and they provide a model useful for promoting health and preventing social chaos.

Article 3 is an excerpt from Professor Bronfenbrenner's 1942 doctoral dissertation that presents an initial view of his ecological theory of human development. Findings from a sociometric analysis of an entire population of laboratory elementary school students at the University of Michigan suggested that the evaluation of social status and structure requires envisioning both the individual and the group as developing units. The elements of social status and structure are interdependent and organized into complex patterns, making piecemeal analysis of isolated aspects and attributes insufficient and even misleading.

Developmental psychologists have typically worked in an experimental research tradition that places considerable theoretical and practical limitations on what can be learned about the forces that affect human development. Laboratory settings do not reflect the actual situations in which children develop, so knowledge of how to design programs that can improve outcomes for children and families is constrained. Article 4 reviews studies that accidentally or intentionally documented the role of the social context on specific processes of human development. The dynamic, evolving, interactive effects between the "social ecology" and the "ecology of human development" are shown to vary as a function of the developmental level of the child.

In Article 5, Professor Bronfenbrenner explains his considerable debt to Kurt Lewin. He emphasizes the intellectual prescience of Lewin, perhaps especially with regard to the development of the link between basic science and social policy, a link that is becoming increasingly prominent in contemporary society. Lewin's rich set of ideas—for instance, his stress on the connections between people and settings and his concept of action research—provide a compelling scientific vision for integrating the theoretical and the practical in building better knowledge and healthier societies.

The ecological model discussed in Article 6 relates to the nexus of science and social policy. According to this model, the individual exists at the innermost level of a set of nested structures comprising the ecological environment. Emphasis is placed on the interconnections and developmental significance of the nested structures, which range in their degree of proximity to, but not influence on, the developing person. This theoretical complexity permits scientific detection of systemic influences on human development.

Article 7 is a version of a discussion session, involving Professors Frank Kessel, William Kessen, Sheldon White, and Professor Bronfenbrenner, at the 1983 biennial meetings of the Society for Research in Child Development; it has been edited to show only Professor Bronfenbrenner's part. In the article, Professor Bronfenbrenner extends the discussion that he and Ann Crouter presented in the 1983 *Handbook of Child Psychology* about the evolution of research models in developmental science across the last century. He suggests that we need to specify and integrate in research two kinds of empirical systems—the biopsychological system and the socioeconomic-political system—in order to understand how the complementarity between the systems may enable human development to flourish. He suggests also that these systems are becoming progressively disorganized and fragmented because of the paucity of research integrating them and that the same may be said for developmental science itself. However, he argues that we may be on the verge of overcoming the disorganization and fragmentation of developmental science because we have finally taken as our laboratory the society in which children grow. Consequently, our research may become better able to contribute to positive integration between the systems and to the promotion of healthy human beings and societies.

In Article 8, Professor Bronfenbrenner outlines the limitations of the traditional social address and attribute models of human development in explaining the interactive efforts of biology and ecology. Using Tulkin's (1970) doctoral dissertation as a window, he takes the reader through each component of his emerging person-process-context model, showing how the addition of each component provides greater explanatory power. Finally, he adds a fourth component "time," to the model, arguing that the dimensions of both personal and historical time need to be taken into consideration. Although the full model is scientifically compelling and laden with promise, he suggests that it is still rarely employed, so that little evidence had thus far been found for its scientific validity. This is the future in the title: the full validation of the person-process-context-time model.

In Article 9, Professor Bronfenbrenner questions whether his ideas have been a victim of their own success. He repeats a quip he made earlier about the sad state of developmental research up through the publication of *The Ecology of Human Development*, referring to mainstream developmental research as "the study of the strange behavior of children in strange situations with strange adults for the briefest possible period of time." In that volume, he urged a greater attention to studies of development in context. One of the points in this article is Professor Bronfenbrenner's subsequent regret that his enjoinder to fellow developmentalists was too successful: "We now have a surfeit of studies on 'context without development.'"

In Article 10, Professor Bronfenbrenner discusses what for him has been a lifelong endeavor, to be both creator and critic of his own work. The bulk of this article is devoted to fleshing out specific ways that context mediates developmental processes, drawing on both cross-cultural findings and Stephen Ceci's work with American children and adults. Taking as his starting point Lewin's field theory, Professor Bronfenbrenner shows that class-theoretic approaches lack the dynamism necessary to disentangle nested processes. Here he uses as a window into this issue the literatures about teenage pregnancy and low birth weight, showing how the process that mediates the influence of demographic variables shifts with contextual changes. He repeats this type of analysis in his exploration of other questions, such as the effects of modernity and temperament.

In Article 11, Professor Bronfenbrenner and Professor Stephen J. Ceci propose a version of the bioecological model. They frame this presentation by reconceptualizing the nature-nurture controversy.

Section II, "Using the Ecology of Human Development to Enhance the Human Condition," specifies the several ways in which Professor Bronfenbrenner's ideas may frame programs and policies promoting positive human development. Across the entries in this section, Professor Bronfenbrenner emphasizes the crucial need for communities to work to support the efforts of families to raise healthy children.

Accordingly, the first entry, Article 12, explains the important connections between research conducted within the framework of the bioecological model and applications to policies and programs that would diminish the chaos affecting contemporary children and families. Article 13 depicts features of the contemporary context of child and family life, including the role of peers in moderating child development. Article 14 explains the important challenges to the positive development of children that exist across the range of socioeconomic settings within which they live. Professor Bronfenbrenner emphasizes the stresses that all parents feel in raising healthy children.

In Article 15, Professor Bronfenbrenner draws from his comparative study of childhood in the United States and the former Soviet Union. He demonstrates the unique utility of the bioecological perspective in understanding discrepancies between societal goals for children and the actual practices associated with child rearing.

In Article 16, Professor Bronfenbrenner again uses bioecological theory to address the relation of nature to nurture, here in relation to the issue of the purported heritability of IQ scores. His presentation explains the egregious conceptual and empirical flaws in claims that genes and environment contribute separately to the variance in intelligence.

In Article 17, Professor Bronfenbrenner extends his discussion of the intimate link between the healthy development of parents and their capacity to promote the positive development of children. He offers several provocative ideas for enhancing the development of both parents and children.

A key facet of Professor Bronfenbrenner's conceptual framework is the stress on the importance for healthy child development of a sustained relationship between a caring adult and a young person. In Article 18, he explains the importance of caring in human development and urges colleagues to pursue evidence-based interactions to promote caring. In the final entry, Article 19, he extends the bioecological model to appraise child care practices cross-nationally. He uses this comparative approach to formulate important proposals to enhance child care policy in the United States.

Conclusion

Ultimately, Urie Bronfenbrenner has, across more than six decades of singularly prolific and significant scholarship, given the world a gift of hope and power. We may remain hopeful that we can, through our own energies and active contributions to our world, optimize our lives and the lives of others with whom we share the fragile ecology supporting our existence. If we pursue the path of science and program and policy applications to which Bronfenbrenner's vision has directed us, we can as well sustain a humane and health-promoting ecology for future generations. Such a contribution may be Urie Bronfenbrenner's greatest legacy. It may be the frame within which human decency and social justice may prosper.

References

Baltes, P. B. (1997). On the incomplete architecture of human ontogeny: Selection, optimization, and compensation as foundations of developmental theory. *American Psychologist, 52,* 366–380.

Baltes, P. B., Lindenberger, U., & Staudinger, U. M. (1998). Life-span theory in developmental psychology. In W. Damon (Series Ed.) & R. M. Lerner (Vol. Ed.), *Handbook of child psychology: Vol. 1. Theoretical models of human development* (5th ed., pp. 1029–1144). New York: John Wiley.

Brandtstädter, J. (1998). Action perspectives on human development. In W. Damon (Series Ed.), & R. M. Lerner (Vol. Ed.), *Handbook of child psychology: Vol. 1. Theoretical models of human development* (5th ed., pp. 807–863). New York: John Wiley.

Brandtstädter, J. (1999). The self in action and development: Cultural, biosocial, and ontogenetic bases of intentional self-development. In J. Brandtstädter & R.M. Lerner (Eds.), *Action and self-development: Theory and research through the life-span* (pp. 37–65). Thousand Oaks, CA: Sage.

Bronfenbrenner, U. (1963). Developmental theory in transition. In H. W. Stevenson (Ed.), *Child psychology: Sixty second yearbook of the National Society for the Study of Education,* part 1 (pp. 517–542). Chicago: University of Chicago Press.

Bronfenbrenner, U. (1970). *Two worlds of childhood: US and USSR.* New York: Russell Sage Foundation.

Bronfenbrenner, U. (1974). Developmental research, public policy, and the ecology of childhood. *Child Development, 45,* 1–5.

Bronfenbrenner, U. (1977). Toward an experimental ecology of human development. *American Psychologist, 32,* 513–531.

Bronfenbrenner, U. (1979). *The ecology of human development: Experiments by nature and design.* Cambridge, MA: Harvard University Press.

Bronfenbrenner, U. (1989). Ecological systems theory. In R. Vasta (Ed.), *Six theories of child development: Revised formulations and current issues* (pp. 185–246). Greenwich, CT: JAI.

Bronfenbrenner, U. (1994). Ecological models of human development. In T. Husen & T. N. Postlethwaite (Eds.), *International encyclopedia of education* (2nd ed., Vol. 3, pp. 1643–1647). Oxford, UK: Pergamon/Elsevier Science.

Bronfenbrenner, U. (2001). The bioecological theory of human development. In N. J. Smelser & P. B. Baltes (Eds.), *International encyclopedia of the social and behavioral sciences* (Vol. 10, pp. 6963–6970). New York: Elsevier.

Bronfenbrenner, U., & Ceci, S. J. (1993). Heredity, environment, and the question "How": A new theoretical perspective for the 1990s. In R. Plomin & G. E. McClearn (Eds.), *Nature, nurture, and psychology* (pp. 313–324). Washington, DC: American Psychological Association.

Bronfenbrenner, U., & Ceci, S. J. (1994). Nature-nurture reconceptualized in developmental perspective: A bioecological model. *Psychological Review, 101,* 568–586.

Bronfenbrenner, U., & Crouter, A. C. (1983). The evolution of environmental models in developmental research. In P. H. Mussen (Series Ed.) & W. Kessen (Vol. Ed.), *Handbook of child psychology: Vol. 1. History, theory, and methods* (4th ed., pp. 357–414). New York: John Wiley.

Bronfenbrenner, U., McClelland, P., Wethington, E., Moen, P., & Ceci, S. J. (1996). *The state of Americans: This generation and the next.* New York: Free Press.

Bronfenbrenner, U., & Morris, P. A. (1998). The ecology of developmental process. In W. Damon (Series Ed.) & R. M. Lerner (Vol. Ed.), *Handbook of child psychology: Vol. 1. Theoretical models of human development* (5th ed., pp. 993–1028). New York: John Wiley.

Damon, W. (Ed.). (1998). *Handbook of child psychology* (5th ed.). New York: John Wiley.

Elder, G. H., Jr. (1998). The life course and human development. In W. Damon (Series Ed.) & R. M. Lerner (Vol. Ed.), *Handbook of child psychology: Vol. 1. Theoretical models of human development* (5th ed., pp. 939–991). New York: John Wiley.

Ford, D. L., & Lerner, R. M. (1992). *Developmental systems theory: An integrative approach.* Newbury Park, CA: Sage.

Gottlieb, G. (1997). *Synthesizing nature-nurture: Prenatal roots of instinctive behavior.* Mahwah, NJ: Lawrence Erlbaum.

Damon, W. (Series Ed.), & Lerner, R. M. (Vol. Ed.). (1998). *Handbook of child psychology: Vol. 1. Theoretical models of human development* (5th ed.). New York: John Wiley.

Lerner, R. M. (2002). *Concepts and theories of human development* (3rd ed.). Mahwah, NJ: Lawrence Erlbaum.

Looft, W. R. (1972). The evolution of developmental psychology. *Human Development, 15,* 187–201.

Magnusson, D. (1999a). Holistic interactionism: A perspective for research on personality development. In L. A. Pervin & O. P. John (Eds.), *Handbook of personality: Theory and research* (2nd ed., pp. 219–247). New York: Guilford.

Magnusson, D. (1999b). On the individual: A person-oriented approach to developmental research. *European Psychologist, 4,* 205–218.

Mussen, P. H. (Ed.). (1970). *Carmichael's manual of child psychology* (3rd ed.). New York: John Wiley.

Sameroff, A. J. (1983). Developmental systems: Contexts and evolution. In P. H. Mussen (Series Ed.) & W. Kessen (Vol. Ed.), *Handbook of child psychology: Vol. 1. History, theory, and methods* (4th ed., pp. 237–294). New York: John Wiley.

Thelen, E., & Smith, L. B. (1998). Dynamic systems theories. In W. Damon (Series Ed.) & R. M. Lerner (Vol. Ed.), *Handbook of child psychology: Vol. 1. Theoretical models of human development* (5th ed., pp. 563–633). New York: John Wiley.

Making Human Beings Human: An Introduction

The main thesis of this volume is that, to a greater extent than for any other species, human beings create the environments that shape the course of human development. Their actions influence the multiple physical and cultural tiers of the ecology that shapes them, and this agency makes humans—for better or for worse—active producers of their own development.

Human Development is a field of inquiry in which major scientific advances have occurred in the past two decades—advances that have significantly expanded existing knowledge and have opened up previously unrecognized domains of scientific investigation. The findings generated by the new theoretical perspectives and research strategies indicate that the major social changes taking place recently in modern industrialized societies, especially the United States, may have altered environmental conditions conducive to human development to such a degree that the process of making human beings human is being placed in jeopardy.

The new scientific advances, and their implications, are generally unknown not only to the general public but also to most policy makers, practitioners, and even to many developmental researchers. The reason for this lack of awareness is that the advances have been occurring simultaneously in disparate disciplines and in unconnected branches of the same discipline. For example, the findings brought together in this volume come from such diverse domains as human genetics, demography, developmental biology, cognitive psychology, structural sociology, statistical modeling, education, and public policy studies. Especially when viewed in relation to each other, these findings, and the theoretical ideas that underlie them, offer new perspectives for understanding the interplay of biological, social, economic, and ideological forces that shape the development of human beings. The evolving perspectives are reflected in the emergence of new bodies of developmental theory and research that represent syntheses across disciplinary lines. The syntheses are found in newly established fields as the ecology of human development, bioecological theory, and life span or life course development. The complementary nature of these approaches, and of the research results they have generated, are only now beginning to be realized.

The *bioecological theory of human development*, together with its corresponding research designs, is an evolving theoretical system for the scientific study of human development over time. Within the bioecological theory, human development is defined as the *phenomenon of continuity and change in the biopsychological characteristics of human beings, both as individuals and as groups*. This process extends over the life course, across successive generations, and through historical time, both in the past and in the future.

The recognition that developmental processes are profoundly affected by events and conditions in the larger environment accords major importance to public policies and practices that influence the nature of the environment and, as a result, have significant effects, often unintended, on the development of children growing up in families, classrooms, and other settings. This state of affairs has implications for both science and public policy. On the one hand, it argues for greater attention by developmental researchers to the indirect effects, both existent and potential, of public policies on developmental processes. On the other hand, it emphasizes the need on the part of policy makers to acquire knowledge and understanding of how policies, and the ways in which they are implemented, affect the capacity of families, schools, and other socialization settings to function effectively as contexts of human development.

Although, in practice, the theory and its supporting data cannot be separated from the applications that both derive from and, in turn, influence it, for reasons of pedagogy it is useful to organize this volume into two main sections. The first section, "On the Nature of Bioecological Theory and Research," presents the key features and theoretical and empirical implications of the bioecological model. It briefly specifies the key issues of human development addressed by the bioecological model and then presents the most recently published (2001) formulation of the model, followed by key excerpts from my writing in chronological order. These excerpts illustrate the evolution of the theory that has resulted in the most recent instantiation of the model. In addition, a piece about bioecological theory by Robert and Beverly Cairns is included in this section because of its importance for understanding the theory's scholarly and social contributions. Each excerpt in Section I is preceded by a brief description of the nature and purpose of the publication from which the excerpt is drawn.

The second section, "Using the Ecology of Human Development to Enhance the Human Condition," concerns applications synthetically linked to the theoretical and research component of the perspective. Here the excerpted material provides illustrations of how bioecological theory and data may address critical issues affecting children's and families' welfare and likelihood of positive development. This section of the book is organized much like the first section. It begins with a brief overview of the issues of application to policy and programs to which the excerpts in the section are directed. The first excerpt in the section is derived from my most recent statement about how the challenges to healthy structure and function confronting the contemporary American family encapsulate the use of bioecological theory and research in devising applications that maximize the capacities of humans to promote their own positive development. The succeeding excerpts in this section are presented chronologically, and each excerpt is preceded by a brief overview of its purpose.

An afterword by Stephen F. Hamilton and Stephen J. Ceci, my colleagues in the Department of Human Development in Cornell University's College of Human Ecology, concludes the volume. This piece places bioecological theory, research, and application in the scholarly and societal context to which it aspires. The ecology of human development perspective is, I believe, a productive means to advance the scientific study of human development in a manner that informs and is informed by the people and social institutions striving to actualize humans' unique potential to enhance their own and future generations' positive and healthy development.

As I learned from Kurt Lewin more than six decades ago, there is nothing more practical than a good theory, and my hope is that the perspective I have developed will be seen as the most practical theory of all. I hope it will give all individuals greater understanding of what they can do to produce a better, more hopeful future for themselves, their children, and the people of the world.

Photo © 1995 by Dede Hatch.

SECTION 1

On the Nature of Bioecological Theory and Research

In Section I of *Making Human Beings Human*, I put forward the history of my thinking about the bioecological theory of human development, often accompanied by my own criticisms of its shortcomings and identification of remaining research challenges. In several of these early articles, I describe the precursors of current bioecological theory (as do Cairns and Cairns in their article), propose new research designs to address the complexity inherent in bioecological theory, and provide the theory's defining principles. Working within what is commonly associated with the European tradition, I provide readers with a mental journey through theorems, propositions, corollaries, and postulates.

Reading the articles in Section I from the most recent to the least recent gives a glimpse into the struggles I faced in crafting this theory. I hope, however, that a close reading reveals a continuity of themes and arguments, even when the terminology itself changed (or was replaced). For example, the terms *micro-*, *macro-*, *meso-*, and *exosystem* that I used in *The Ecology of Human Development* (1979) were sometimes replaced in my later writings by more general language, such as *interconnected systems*; my early doubts about the availability of research paradigms that could analyze the synergistic interaction between heredity and environment have resurfaced in myriad ways in later publications. I hope readers find not only continuity in my own thinking but also an accumulation of evidence for the usefulness of the foundational principles of bioecological theory.

1

Article 1

The Bioecological Theory of Human Development

The bioecological theory of human development reached maturity 10 years after the publication of "Ecological Systems Theory" (Article 10 of this volume), which had called the future of the "ecology of human development" into question as a discipline. The following successor to that article accepts the bioecological theory as a paradigm for the future and specifies its defining properties.

The bioecological model, together with its corresponding research designs, is an evolving theoretical system for the scientific study of human development over time. Within the bioecological theory, development is defined as the *phenomenon of continuity and change in the biopsychological characteristics of human beings both as individuals and as groups. The phenomenon extends over the life course across successive generations and through historical time, both past and present.*

Source: Bronfenbrenner, U. (2001). The bioecological theory of human development. In N. J. Smelser & P. B. Baltes (Eds.), *International encyclopedia of the social and behavioral sciences* (Vol. 10, pp. 6963–6970). New York: Elsevier. Reprinted with permission from Elsevier Science Ltd.

Defining Properties of the Bioecological Model

The term *evolving* highlights the fact that the model, along with its corresponding research designs, has itself undergone a process of development over its own "life course." Another defining property of the bioecological model specifies that it deals with two closely related but nevertheless fundamentally different developmental processes, each taking place over time. The first defines the phenomenon under investigation: namely, that of continuity and change in the biopsychological characteristics of human beings. The second focuses on the development of the scientific tools—the theoretical models and corresponding research designs required for assessing the continuity and change.

These two tasks cannot be carried out independently, for they are the joint product of emerging and converging ideas, based on both theoretical and empirical grounds—a process called "developmental science in the discovery mode" (Bronfenbrenner & Evans, 2000, pp. 999–1000). In the more familiar "verification mode," the aim is to replicate previous findings in other settings to make sure that the findings still apply. By contrast, in the discovery mode, the aim is to fulfill two broader but interrelated objectives:

1. Devising new alternative hypotheses and corresponding research designs that not only call existing results into question but also stand a chance of yielding new, more differentiated, more precise, replicable research findings and thereby producing more valid scientific knowledge.

2. Providing scientific bases for the design of effective social policies and programs that can counteract newly emerging developmentally disruptive influences. This has been an explicit objective of the bioecological model from its earliest beginnings.

A major challenge to today's bioecological model is to discover how such new working hypotheses and corresponding research designs can be developed for the future. One answer lies in the possibility that, despite historical change, some elements of the model, and their interrelationships, may remain constant across both time and space. From this perspective, today's model has several distinctive defining properties that become the foundation for the rest. Some are of relatively recent origin; others date back to the model's earliest formal beginnings. Each is expressed here in the form of a proposition.

Proposition I

An early critical element in the definition of the ecological model is *experience*. The term is used to indicate that the scientifically relevant features of any environment for human development include not only its objective properties but also the way in which these properties are subjectively experienced by the persons living in that environment. This equal emphasis on an experiential as well as an objective view springs neither from any antipathy to behavioristic concepts nor from a predilection for existential philosophical foundations. It is dictated simply by a hard fact. Very few of the external influences significantly affecting human behavior and development can be described solely in terms of objective physical conditions and events.

A critical term in the foregoing formulation is the word *solely*. In the bioecological model, both objective and subjective elements are posited as driving the course of human development; neither alone is presumed sufficient. Moreover, these elements do not always operate in the same direction. It is therefore important to understand the nature of each of these two dynamic forces, beginning on the *phenomenological* or *experiential* side. Both of the underlined terms are relevant because, while related to each other, they are typically applied to somewhat different spheres. The former is more often used in relation to how the environment is perceived and changed by human beings at successive stages of the life course, beginning in early infancy and proceeding through childhood, adolescence, adulthood, and, ultimately, old age.

By contrast, *experience* pertains to the realm of subjective feelings: for example, anticipations, forebodings, hopes, doubts, or personal beliefs. These, too, emerge in early childhood, continue through life, and are characterized by both stability and change. They can relate to self or to others, and especially to family, friends, and other close associates. They can also apply to the activities in which one engages: for example, those that one most or least likes to do. But the most distinctive feature of such experiential qualities is that they are "emotionally and motivationally loaded," encompassing both love and hate, joy and sorrow, curiosity and boredom, desire and revulsion, often with both polarities existing at the same time but usually in differing degrees. A significant body of research evidence indicates that such positive and negative subjective forces, evolving in the past, can also contribute in powerful ways to shaping the course of development in the future.

But these are not the only powerful forces at work. There are others that are more objective in nature. This does not mean, however, that they are necessarily either more or less influential, mainly because the two sets of forces are interdependent and affect each other. Like their subjective counterparts, these more objective factors also rely for their assessment on corresponding theoretical models and associated research designs that have evolved over time. These more objective relationships are documented below in the form of two propositions (Bronfenbrenner & Evans, 2000; Bronfenbrenner & Morris, 1998). The first specifies the theoretical model and provides concrete examples; the second foreshadows the corresponding research designs for their assessment.

Proposition II

Over the life course, human development takes place through processes of progressively more complex reciprocal interaction between an active, evolving biopsychological human organism and the persons, objects, and symbols in its immediate external environment. To be effective, the interaction must occur on a fairly regular basis over extended periods of *time*. Such enduring forms of interaction in the immediate environment are referred to as *proximal processes*. Examples of such processes include feeding or comforting a baby; playing with a young child; child-child activities; group or solitary play; reading, learning new skills; athletic activities; problem solving; caring for others; making plans; performing complex tasks; and acquiring new knowledge and know-how.

For the younger generation, participation in such interactive processes over time generates the ability, motivation, knowledge, and skill to engage in such activities both with others and on one's own. For example, through progressively more complex interaction with their parents, children increasingly become agents of their own development, to be sure only in part.

In sum, *proximal processes* are posited as the primary engines of development. The next defining property speaks to the corresponding research designs.

Proposition III

The form, power, content, and direction of the proximal processes producing development vary systematically as a joint function of the characteristics of the *developing person* (including *genetic inheritance*); of the *environment*—both immediate and more remote—in which the processes are taking place; of the nature of the *developmental outcomes* under consideration; and of the continuities and changes occurring in the environment over *time*, through the life course, and during the historical period in which the person has lived.

Propositions II and III are theoretically interdependent and subject to empirical test. An operational research design that permits their simultaneous investigation is referred to as a *process-person-context-time model* (PPCT for short).

In the corresponding research designs for the bioecological model, the element of *time* has special importance. To show that development has actually occurred, the research design must demonstrate, or at least make plausible, that the elements in the design, and their dynamic relationships to each other, have influenced the biopsychological characteristics of the developing person over an extended period of time. For example, a rich data archive generously made available by Small and Luster (1990) from their statewide studies of youth at risk in Wisconsin has made possible some reanalyses of working hypotheses derived from the newly emerging formulations.

Parental monitoring was defined as "the effort by parents to keep informed about and set limits on their children's activities outside the home." Higher levels of academic performance require mastery of progressively more complex tasks and hence are more difficult to achieve. The relation between parental monitoring and school grades shows a declining curvilinear trend. This effect, however, is far stronger for girls than for boys, particularly in families with two biological parents.

Both of these results are consistent with two working hypotheses derived from the bioecological model. The first stipulates that proximal processes (in this instance, parental monitoring) are likely to have greater impact in two-parent families than in those in which the mother is a single parent or the father is a step-parent. The second hypothesis posits a stronger and longer-lasting influence of the family on the development of females than of males.

In addition, a distinctive feature of the pattern for girls is that the curve markedly flattens at higher levels of monitoring and, in the case of daughters of single-parent mothers, even becomes a turnaround. This finding suggests that under such circumstances the demands on the girls may become so great that the existing proximal processes are not equal to the task and, as a result, bring fewer educational returns. Finally, an analysis of data on students whose mothers had no more than a high school education revealed a similar pattern, but the constructive influence of monitoring was appreciably weaker, and its greater benefit to girls was reduced. Nevertheless, daughters of mothers with less than a high school education both in single-parent and in stepfather families still had higher grade point average (GPA) scores than did sons. Moreover, within each level of mother's education statistically significant differences by family structure were found in school achievement, with students growing up in two-parent families receiving the highest grades and those from single-parent families the lowest.

Also, a second analysis was carried out assessing the influence of the mother's educational level on the effects of her parental monitoring. Because, for a number of reasons, the addition of this parameter makes the interpretation of the findings in graphic form rather complex, the main results are summarized below.

1. The effect of parental monitoring on students' GPA was clearly greatest for those who were living with both biological parents and whose mothers had had some education beyond high school. Also, the extent and positive effect of mothers' monitoring was greatest at the beginning of high school and decreased gradually thereafter.

2. The constructive influence of mothers with *education beyond high school* both in "mother-only" families and in those with "own mother and stepfather" was considerably less and declined more rapidly.

3. The results of parental monitoring by mothers with less than a high school education were also positive but not as strong. Mothers from families with two biological parents were again the most effective monitors, but less so than those with some education beyond high school. The means for the three types of family structures were in the same order but also closer together.

The interpretation of these findings is confounded by the absence of separate statistics for males and females, a condition arising from the low frequencies of subjects of both genders among children in families other than those consisting of two biological parents.

In conclusion, two qualifications are required regarding the scientific validity of the reported findings. First and foremost, most of the reported research was conducted a decade ago and may not, in all instances, apply to the outcome of parent-child monitoring in the present year, 2001. Second, it is not always the case that separated or single-parent families put the future development of their children at risk. In some instances, such family forms lead to new relationships and structures that make possible a constructive change in the course of their children's development.

To turn to a related issue: although proximal processes function as the engines of development, the energy that drives them comes from deeper sources that take us back to the experiential world of Proposition I. Both the subjective and the objective forces exert an especially strong influence on development during the formative years (from early infancy to young adulthood). A substantial body of research over the past century indicates that, two or three decades ago, these forces lay mainly within the family, with parents acting as the principal caregivers and sources of emotional support for their children, and with other adult family members living in the home being next in line. To a lesser extent, other relatives, family friends, and neighbors also functioned in this role.

There has been a marked change in this pattern, however, over the past three decades. Parents, and other adult family members as well, have been spending increasing amounts of time commuting to and working at full-time jobs (in which overtime is increasingly often required or expected).

The nature of this trend and its relevance for human development are conveyed in the propositions that follow. (For brevity's sake, the term *child* is used below to encompass the entire period from infancy through young adulthood.)

Proposition IV

In order to develop—intellectually, emotionally, socially, and morally—a child requires, for all of these, the same thing: participation in *progressively more complex activities*, on a regular basis over an extended period of time in the child's life, with one or more persons with whom the child develops *a strong, mutual emotional attachment, and who are committed to the child's well-being and development, preferably for life* (Bronfenbrenner & Evans, 2000; Bronfenbrenner & Morris, 1998). The prerequisites stipulated in Proposition IV then lead to the developmental consequences described in the next proposition.

Proposition V

The establishment of a strong mutual emotional attachment leads to *internalization* of the parent's activities and expressed feelings of affection. Such mutual ties, in turn, motivate the child's interest and engagement in related activities in the immediate physical, social, and—in due course—symbolic environment that invite exploration, manipulation, elaboration, and imagination. The next proposition broadens the family circle.

Proposition VI

The establishment and maintenance of patterns of progressively more complex interaction and emotional attachment between parent and child depend in substantial degree on the availability and involvement of another adult, a *third party*, who assists, encourages, spells off, gives status to, and expresses admiration and affection for the person caring for and engaging in joint activity with the child. It also helps, but is not absolutely essential, that the third party be of the opposite sex from that of the other person caring for the child because this is likely to expose and involve the child in a greater variety of developmentally instigative activities and experiences (Bronfenbrenner, McClelland, Wethington, Moen, & Ceci, 1996). Where this is an attachment to two or more parent figures, each can serve as a third party to the other.

The research evidence for this proposition came mainly by default. It was produced by demographic data documenting a rapid rise in the proportion of single-parent households. The trend began in the 1980s and then continued at an even faster rate through most of the 1990s. The overwhelming majority of such homes were those in which the father was absent and the mother bore primary responsibility for the upbringing of the children.

A large number of investigations of developmental processes and outcomes in families of this kind have since been conducted across a range of cultural and social class groups. In general, the findings lead to two complementary conclusions.

First, even in families living in favorable socioeconomic circumstances, children of single-parent mothers or fathers for whom no other person is acting reliably in a "third-party" role are at greater risk for experiencing one or more of the following developmental problems: hyperactivity or withdrawal; lack of attentiveness; difficulty in deferring gratification; poor academic achievement; school misbehavior; and frequent absenteeism.

Second, at a more serious level, such children are at greater risk for a so-called "teenage syndrome" of behaviors that tend to be associated together: dropping out of school; involvement in socially alienated or destructive peer groups; smoking; drinking; frequent sexual experience; adolescent pregnancy; a cynical attitude toward work; and—in the more extreme cases—drugs, suicide, vandalism, violence, and criminal acts. Most of these effects are more pronounced for boys than for girls (Bronfenbrenner et al., 1996).

Not all single-parent families, however, exhibited these disturbed relationships and their disruptive effects on children's development. Systematic studies of the exceptions have identified what may be described as a general "immunizing" factor. For example, children of single parents were less likely to experience developmental problems especially in families in which the mother (or father) received strong support from other adults living in the home. Also helpful were nearby relatives, friends, neighbors, members of religious groups, and, when available, staff members of family support and child care programs. What mattered most was not only the attention given to the child—important as this was—but also the assistance provided to the single parent or by others serving in the supportive roles cited in Proposition VI. It would seem that, in the family dance, "it takes three to tango."

But dancing is not the whole story. By the 1980s, theory and research in the ecology of human development had documented an accelerating trend toward greater permissiveness in styles of child rearing in American families. At the same time, successive scientific investigations had revealed progressively greater developmental advantage for strategies that placed increased emphasis on parental discipline and demand. The interpretation that emerged from analyses of the available data suggested that widespread application of these research findings could serve as an effective response to the developmentally disruptive changes taking place in contemporary society.

At this point, it is important to mention two other bodies of research that contributed significantly to the development of bioecological theory and its corresponding research designs. The first is now of long standing. A quarter-century ago, the sociologist Glen H. Elder Jr., in his classic volume *Children of the Great Depression* (1974, 1999), extended the concept of development beyond the formative years to encompass the entire life course.

The second addition has yet to be fully exploited. In 1994, Bronfenbrenner and Ceci, taking the bioecological model as their point of departure, suggested an empirically testable alternative to the established scientific paradigm used in behavior genetics. The proposed alternative model (a) allows for nonadditive synergistic effects; (b) employs direct measures of the environment; and (c) proposes *proximal processes* as mechanisms of person-environment interaction through which genotypes for developmental competence are transformed into phenotypes. The model predicts that (a) estimates of heritability (h^2) for developmental competence increase markedly with the magnitude of proximal processes; (b) heritability measures the proportion of variation in individual differences that are attributable only to *actualized* genetic potential, with the degree of *unactualized* potential remaining unknown; and (c) actualized genetic potential (h^2) will vary with the quality of the environment and will increase as that quality is improved (for example, through providing job opportunities, health services, and intervention programs in low-income neighborhoods).

The authors also suggested that high levels of such patterns of parental behavior as "neglect, abuse, or domination" can serve as powerful mechanisms for actualizing genetic potentials for developmentally maladaptive behaviors that both disrupt proximal processes and produce developmental disarray.

The Bioecological Model in the Discovery Mode: Future Perspectives

This section is based on propositions and working hypotheses derived from the bioecological model for which, as yet, there are few empirical data. It begins with future prospects for addressing the second stated goal of the bioecological model, that of "providing needed scientific bases for the design of effective social policies and programs that can counteract newly emerging developmentally disruptive influences."

In accord with the latter objective, the section begins with an unorthodox proposal. By and large, thus far, theory and research on human development have been concerned with the influence of the older generation on the development of the younger. In the proposition that follows, the direction is reversed. It should be noted that the basic idea underlying this proposition is not new and is foreshadowed both in the theory of Vygotsky (1978) and in the contemporary "action" theory of Brandtstadter (1998, 1999).

Proposition VIII

The psychological development of parents is powerfully influenced by the behavior and development of their children. This phenomenon occurs through the life course; is more evident during the formative years, when most children are living at home in the care of their parents; and often becomes especially pronounced during adolescence, when the young begin to strive for independence both as individuals and as members of peer groups. Such behavior is particularly likely to occur among those adolescents or youth who have comparatively little contact with their parents or other caring adults earlier in life. Although many studies have focused on the development of such alienated young people, the impact of the latter's behavior on the subsequent development of their parents has yet to receive the systematic investigation that it deserves. The converse of the foregoing proposition—the influence of the successful transition of children through adolescence and young adulthood on the constructive development of their parents—has regrettably received even less scientific attention.

Proposition IX

Over the life course, the process of attachment exhibits a turnaround. In the beginning, it is the children who are the beneficiaries of the parents' irrational commitment, whereas toward the end the roles are reversed. Then it is the elderly parents who receive the love and care of their now middle-aged children. If, however, there was no attachment at the beginning, there may be no attachment at the end.

In this regard, developmental science has yet to address a curious omission with respect to both theory and research design. Resort to search engines in psychology and related fields has thus far failed to identify any investigations of the influence of parent-child attachment in the future development of the *parent* in contrast to that of the child.

This is not quite the case, however, for the next proposition in the discovery mode. The theoretical model, the corresponding research design, and half of the necessary empirical data are already available. The only problem is to find or conduct a study that meets the following requirements.

Proposition X

If an investigation conducted in the past meets the requirements of the bioecological model, including assessment of developmental outcomes "over an extended period of time," then *replication* of the study at a later point in time would reveal whether the processes under investigation were still valid or had been nullified or superseded by subsequent historical changes. When the latter occurs, the investigator is confronted with the challenge of proposing alternative working formulations for explaining the observed phenomena.

At the conclusion of this article, we move from the domain of theory and research design to the world of reality and action. In the bioecological model, these two worlds have never been far apart. Especially over the last three decades, they have become ever closer to each other. At a more general level, the findings from both domains reveal what has been referred to as "growing chaos" in the lives of children, youth, families, schools, the world of work, and the ever-greater commuting in between.

The most recent report of this phenomenon contains the following summary about the nature of "chaos" and its developmental consequences (Bronfenbrenner & Evans, 2000):

> Chaos integrates the various elements involved, and foreshadows the role [of chaos] in the bioecological model in terms of what is called a "chaotic system." Such systems are characterized by frenetic activity, lack of structure, unpredictability in everyday activities, and high levels of ambient stimulation. Background stimulation is high, and there is a general lack of routinization and structure in daily life. The environment is also a major source of interruption of proximal processes in the form of residential noise, crowding, and classroom design. (p. 121)

At the turn of the century, we are left with a troubling question: From the perspective of the bioecological model, what is the prospect for the future development of our species? Today the answer to that question lies in the willingness of the United States and other economically developed countries to heed the emerging lessons of developmental science. At the moment, it is difficult to know what the answer will be. The future could go either way.

Given this alternative, surely it becomes the responsibility of developmental science to communicate such knowledge as we possess and to do so in words that can still find an echo. Here is a first draft.

In the United States it is now possible for a youth, female as well as male, to graduate from high school, or a university, without ever caring for a baby; without ever looking after someone who was ill, old, or lonely; and without comforting or assisting another human being who really needed help. The developmental consequences of such a deprivation of human experience have not as yet been scientifically researched. But the possible social implications are obvious, for—sooner or later, and usually sooner—all of us suffer illness, loneliness, and the need for help, comfort, and companionship. No society can long sustain itself unless its members have learned the sensitivities, motivations, and skills involved in assisting and caring for other human beings.

References

Brandtstadter, J. (1998). Action perspectives on human development. In W. Damon (Series Ed.) & R. M. Lerner (Vol. Ed.), *Handbook of child psychology: Vol. 1. Theoretical models of human development* (5th ed., pp. 807–863). New York: John Wiley.

Brandtstadter, J. (1999). The self in action and development: Cultural, biosocial, and ontogenetic bases of intentional self-development. In J. Brandtstadter & R. M. Lerner (Eds.), *Action and self-development: Theory and research through the life span* (pp. 37–65). Thousand Oaks, CA: Sage.

Bronfenbrenner, U., & Ceci, S. J. (1994). Nature-nurture reconceptualized: A bio-ecological model. *Psychological Review, 101*(4), 568–586.

Bronfenbrenner, U., & Evans, G. W. (2000). Developmental science in the 21st century: Emerging theoretical models, research designs, and empirical findings. *Social Development, 9*(1), 115–125.

Bronfenbrenner, U., McClelland, P., Wethington, E., Moen, P., & Ceci, S. J. (1996). *The state of Americans: This generation and the next.* New York: Free Press.

Bronfenbrenner, U., & Morris, P. A. (1998). The ecology of developmental processes. In W. Damon (Series Ed.) & R. M. Lerner (Vol. Ed.), *Handbook of child psychology: Vol. 1. Theoretical models of human development* (5th ed., pp. 993–1028). New York: John Wiley.

Elder, G. H., Jr. (1974). *Children of the Great Depression.* Chicago: University of Chicago Press.

Elder, G. H. (1999). *Children of the Great Depression* (25th Anniversary Edition). Chicago: University of Chicago Press.

Small, S., & Luster, T. (1990, November, 27). *Youth at risk for parenthood.* Paper presented at the Creating Caring Community Conference, Michigan State University, East Lansing.

Vygotsky, L. S. (1978). *Mind and society: The development of higher psychological processes.* Cambridge, MA: Harvard University Press.

Article 2

Social Ecology
Over Time and Space

R. B. Cairns and B. D. Cairns

This article documents the evolution of Bronfenbrenner's theories—first of human development and then of the ecology of human development. Robert and Beverly Cairns draw on Bronfenbrenner's doctoral dissertation to state their case for enlarging existing theories in the ecology of human development.

Social development applies not only to the individual but to the social organization of which he is a part. Variations occur not only in the social status of a particular person within the group, but also in the structure of the group itself—that is, in the frequency, strength, pattern, and basis of the interrelationships which bind the group together and give it distinctive character. Social status and structure are of course interdependent, but attention must be given to both of these variables if the process of social development is to be properly understood. (Bronfenbrenner, 1943, p. 363)

Source: Cairns, R. B., & Cairns, B. D. (1995). Social ecology over time and space. In P. Moen, G. H. Elder Jr., & K. Luscher (Eds.), *Examining lives in context: Perspectives on the ecology of human development* (pp. 397–421). Washington, DC: American Psychological Association. Copyright 1995 by the American Psychological Association. Reprinted with permission.

In lectures and writing, Urie Bronfenbrenner often identifies an overlooked paper, person, or idea to make insightful points about the present. By example, he reminds us that certain contributions are simply so insightful that they cannot be overlooked. If rediscovered, they demand to be cited with appropriate credit. In that spirit, it seems appropriate to begin by commenting on a remarkable series of articles that was first published 50 years ago (Bronfenbrenner, 1943, 1944a, 1944b). In his first scientific publications, Urie Bronfenbrenner succinctly expressed many of the key ideas basic to the development of modern social ecology.

The need for an integrated developmental science to understand social ontogeny has been recognized for over a century. The vision has become increasingly clear from the contributions of Baldwin (1897), Mead (1934), Bronfenbrenner (1979), and Magnusson (1988) in human social behavior, and Schneirla (1966) and Kuo (1967) in nonhuman comparative study. However, the pragmatics of the new science have not been as easily achieved as the vision. The methods that are required call for inventiveness, creativity, and an enormous investment in careful, laborious, and detailed analysis. It has been easier to adopt the vision than to invent the methods.

First it seems appropriate to take a second look at some of the ideas that were expressed 60 years ago and the technical advances that were achieved in the early work of Urie Bronfenbrenner.

At the beginning of the first article in the series, Bronfenbrenner (1943) specifies why the social development of individuals cannot be divorced from the social networks in which they are embedded. Virtually all contemporary discussions now acknowledge the integrative nature of social development and adopt the perspective that influences without and within simultaneously affect individual development. Bronfenbrenner's emphasis on the role of social ecology has helped change the face of modern social science. Yet even modern practitioners still have a way to go to catch up with the early science that the young Bronfenbrenner envisioned. There remain today serious gaps in the integration across levels. For the most part, investigators of communities and neighborhoods continue to live in different worlds than investigators of peer groups and social networks, and researchers of individual development still [1995] have a hard time reaching beyond the dyad and the family.

There is also the problem of time and timing. In the course of development, individuals inevitably grow, mature, and change. In the same time frame, changes occur in their societies, their communities, their social networks, their families, and their personal relationships. The secrets of social development require the researcher to track these simultaneous developmental changes in persons and social contexts and to determine the interrelations among them.

To quote from an article by Bronfenbrenner based on his doctoral dissertation:

> It will be noted that the questions are all phrased positively: that is, the children were not asked to name those whom they would dislike as companions. Despite the fact that they might contribute valuable information concerning the degree and character of social rejection, negative questions were avoided because of their possible effect, by calling attention to the less-favored children in each group of fostering discrimination and thus causing even more severe social maladjustment. (Bronfenbrenner, 1944a, p. 43)

In the results, we find 24 carefully framed generalizations, including 3 on the nature of social group status (e.g., a distinction between rejected and neglected children) and 4 on the structure of children's social groups (e.g., the nature of gender, age segregation, and group coherence). Among other things, Bronfenbrenner (1994a) concluded that the "classroom groups of older children show greater social solidarity than younger age groups," that in social groups the "sex cleavage becomes very pronounced" as children enter middle and late childhood, and [that] "all of the above developmental trends are interdependent" (p. 74). If this sounds familiar, it should be. This is virtually exactly what Maccoby (1960) and others (e.g., Cairns & Kroll, 1994; Cairns, Perrin, & Cairns, 1985) have observed in their work on the social groups of children.

To ensure that readers do not miss the point, Bronfenbrenner ended the article with the following summation:

> In sum, the proper evaluation of social status and structure requires the envisagement both of the individual and the group as developing organic units. Piecemeal analysis, fixed in time and space, of isolated aspects is insufficient and even misleading, for the elements of social status and structure are interdependent, organized into complex patterns, and subject both to random and lawful variation. (Bronfenbrenner, 1944a, p. 75)

On this score, it has been proposed that stability and continuity in social patterns arise because of the network of correlation between internal and external conditions. These correlations follow directly from the bidirectional influences between actions and the internal states that the actions help produce (Cairns & Cairns, 1994; Cairns, Gariepy, & Hood, 1990).

This line of reasoning seems consistent with and extends Bronfenbrenner's assertion that "piecemeal analysis, fixed in time and space, of

isolated aspects and attributes is insufficient and even misleading"
(Bronfenbrenner, 1944a, p. 75). We would add that it is insufficient
and even misleading because it leaves out the feedback that exists between
behavior and biology, between individuals and peers, and between parents
and their offspring. The work underscores that the concept of development should be extended to include developmental changes across
generations.

At first blush, this line of research and the results that have been
generated may seem to be distant from the major concerns of social ecology. It is true that they have been virtually lost in the space between contemporary sciences. But are the findings really so far removed from social
ecology? In this regard, we believe that they constitute one of the most
powerful and convincing cases for Bronfenbrenner's (1943) assertion that
"social development applies not only to the individual but to the social
organization of which he is part" (p. 363).

The following illustration concerns one of the intermediate
circles in the social ecology diagram, the sociometric group, to which
Bronfenbrenner (1944a) devoted his early paper. It is almost as if we
picked up where he left off and we had to begin with the same issues of
mathematics and statistics (Cairns, Gariepy, & Kindermann, 1990; Cairns
et al., 1985). The problems arise, as Bronfenbrenner (1943) identified,
when the research focus shifts the unit of developmental analysis from a
person to a group or a network. Curiously enough, despite clear recognition of the problem and guides to isolate its solution by Bronfenbrenner
(1943), the task has been attempted only rarely in recent developmental
and social studies. This holds despite the strong assumptions in the
contemporary social development literature on the effects of peer groups
and the power and stability of their influence. And where it has been
attempted, the focus has been on the stability of social status rather than
the stability of the actual social network and its structure.

Although Bronfenbrenner's early papers on methodology have been
virtually lost, the insights on social development reflected in them seem
to have gained hegemony in social development. This raises broader
questions: Why has empirical progress on basic issues of social development been so hard to achieve, and why has it been so rarely recognized,
once the hard-won gains have been made? It is one thing to adopt an
overarching framework; it is quite another to go beyond the rhetoric and
rigorously assess the logical implication of the orientation.

Few would now debate the assertion that it is folly to proceed with
piecemeal analysis that is fixed in time and space. Nevertheless, such
piecemeal, variable-oriented research remains dominant in our major

developmental journals. If anything, there seems to be less journal space given to integrative study in the 1990s than there was in the 1940s. To be sure, here are implicit and explicit pressures to report findings in terms of multivariate analyses (e.g., multivariate analysis of variance, multiple logistic regression, structural modeling equations [LISREL], and random effect models [hierarchical linear modeling; HLM]). The prevalence of these procedures implies that the problem of integration can be solved by statistical manipulation. That is a myth. The tough tasks of social developmental research must be addressed before analysis: in the research design, measurement, and conceptualization.

One other historical footnote is in order. In addressing the problem of how to measure intelligence, Binet and Henri (1895) argued that, even if one succeeded in splitting the mind into mental elements, one would not know how to put them back together. That insight and procedures it stimulated paved the way for the various families of intelligence or ability tests, arguably the most influential contribution of psychology to society in the twentieth century. An integrative approach is even more important for social development than for cognitive development, to understand the interdependence of events within and without the individual (Bronfenbrenner & Ceci, 1994; Cairns, Elder, & Costello, in press [1996]).

Both the society and the science should benefit from an enlarged vision of what can be accomplished within the next decade through intensive developmental study. Part of the vision should be to extend the methods and analyses that capture the integrated nature of social development. Appropriate procedures have already been established; they must now be vigorously exploited (Magnusson & Bergman, 1990b). A related goal should be to determine how these methods, and the ideas that give rise to them, can be used to promote health and prevent chaos in human societies. All this is to suggest that the original statement of Bronfenbrenner on social development (1943) was on target. The discipline needs to enlarge the vision, update the methods, and continue to work on the making of the science.

References

Baldwin, J. M. (1897). *Social and ethical interpretations in mental development: A study in social psychology.* New York: Macmillan.
Binet, A., & Henri, V. (1895). La psychologie individuelle. *L'annee psychologique, 2,* 411–465.

Bronfenbrenner, U. (1943). A constant frame of reference for sociometric research. Part I. *Sociometry, 6,* 363–397.

Bronfenbrenner, U. (1944a). A constant frame of reference for sociometric research: Part II. Experiment and inference. *Sociometry, 7,* 40–75.

Bronfenbrenner, U. (1944b). The graphic presentation of sociometric data. *Sociometry 7,* 283–289.

Bronfenbrenner, U. (1979). *The ecology of human development: Experiments by nature and design.* Cambridge, MA: Harvard University Press.

Bronfenbrenner, U., & Ceci, S. J. (1994). Nature-nurture reconceptualized: A bio-ecological model. *Psychological Review, 101,* 568–586.

Cairns, R. B., & Cairns, B. D. (1994). *Lifelines and risks: Pathways of youth in our time.* New York: Cambridge University Press.

Cairns, R. B., Elder, G. H., Jr., & Costello, E. J. (Eds.). (In press [1996]). *Developmental science* (Cambridge Studies in Social and Emotional Development). New York: Cambridge University Press.

Cairns, R. B., Gariepy, J. L., & Hood, K. E. (1990). Development, microevolution, and social behavior. *Psychological Review, 97,* 49–65.

Cairns, R. B., Gariepy, J. L., & Kindermann, T. (1990). *Identifying social clusters in natural settings.* Unpublished manuscript, University of North Carolina.

Cairns, R. B., & Kroll, A. B. (1994). A developmental perspective on gender differences and similarities. In M. L. Rutter, D. F. Hay, & S. Baron-Cohen (Eds.), *Developmental principles and clinical issues in psychology and psychiatry* (pp. 330–372). Oxford, UK: Blackwell Scientific Publishers.

Cairns, R. B., Perrin, J. E., & Cairns, B. D. (1985). Social structure and social cognition in early adolescence: Affiliative patterns. *Journal of Early Adolescence, 5,* 339–355.

Kuo, Z. Y. (1967). *The dynamics of behavioral development: An epigenetic view.* New York: Random House.

Maccoby, E. (1960). Gender and relationships: A developmental account. *American Psychologist, 46,* 513–520.

Magnusson, D. (1988). *Individual development from an interactional perspective.* Hillsdale, NJ: Lawrence Erlbaum.

Magnusson, D., & Bergman, L. R. (Eds.). (1990a). *Data quality in longitudinal research.* Cambridge, UK: Cambridge University Press.

Magnusson, D., & Bergman, L. R. (1990b). A pattern approach to the study of pathways from childhood to adulthood. In. L. N. Robins & M. Rutter (Eds.), *Straight and devious pathways from childhood to adulthood* (pp. 101–115). Cambridge, UK: Cambridge University Press.

Mead, G. H. (1934). *Mind, self, and society.* Chicago: Chicago University Press.

Schneirla, T. C. (1966). Behavioral development and comparative psychology. *Quarterly Review of Biology, 41,* 283–302.

Social Status, Structure, and Development in the Classroom Group

The roots of the ecology of human development can be found in this
excerpt, drawn from my 1942 doctoral dissertation.

Sociometric Technique

The emphasis of modern developmental theory on the socioemotional
aspects of human growth has imposed the necessity of devising techniques for evaluating the degree and character of social development. The
problem has been complicated by the fact that social development applies
not only to the individual but also to the social organization of which
he is a part. Variations occur not only in the social status of a particular
person within the group but also in the structure of the group itself—that
is, in the frequency, strength, pattern, and basis of the interrelationships
which bind the group together and give it distinctive character. Social
status and structure are of course interdependent, but attention must be
given to both of these variables if the process of social development is to
be properly understood.

Source: Bronfenbrenner, U. (1942). *Social status, structure, and development in the
classroom group*. Unpublished doctoral dissertation, University of Michigan.

One of the most ingenious devices for the study of social status and structure is the sociometric test. This technique permits the analysis of a person's position within the group; it also makes possible an analysis of the framework of the group organization—an identification of persons dominant in the group structure, of cliques, of cleavages, and of patterns of social attraction and repulsion.

It is to be expected that so revealing a technique would be widely accepted and would yield valuable results in the study of social phenomena—particularly in the investigation of social development as indicated by change in status and structure. Moreover, in the light of the emphasis upon the individual found in modern psychological and sociological thought, it is to be expected that the results obtained through sociometric research would be evaluated not only in terms of the technique itself but also in relation to other experimental and clinical data, with the aim of securing a better understanding of the human organism and its growth.

While it has been the writer's observation that neither of the expectations has been fully realized, the first is the one which receives major emphasis, for the conclusion was reached that among the principal obstacles to a more fruitful utilization of the sociometric method are certain technical inadequacies. It is the purpose of this paper to indicate the specific character of these inadequacies, to suggest means for overcoming them, and to apply the more refined techniques which have been developed in an illustrative and exploratory study.

Principles and Methods

Definition

The approach to social relationships adopted and developed in the present thesis is that outlined by Moreno (1934) in the monograph *Who Shall Survive?* In this volume, the technique and its theoretical bases and interpretations are treated collectively under the term *sociometry*. As defined by Moreno (1934), sociometry is "the mathematical study of psychological properties of populations, the experimental techniques of and the results obtained by application of quantitative methods" (p. 437). In view of discussions by Franz (1939), Moreno (1934, 1941), and Jennings (1941), the writer has been led to rephrase the original definition in somewhat more specific terms as follows: *Sociometry is a method for discovering, describing, and evaluating social status, structure, and development through estimating the degree of acceptance or rejection between individuals in groups.* The significance of this definition, its implications and applications, will become evident in succeeding chapters which present in effect a methodological biography and critique of sociometric research.

Conditions of Experiment

Purpose of the Experiment. It was pointed out earlier that, largely because of technical limitations, several of the broader problems arising in sociometric work have not as yet been systematically investigated. These problems include the longitudinal study of change in social status and structure and the comparison and evaluation of sociometric groups. It was further indicated that the organismic approach implies a reorientation and expansion of sociometric research. Calling for an interchange of whole and part, it demands that the treatment of the child as an item in sociometric study be replaced by the consideration of the sociometric result as an item in child study.

The investigations about to be described were undertaken with the above problems and approaches in mind. Since they deal with untried and extensive techniques and materials, the studies are necessarily illustrative and exploratory in character. Consequently, the experiments to be reported are significant not in terms of yielding conclusive results but rather in terms of defining problems, providing specific approaches for their solution, revealing pitfalls, eliminating blind alleys, illustrating the general scope and character of results that may be obtained, suggesting hypotheses, and delineating areas for subsequent intensive investigation. Specifically, an attempt was made in these experiments to pave the way for the longitudinal study of sociometric status, structure, and development in groups of varying size and for the analysis of results in the light of data from other fields both with regard to general trends and with reference to the individual as the final and most important clinical entity.

Subjects and Groups. A sociometric analysis was made of the entire population of the laboratory elementary school at the University of Michigan. This population included children from the nursery to the sixth-grade level, but inasmuch as the four upper grades had been combined into two classes, there were but six separate social groups in all: Nursery, Kindergarten, Grade I, Grade II, Grade III–IV, and Grade V–VI. The groups ranged in size from 14 to 33. The demands of the war had created greater family mobility in the university community so that withdrawals and new entrants were more frequent than they had been in previous years.

Conclusions

In the light of the discussion and evidence submitted in the course of this paper, certain generalizations appear warranted. The generalizations are of two general types: those pertaining to technique and those pertaining to experimental results.

Technique

Conclusions with regard to technique may be regarded as fairly well established. They include the following:

1. Social status, structure, and development may be studied effectively by means of refined mathematical techniques adapted for use in diverse sociometric situations.

2. The concept of deviation from chance expectancy provides a basis for deriving indices which may be used for the estimation and comparison of social status, of the degree of coherence within social groups, and of the extent of group cleavage on the basis of such factors as sex, age, race, nationality, or similar attributes.

3. Definition of sociometric status and structure in terms of deviation from chance expectancy (e.g., neglectees and stars) permits identification of trends otherwise obscured.

4. Certain of the techniques developed may be divested of their mathematical complexities and are thus adaptable for general use by teachers, psychologists, and social workers. Specifically, within established limits, raw sociometric scores may be legitimately utilized for the comparative and longitudinal study of individual status and group coherence.

Experimental Results

The generalizations derived from the experimental results are, for the most part, to be regarded as suggestive rather than final. They represent conclusions to be verified and principles to be taken into account in subsequent definitive research. The generalizations may be conveniently classified under the three major topics of the study: status, structure, and development.

Finally, taking into account all the experimental evidence, two principles emerge as paramount in the sociometric study of social status, structure, and development.

1. To be meaningful and valid, sociometric research must be accompanied by careful clinical observation; only thus may the full significance of sociometric results be known. This generalization applies equally to the study of individuals and groups.

2. The proper evaluation of social status and structure requires the envisagement of both the individual and the group as developing organic units. Piecemeal analysis, fixed in time and space, of isolated aspects and attributes is insufficient and even misleading, for the elements of social status and structure are interdependent, organized into complex patterns, and subject both to random and lawful variation.

References

Franz, J. G. (1939). Survey of sociometric technique. *Sociometry, 2,* 76–92.
Jennings, H. H. (1941). Sociometry and social theory. *American Sociological Review, 6,* 512–522.
Moreno, J. L. (1934). *Who shall survive? A new approach to the problem of human interrelations.* New York: Nervous and Mental Disease Publishing.
Moreno, J. L. (1941). *Foundations of sociometry* (Sociometry Monograph No. 4). Oxford, UK: Beacon House.

Article 4

The Social Ecology of Human Development

A Retrospective Conclusion

This article documents the dynamic evolving interactive effect between social ecology and the ecology of human development. The article evaluates studies [before 1973] of the role of social context in affecting specific processes of human development and investigations that did not explicitly address this relationship but contained relevant information.

M y topic is "the social ecology of human development." I speak to that topic from the peculiarly narrow perspective of a developmental psychologist. I say "peculiarly narrow" because from its beginnings less than a century ago the systematic psychological study of human development has been concerned primarily with process rather than with social content. More importantly, influenced by the comparative simplicity of the laboratory setting, investigators have typically employed an experimental model that is empirically limited in at least four major respects.

First, the system usually involves or at least considers only two persons, an experimenter and a child, usually referred to as a subject. Second, the process taking place is ordinarily conceived of as unidirectional. That is,

Source: Bronfenbrenner, U. (1973). The social ecology of human development: A retrospective conclusion. In F. Richardson (Ed.), *Brain and intelligence: The ecology of child development* (pp. 113–123). Hyattsville, MD: National Educational Press.

one examines the influence of the experimenter on the subject but not the reverse. Third, the experimenter is typically a stranger, usually a graduate student with no previous relationship with the child. And finally, and perhaps most importantly, the two-person system exists, or at least is treated as if it exists, in isolation from any other social system that could encompass or accompany it. These four features, so common to research practice, are hardly characteristic of the situations in which children actually develop. Thus, in family, preschool, play group, or classroom there are usually more than two people; the child also influences those who influence him; the other participants are typically not strangers but have enduring and diverse relationships and roles vis-à-vis the child; and finally, the behavior of all of these participants is profoundly affected by other social systems in which they have roles and responsibilities. It is my contention that this impoverished context in which our research has often been carried out places severe theoretical and practical limitations on what we can learn about the forces that affect human development or about the manner in which these forces can be structured and mobilized to enhance that process. Knowledge of what might be called the ecology of human development is especially essential for the design of programs intended to foster the child's cognitive emotional or social growth. Fortunately we are not completely without evidence in this sphere. Data are available from two sources.

First, although they are still a minority, there are a number of studies that have focused directly on the role of the social context in facilitating or impeding specific processes of human development. Second, and far more numerous, are investigations that did not explicitly select such factors for study but, sometimes quite accidentally, contained information that is relevant: for example, a study that required more than one experimenter or that involved persons who took different roles in relation to the child.

To turn to the task at hand, it is obvious that the optimal ecological situation for a child varies as a function of his developmental level. Accordingly, I propose to discuss the role of context in some detail at one level and in lesser detail at another. The first period is infancy, age zero to three for present purposes; and the second, early childhood, age four through preadolescence.

To illustrate the basis for developing generalizations, I begin with some concrete illustrations of the kinds of studies on which I have drawn. The first example is a 25-year-old study now well known but before 1965 seldom cited and looked at somewhat askance. I refer to Harold Skeel's research with two groups of mentally retarded, institutionalized children who constituted the experimental and control groups in an experiment he had initiated 30 years earlier (Skeels, 1966; Skeels & Dye, 1939; Skeels, Updegraff, Wellman, & Williams, 1938). When the children were three years of age, 13 of them were placed in the care of female inmates in a state institution for the mentally retarded, with each child being assigned to a different ward. A control group was allowed to remain in the original institutional environment, a children's orphanage. During the formal experiment period, which averaged a year and a half, the experimental group showed a gain in IQ of 28 points, from 64 to 92, whereas the control group dropped 26 points. Upon completion of the experiment, it became possible to place the institutionally mothered children in legal adoption. Thirty years later, all 13 children in the experimental group were found to be self-supporting; all but two had completed high school, with four having one or more years of college. In the control group, all were either dead or still institutionalized. There is a dramatic incident connected with this study. At the time Skeels was severely criticized by a leading child psychologist of the period, Florence Goodenough of the Institute of Child Welfare of the University of Minnesota. Although the fact is not recorded in Skeels's account, one of his mentally retarded "unadoptable" children ultimately received a master's degree, as noted below.

The question arises: What accounted for the dramatic gains? Skeels reports that the mentally retarded women in the institution spent a great deal of time with the children: playing, talking, and training them in every way. But these are not systematic data. More specific evidence of what might be going on comes from one of the few explicitly ecological studies that I have been able to find in the literature. I refer to the research by the Gewirtzes on the relation of the behavior of caretakers to behavior of children in three settings in Israel—in an institution, in a kibbutz, and in the family (Gewirtz & Gewirtz, 1969). The children were all six months of age. The authors made detailed systematic observations, on a time sampling basis, of the same two classes of behavior, vocalization and smiling, as manifested by both the infants and their caretakers. Although the Ns are small and there are no inferential statistics, the results are instructive.

The data reported are means for 11 waking hours of observation. The average number of vocalizations for caretakers in the institution was 83; in the kibbutz, the corresponding figure was 175. I might add parenthetically, for those who have the mistaken notion that the kibbutz is a place where children are not brought up by parents, that 81 percent of these adult vocalizations were by the child's own mother. In a similar vein, we carried out a study in 36 kibbutzim; the average amount of time that 12-year-old children reported having spent with one or the other or both of their parents was four and one-half hours every weekday and even more on the Sabbath and holidays.

In the Gewirtz study, the figure for vocalization to the youngest child in the family was 171. Now we come to an even more interesting question: What are the corresponding data for vocalizations by the children? They are, respectively, 307, 365, 377, and 503. Note the association between the two sets of numbers. The investigators provide another instructive statistic: this is the percentage of a child's vocalizations which occurred in an interactive sequence—the percentage that was associated with some utterance by an adult. Here are the percentages: 10, 20, 22, and 36. Again note the correlation with adult-initiated vocalization. In other words, the child's response is a function of the adult's response. These differences across settings are not very large, but, and this is the important fact, they are already apparent at six months. Finally, the differences for children are smaller than those for the adults. As data from a number of studies, including the Skeels study I just reported, indicate, the older the child (or, more accurately, the longer a child stays in the setting), the greater the setting differences become. In other words, there is magnification of differences over time. This is particularly notable in the data comparing the first child with later children.

The results on smiling are similar. The figures for the institution are again lowest for both adult and infant behavior. The single child gets and gives more smiles than the youngest child, but, interestingly enough, the kibbutz surpasses the family: the children there both get and give more smiles than those in family settings. Thus, while family and kibbutz manifest high levels of both vocalization and smiling, the kibbutz turns out to be primarily a smiling environment, while the family, especially for the single child, emerges as a vocalizing environment.

In summary, the results suggest that children become isomorphic with their social environment, their ecological setting, as a function of the interaction that takes place among the participants in that ecological setting. Many questions remain unanswered. For example, in the Gewirtz study, modality was held constant: vocalization by caretaker versus vocalization by child; smiling by caretaker versus smiling by child. Suppose you crossed modalities, what would happen then? Is reinforcement through one modality more powerful than through another? I know of no published research on this question, but one of my undergraduate students, Gloria Dragsten, reports some provocative observations. Working as a baby-sitter, she reinforced vocalization in three different ways. First, when the infant vocalized, she responded by a sound: "chicca, chicca, chicca." Second, she didn't make any sounds whatsoever but simply stuck out her tongue. And third, in order not to be seen or heard, she would get behind the child and tickle it from the back. In other words, touch, vision, and sound. Although her data were very limited, they nevertheless showed a consistent pattern: auditory reinforcement was clearly more effective than visual or tactual, at least for producing vocal responses.

The Gewirtz study and this modest follow-up would seem to suggest that it is the adult who determines behavior of the child, that infants are initially similar and become different as a function of exposure to different social environments. But this is not quite so. Consider a study by Karelitz, Fisichelle, Costa, Karelitz, and Rosenfeld (1964) which related infant crying during the first four to 10 days of life with Stanford Binet IQ at three years of age; the correlation was .45. Now, one doesn't put much faith in a correlation like that unless one finds support from other studies. In this instance, however, such support is at hand. It comes from a study by Moss (1967). Moss investigated interaction of mothers with their infants at two different age levels—three weeks and three months—and found striking differences in pattern. At three weeks, it was the infant who gave the process both its impetus and direction. At the core of the interaction was the infant's cry. In Moss's words,

> It is the infant's cry that is determining the maternal behavior. Mothers describe the cry as a signal that the infant needs attention and they often report their nurturant actions in response to the cry. Furthermore, the cry is a noxious and often painful stimulus that probably has biological utility for the infant, propelling the mother into action for her own comfort as well as out of concern for the infant. . . . Thus we are adopting the hypothesis that . . . the cry acts to instigate maternal intervention. (pp. 28–29)

By three months, however, the initiative has passed to the mother, paradoxically as a function of the infant's own activity.

> We propose that maternal behavior initially tends to be under the control of the stimulus and reinforcing conditions provided by the young infant. As the infant gets older, the mother, if she behaved contingently toward his signals, gradually acquires reinforcement value which in turn increases her efficacy in regulating infant behaviors. . . . Thus, at first the mother is shaped by the infant and this later facilitates her shaping the behavior of the infant. We would therefore say that the infant through his own temperament or signal system contributes to establishing the stimulus and reinforcement value eventually associated with the mother. According to this reasoning, the more irritable infants (who can be soothed) whose mothers respond in a contingent manner to their signals should become more amenable to the effects of social reinforcement and manifest a higher degree of attachment behavior. (pp. 29–30)

Notice what is going on. Here, as I see it, is the true importance, the true compelling power of genetic factors in psychological development. Genetically mediated differences in susceptibility and in behavior, often not of great magnitude initially, in fact determine what aspects of the environment can affect the child by determining the kinds of reinforcements that are offered to the child. Thus, in significant measure it is the infant who shapes his own environment. Notice that this most potent component, the actual shaping of the environment, can operate, at least at this early age level, only through the intervention of other people. In other words, this most important component requires and operates through a social ecology, indeed one that is highly specific in its structural and functional properties. For example, we may take a study by Sandler and Julia (1966) which compared the behavior of infants during the first 10 days of life in a rooming-in arrangement versus a nursery. They found that in the rooming-in situation the infants quieted much more readily; they were more responsive to attention.

In order to understand the implications of this finding for subsequent development, I call your attention to some interesting sex differences that emerged in Moss's research. Moss found that, from the very beginning at three weeks of age, female infants were more easily soothed and more responsive to maternal intervention than male infants. This implies that mothers receive more positive reinforcement from female infants than from male infants and, as Moss's data indicate, this in turn leads mothers to respond more contingently to female infants than to male infants, with the result that females become "more easily socialized." Again these are not isolated findings. James Garbarino (1973) has found at least half a dozen studies pointing in the same direction. In some instances where the data had not been analyzed separately in terms of sex, he did the analysis himself. Here is an example from the Karelitz study I mentioned earlier: the overall correlation between infant crying and IQ at age three was .45. Garbarino analyzed the data separately for female infants and male infants; the correlations were .54 versus .30. Contrary to folklore or to psychoanalysis (and the two nowadays are not easily distinguished), in this perspective it is not the female whose personality development is mysterious, but the male.

In any case, it is again clear that we are not dealing with a one-way process. It is interactive at two levels. First, it involves an interaction between genetically determined biological characteristics and environmental events. Second, such interplay becomes possible only through a social process in which not only does the adult, typically the mother, shape the behavior of the infant, but the infant also shapes the behavior of the adult. Indeed, it is the infant who gives the impetus to the process, in terms of not only energy but direction. This brings us to our next and final example—at least for the period of infancy—and one that brings us closer to implications for programs.

I refer to Frank Palmer's research (Palmer & Rees, 1969) on the effects of intervention with a sample of 180 two-year-old boys living in Harlem. The experimental groups were exposed to two treatment conditions labeled "concept training" and "discovery."

> Under both conditions, the child interacted with the instructor on a one-to-one basis, meeting with him for two one-hour sessions a week over an eight-month period. The children assigned to the concept training group were systematically taught concepts selected to increase their ability to make discriminations along dimensions of size, texture, position, form, quantity, etc.

The purpose of the other experimental condition, the discovery group, was to allow us to distinguish between effects due to interacting with adults on a one-to-one basis and playing with materials not normally available and effects due to the teaching of specific concepts. Thus, no attempt was made to teach concepts to the children in the discovery group. The same materials and toys used with the concept group were used with these children, but they were in a free play setting. The instructor was told to speak only if the child asked a question and to play with him as though they were in a typical nursery school. "In both conditions the child was provided with the opportunity for uninterrupted, mutual interaction with an adult in a situation providing increasingly complex stimuli requiring increasingly complex responses."

After eight months of training, both experimental groups outdid their controls. Moreover, children from a lower socioeconomic background in the experimental group outperformed the middle-class children in the control group, and the gains were retained when the groups were retested a year later. Finally, contrary to the investigators' expectations at the time of testing, immediately after the eight months of training, the discovery group emerged as superior to the concept training group on the Peabody Picture Vocabulary Test. The control group was superior on concept measures. There was no difference on other measures. Testing one and two years after the program ended saw all differences between training and discovery washed out, although both groups remained superior to the nonparticipating control. Palmer and Rees offer the following interpretation of this result:

> It appears that what is taught is not as important as the condition under which it is taught; specifically, the adult-child, one-to-one relationship. . . . Any well-conceived instructor training program may have equally beneficial

effects provided training is introduced early enough in the child's life and there is a systematic, uninterrupted relationship between instructor and child over an extended period of time.

In this writer's view, however, this conclusion beclouds the critical difference between the two groups. According to the investigators' own statements, children in both groups experienced an uninterrupted one-to-one relationship. The crucial difference between them had to do with the fact that in the concept training group the initiative lay overwhelmingly with the instructor, whereas in the discovery group the instructor could be responsive to the child. In other words, the discovery treatment permitted and encouraged a two-way process in which the adult and the child could reinforce each other, imitate each other, and develop a mutual attachment which in turn enhanced their influence on each other's behavior.

We are now in a position to summarize our conclusions in the form of a single integrating principle: In the early years of life, *the psychological development of the child is enhanced through his involvement in progressively more complex, enduring patterns of reciprocal contingent interaction with persons with whom he has established a mutual and enduring emotional attachment.*

Before proceeding to a second major principle, it is important to make explicit one of the implications of the foregoing principle at a more down-to-earth level. The principle, it will be observed, makes rather exacting demands on the adult participants. Anyone who proposes to provide the child with the specified conditions had better realize what he is getting into. In this connection, the author is reminded of a reply made by a Soviet colleague to the question of why the Russians were discontinuing, as they are, their planned expansion of boarding institutions for the care and education of children. His answer: "You can't pay a woman to do what a mother will do for free."

To make the same point more explicitly, the only person who will be willing to do all the things that need to be done in order to foster the development of a young child is likely to be someone who has an irrational attachment to that child. There are of course other less pejorative terms for "irrational attachment," the most common one being "love."

But in a scientific paper, one should eschew subjective terms. Accordingly, we shall remain operational and speak not of love but of its functional manifestation in adult-infant interaction, namely, the presence of a reciprocal system involving reinforcement, modeling, and mutual attachment. Under what kinds of conditions is such a system most likely to develop? There are two investigations that shed some light on this issue. The first is a comparative study of maternal behavior and infant development in two types of family structures, referred to as *monomatric* and *polymatric* (Caldwell et al., 1963). In the former, the baby was cared for by only one person—his mother; in the latter, there was more than one mother figure available to the child, such as a maternal grandmother, aunt, or older sister. The sample was drawn from mothers attending a prenatal clinic operated by a city health department. The investigators used a variety of methods to study mother-infant interaction, including observations and developmental scales. By the time the infants were six months of age, there were marked differences in the behavior of the mothers in the two types of family structure, and some differences were greater for the infants than for their mothers. The results of the study are summarized by the authors as follows:

> The infant whose early social experiences are monitored principally by one female caretaker finds it somewhat easier to learn to relate to other people, is slightly more comfortable and active in strange and possibly frightening surroundings, and exhibits more positive affect in interactive sequences with his mother. (p. 658)

Through an analysis of interview data obtained from mothers before their babies were born, the investigators established differences in the personality characteristics of mothers who were later to provide polymatric versus monomatric environments for their children, with others in the former group being rated as more hostile, dominant, and dependent in their interpersonal relations.

The impact of situational and structural factors on maternal care is even more explicitly demonstrated in the previously cited studies of Skeels and the Gewirtzes.

We are now in a position to state a second major principle regarding the conditions which foster human development in the early years. We have already noted the critical role played by the child's involvement in a reciprocal system of interaction and attachment. We can now affirm that *the extent to which such a reciprocal system can be developed and maintained depends on the degree to which other encompassing and accompanying social structures provide the place, time, example, and reinforcement to the system and its participants.*

This second principle carries powerful implications for the development of programs and public policy affecting the welfare of young children. But before considering these implications, we do well to examine how the conditions necessary for the child's development change as he becomes older. So far, all the evidence we have examined underscores the importance of the mother-child relationship. What about fathers? Is there any evidence that two parents are better than one?

Indirect evidence bearing on this issue comes from an analysis my students and I have been carrying out on data from a seemingly irrelevant source: experiments carried out with preschool children in the laboratory and not involving parents at all. In examining this large body of data, we were concerned, not with the problem pursued by the original investigator, but with a seemingly incidental matter: Who were the experimenters in the study, and what difference did this make to the performance of the children? Although the analysis is not yet complete, several trends are beginning to emerge:

1. Whatever the purpose of the experiment (learning, discrimination, retention, persistence, etc.), children tend to perform better when there are two experimenters present than when there is one.

2. Performance is enhanced if one of these two persons functions as a model (that is, he provides an example of the behavior to be engaged in by the child) and the second acts as a reinforcer (that is, he in some way rewards the child for desired performance; such reward may be nothing more than a nod, smile, or "uh-huh").

3. The child's performance is likely to be somewhat better when the model is of the same sex as the child and the reinforcer is of the opposite sex.

4. The results are more effective when the reinforcer reinforces not only the child but the model who is exhibiting the desired behavior.

Where does the child find himself in a situation in which he is exposed to an adult model of the same sex and an adult reinforcer of the opposite sex who reinforces not only the child but the same-sex model?

Additional evidence comes from direct studies of the family itself. For example, a growing body of research on the effects of father absence, both complete and temporary, reveals deleterious effects on the psychological development of the child. Absence is especially critical during the preschool years, affects boys more than girls, and operates not only directly on the child but indirectly by influencing the behavior of the mother. Children from father-absent homes, at least initially, are more submissive, dependent, effeminate, and susceptible to group influence, with the latter course of development being determined by the character of the group in which the child finds himself. Thus in lower-class families, where father absence is particularly common, the initially passive and dependent boy readily transfers his attachment to the gang, where, to earn and keep his place, he must demonstrate his toughness and aggressiveness (Bronfenbrenner, 1967).

Similar but not so extreme effects are likely to occur in homes in which the father is present but plays a subordinate role. In a study of the relation between parental role structure and child's behavior (Bronfenbrenner, 1961a, 1961b), it was found that matriarchal families, in which primarily the mother held the power of decision, tended to produce children who "do not take initiative" and "look to others for direction in decision." Similar results were obtained for patriarchal families. In contrast, responsibility and leadership tended to be maximized in a differentiated family structure in which both parents took active but somewhat differing roles in relation to the child. Specifically, children tended to be more responsible in families in which the father was the principal companion and disciplinarian for the boy, and the mother for the girl.

In short, a three-person model including two adults of opposite sex appears to be more effective for socialization than a two-person, mother-child model. Although there is a need for additional evidence, it appears likely that, in the beginning, the father functions primarily as a source of support and stand-in for the mother, who provides the primary dependency relationship so essential for the child's further development. But already in the preschool years, the father exerts an important direct influence on the development of the young child, especially when he is a boy.

The fact that the structure most conducive to a child's development turns out to be the family is hardly surprising. The family is, after all, the product of a million years of evolution and should therefore have some survival value for the species. But the family is not all-determining.

Let me just give you one example which came as a surprise to me. One of our doctoral students, Michael Siman (1973), is just completing a thesis in which he did something that, so far as I know, has never been done before. Working with a large sample of teenagers (ages 12 to 17), most of them from middle- and lower-middle-class homes in New York City, he went to a great deal of trouble to identify and study the actual peer groups in which these adolescents spend so much of their time. There were 41 such peer groups in all. Siman was interested in determining the relative influence of parents versus peers on the behavior of the teenager. Three classes of behavior were studied:

1. *Socially constructive activities* such as taking part in sports, helping someone who needs help, telling the truth, and doing useful work for the neighborhood or community without pay

2. *Neutral activities* such as listening to records and spending time with the family

3. *Antisocial activities* such as "playing hooky," "doing something illegal," and hurting people

Siman also obtained information on the extent to which each teenager perceived these activities to be approved or disapproved by his parents and by the members of his peer group. The results are instructive. In the case of boys, for example, he finds that for all three classes of behavior, peers are substantially more influential than parents. In fact, in most cases, once the attitudes of the peer group are taken into account, the attitudes of the parents make no difference whatsoever. The only exceptions are in the area of constructive behavior, where the parent does have some secondary influence in addition to the peer group. But in the neutral and especially the antisocial sphere, the peer group is all-determining. When it comes to such behaviors as doing something illegal, smoking, or aggression, once the attitude of the peer group is taken into account, the parents' disapproval carries no weight.

What we are seeing here, of course, are the *roots of alienation* and its milder consequences. The more serious manifestations are reflected in the rising rates of youthful drug abuse, delinquency, and violence documented in charts and tables specially prepared for the White House Conference on Children (*Profiles of Children,* 1970, pp. 78, 79, 108, 179, 180). According to these data the proportion of youngsters between the ages of 10 and 18 arrested for drug abuse doubled between 1964 and 1968; since 1963, juvenile delinquency has been increasing at a faster rate than the juvenile population; over half the crimes involve vandalism, theft, or breaking and entry; and if the present trends continue, one out of every nine youngsters will appear in juvenile court before age 18. These figures index only detected and prosecuted offenses. How high must they run before we acknowledge that they reflect deep and pervasive problems in the treatment of children and youth in our society?

What accounts for the growing alienation of children and youth in American society? Why is it that the parents have so little influence? There are those who are quick to put the blame on the parents themselves, charging them with willful neglect and inadequate discipline. But to take this view is to disregard the social context in which families live and thereby to do injustice to parents as human beings. Although there is no systematic evidence on the question, there are grounds for believing that parents today, far from not caring about their children, are more worried about them than they have ever been in the course of recent history. The problem, as indicated by Siman's data, is that many parents have become powerless as forces in the lives of their children. The crux of the matter is this: parents aren't effective because the ecological situation doesn't permit them to be. The ecological settings in which parents and others concerned with children live in our society are such that there is no time, place, example, or reinforcement for interaction with children. We live in an age-segregated society in which children and adults lead separate lives. This hard fact carries with it an important implication: for programs to be effective, they must break down these age barriers. We have to put people back into programs. This requirement applies to day care; it applies to the schools that are becoming stockades; it applies to every place where children are found in American society.

References

Bronfenbrenner, U. (1961a). The changing American child: A speculative analysis. *Merrill-Palmer Quarterly, 7*, 73–84.

Bronfenbrenner, U. (1961b). Toward a theoretical model for the analysis of child relationship in the social context. In J. C. Glidewell (Ed.), *Parental attitudes and child behavior* (pp. 96–109). Springfield, IL: Charles C Thomas.

Bronfenbrenner, U. (1967). The psychological costs of quality and equality in education. *Child Development, 38*, 909–925.

Caldwell, B. M., Hersher, L., Lipton, E. L., Richmond, J. B., Stern, G. A., Eddy, E., Drachman, R., & Rothman, A. (1963). Mother-infant interaction in mono-matric and polymatric families. *American Journal of Orthopsychiatry, 33*, 653–664.

Garbarino, J. (1973). *The impact of anticipated reward upon cross-age tutoring.* Unpublished doctoral dissertation, Cornell University.

Gewirtz, H. B., & Gewirtz, J. L. (1969). Caretaking settings, background events and behavior differences in four Israeli childrearing environments: Some preliminary trends. In B. M. Foss (Ed.), *Determinants of behavior* (Vol. 4, pp. 229–295). London: Methuen.

Karelitz, S., Fisichelle, V. R., Costa, J., Karelitz, R., & Rosenfeld, L. (1964). Relation of crying activity in early infancy to speech and intellectual development at age three. *Child Development, 35*(3), 769–777.

Moss, H. A. (1967). Sex, age, and state as determinants of mother-infant interaction. *Merrill-Palmer Quarterly, 13*(1), 19–36.

Palmer, F. H., & Rees, N. H. (1969, March 27). *Concept training in two-year olds: Procedure and results.* Paper presented at the biennial meeting of the Society for Research in Child Development, Santa Monica, CA.

Sandler, L. W., & Julia, H. (1966). Continuous interactional monitoring in the neonate. *Psychosometric Medicine, 28,* 822–835.

Siman, M. A. (1973). *Peer group influences during adolescence: A study of 41 naturally existing friendship groups.* Unpublished doctoral dissertation, Cornell University.

Skeels, H. M. (1966). Adult status of children with contrasting early life experiences. *Monographs of the Society for Research in Child Development, 31,* Serial #105.

Skeels, H. M., & Dye, H. B. (1939). A study of the effects of differential stimulation on mentally retarded children. *Proceedings and Addresses of the American Association on Mental Deficiency, 44,* 114–136.

Skeels, H. M., Updegraff, R., Wellman, B. L., & Williams, H. M. (1938). *A study of environmental stimulation: An orphanage pre-school project* (University of Iowa Studies in Child Welfare, Vol. 15, No. 4). Iowa City: University of Iowa.

White House Conference on Children. (1970). *Profiles of children.* Washington, DC: Government Printing Office.

Article 5

Lewinian Space and Ecological Substance

Throughout my writing, but especially in this article, I acknowledge my great debt to Kurt Lewin. Lewin became one of my mentors shortly after I had completed my PhD, in 1942, while I was still in my 20s.

I am grateful to you, my colleagues, for giving me an opportunity to acknowledge, at least in small part, an intellectual debt of considerable size and of long standing to Kurt Lewin. As we so often do with a generous benefactor, while making a token repayment on the principal, I shall on the very same occasion be increasing my indebtedness by giving new promissory notes. My purpose in borrowing on Lewin's rich intellectual capital is to finance some additions of my own to his brilliantly conceived theoretical structures—additions, incidentally, that Lewin himself might well have viewed as incompatible with his original designs.

Perhaps you, too, will doubt the soundness of the investment, and on more compelling grounds. After all, Lewinian theory does not exactly dominate today's [1977] psychological scene. And even when Lewin was alive, his ideas were more divergent than mainstream.[1]

Source: Bronfenbrenner, U. (1977, August 26). *Lewinian space and ecological substance*. Acceptance speech on receiving the 1977 Kurt Lewin Memorial Award from the Society for the Psychological Study of Social Issues, American Psychological Association, San Francisco. Published in Bronfenbrenner, U. (1978). Lewinian space and ecological substance. *Journal of Social Issues, 33*(4), 199–212. Copyright © 1978. Reprinted with permission of Blackwell Publishers.

This brings me to my first major thesis—that Lewin was ahead of his time, that only now are we in a position to appreciate the importance, and indeed the necessity, of his mode of thought for advancing the growth of basic science and social policy relating to human behavior and development. In short, I am proposing that Lewinian theory is a set of ideas whose time has come.

The reasons why Lewinian modes of thought now become essential to our science will, I trust, become apparent as I develop my argument. But first, we must reacquaint ourselves briefly with the distinctive properties of Lewin's field-theoretical approach.

I first encountered Lewin's ideas as a Cornell undergraduate, majoring in psychology in the mid-1930s. In that fortress of Titchenorian structuralism, it took a renegade faculty member with a European degree (and we have fortunately always had more than our share of these at Cornell) to suggest to an uncouth sophomore that he read and review the only two chapters by Europeans in the 1931 Murchison *Handbook of Child Psychology*, one by Piaget (1931) and the other by Lewin (1931). I still have a copy of the paper I wrote. It concluded summarily that both were fuzzy thinkers unable to operationalize their ideas, which were basically unscientific in the first place. In the margin was a pencil note by my mentor, Professor Frank S. Freeman.[2]

Freeman wrote: "You judge too quickly; someday you may change your mind." I did change my mind; especially a few years after I had graduated, when I came to know Kurt Lewin in person. We met under somewhat unorthodox circumstances, which are not without historical interest. When people ask me where I got my graduate training, I am sometimes tempted to tell the truth, that I received almost all of it after I had finished my doctoral degree. The day after I got my PhD, I became a private in the U.S. Army and, after a series of more conventional assignments, ended up in a most unconventional war setting—Station S, located in an allegedly secret hideout outside of Washington, D.C., where the Office of Strategic Services operated an assessment center for evaluating candidates for secret service duty overseas. The "assessors" were a remarkable group, selected and directed by Professor Henry A. Murray of Harvard University. They included, among others, several world-class scientists (e.g., Edward C. Tolman, David Levy, Theodore Newcomb) and one outstanding developmental scientist who had escaped from Hitler's Germany. His name was Kurt Lewin. In addition, fortunately for me, there were also four or five young whippersnappers—enlisted men who happened to have PhDs in psychology and were transferred from their regular military units, put into civilian clothes, and assigned to assist the senior professionals. But those of you who knew any of our "bosses" will quickly recognize that they were neither willing nor able to keep us in our place. They welcomed us as colleagues, a great good fortune for us.

We were on 24-hour duty, with weekends off every two weeks. In the late evening, after our assessment duties were over, there were two major voluntary activities for which we most often got together: *singing* and *thinking out loud about human behavior and development*. Lewin, of course, took the lead in both. He knew songs from all over the world in every language, and he sang them with gusto and affection. But beneath the variety, there was also a common theme. For him the songs were always an expression of human relations at the personal, interpersonal, group, and cultural level. He was a lover of diversity in human groups, in this instance as reflected in their songs. And it was this same passion that reappeared at the intellectual level in our animated discussions far into the night. There was an interesting quality in Lewin's line of thought about human behavior: whenever he spoke, it was always to place behavior in *context*—situational, interpersonal, sociological, cultural, historical—and above all, *theoretical*.

For Lewin, theory—and highly abstract theory at that—was what psychology was all about. That is where psychology began and where it always ended. But in between, Lewin invariably came down to earth. Witness his classic reminder: "There is nothing so practical as a good theory."

Moreover Lewin, constantly reminded, lest we be misled, that the space is not physical but *psychological*—consisting of the environment not as it exists in the so-called objective world (where, for us, practical matters are usually thought to reside) but in the mind of the person, in his or her *phenomenological field*—including, as especially significant, the world of imagination, fantasy, and unreality.

Lewin's equation of the psychological with the subjective of course flew in the face of the most sacred tenets of the dominant psychological theory of that time: American behaviorism. Even more heretical from an American perspective was his treatment of motivational forces as emanating not from within the organism but from the environment. Objects, activities, and, especially, other people sent out lines of force, valences and vectors that attracted and repelled, thus steering the behavior of the person.

Where, then, is the person, and what is his or her nature? The first part of this question is more easily answered than the second. Within "the psychological field," Lewin posited the existence of a phenomenological entity identified as the "self." The self consists of so-called "psychical systems," which appear to be somehow isomorphic with the structure of the environment, but, as I have documented elsewhere (Bronfenbrenner, 1951), the nature and origin of this isomorphism remain somewhat vague.

Yet, according to Lewin's own maxim, this is a theory that presumably provides us our surest guide for dealing with practical problems—a theory, mind you, in which the perceived is viewed as more important than the actual, the unreal as more valid than the real, where the motivation that steers the person's behavior inheres in external objects, activities, persons, and groups, and, to the utter confounding of the practical doer, where the content of all these complicated structures remains unspecified.

To understand Lewin's position, we need to see our discipline in historical perspective. At the time of its beginnings, psychology used to be defined as the science of the mind; only later did it become, especially in the United States, the science of behavior. If we take Lewin seriously, we must understand him as telling us to move back in the direction of the original "mental" conception but still leave behavior in the model. This is what he means in urging us to investigate the environment and human activity as they appear in the minds of people. In short, we may view Lewin as proposing a synthesis of the two traditional conceptions of our science.

It is from this broadened conception that our series of paradoxes can be resolved. Let us consider them one by one.

The reason why Lewin does not yet specify the content of the psychological field is that this psychological terrain has still to be explored. It is a scientific task still to be undertaken, and this is where the future of psychology lies. Until substantive data about the nature of the perceived environment begin to become available, we can have only a theory of form and not of content.

We do need, however, to prepare ourselves for investigating the unknown; we need to know where to look as we begin our explorations so that the critical features of the terrain do not elude our gaze. Among the phenomena we must be prepared to encounter are the motivational properties inhering in perceived objects, activities, persons, and events, including those in the domains of unreality. Above all, we must be prepared to see a complex of differentiated regions, some embedded in others, some interconnected, others isolated, but all interacting to steer the behavior and development of the person.

What can all this possibly mean in concrete terms? Does Lewin provide us with any tangible, down-to-earth examples? Does he ever! He does it all the time, from the very beginning, from the very first paper he ever wrote. Its title was "Kriegslandschaft" ("War Landscape"), published at the end of the First World War, after he had spent several years in the army, most of it in the front lines, where he had been wounded in combat. The article, which appeared in the *Zeitschrift für Angewandte Psychologie* (Lewin, 1917), is a marvelous prefiguring of all his basic theoretical concepts. In this extraordinary paper, Lewin describes how the perceived reality changes as one moves nearer to the battlefront. What first appears as a lovely bucolic scene of farmhouses, fields, and wooded areas is gradually transformed. The forested hilltop becomes an observation post, its sheltered side, the location for a gunning emplacement. An unexposed hollow is seen as a probable battalion aid station. Aspects of the natural landscape that were a delight only a few kilometers back are now perceived as ominous: the frightening defile, the camouflage of trees, the hill that hides the unseen enemy, the invisible objective to be taken, the place and time of security after the fray—features of the environment that threaten, beckon, reassure, and steer one's course across a terrain objectively undistinguishable from scenes only a short distance behind the front.

Implementation of these theoretical ideas in actual research is being carried out in a major project on the comparative ecology of human development, being pursued jointly with colleagues in four modern industrialized societies—Britain, Israel, Sweden, and West Germany. The project focuses on the impact of formal and informal support systems on family functioning and the development of the child and is supported by grants from both public and private agencies.

Present circumstances permit only the briefest outline of the nature of this theoretical and empirical work. In the former sphere, consistent with Lewin's topological thinking, the ecological environment is seen as a series of nested and interconnected structures. The innermost of these, referred to as the *microsystem*, is the one most familiar to psychologists. Indeed, most of Lewin's early theorizing and experimentation was concentrated in this domain. But as might be expected, he looked at it from what is still a somewhat unorthodox perspective. For him, there were two critical features of the immediate situation. The first was the concept of *Tätigkeit*, or activity. An activity was distinguished from an act, such as a movement or an utterance, in being *molar* rather than *molecular*—an ongoing process characterized by intention and possessing a momentum of its own, so that the person is captured by a demand for closure. Consistent with this element of intention, a dominant feature of an activity is the perception of a goal and movement toward the goal.

The second feature of the immediate situation that is especially salient in Lewin's theory is the existence *of connections between people in the setting*. Moreover, these interconnections are formulated in terms *not so much of interpersonal feelings as of the relations of the various parties toward each other as members of a group engaged in common, complementary, or relatively independent tasks.*

The next level of the ecological environment is the *mesosystem*, which comprises the relations among two or more settings in which the developing person becomes an active participant. For instance, the mesosystem for an American 12-year-old would typically include connections between home, school, and neighborhood peer group. *In sum, a mesosystem is a system of microsystems.*

These possible interactions are of several types. The most basic is what we have called the *ecological transition*: that is, the move by the developing person into a new and different ecological context. Examples include entering a day care center, moving from preschool to school, going to camp, graduating, finding one's first job, changing jobs, marrying, taking vacations, traveling, moving, changing careers, emigrating, or, to return to the more universal, going to the hospital, coming home again, returning to work. We suggest that each such transition has developmental consequences that involve the person in new activities and types of social structure. Moreover, from the point of view of research design, every transition is in effect a ready-made experiment of nature with a built-in, before-after design.

The next level in our nested structure of the ecological environment is the *exosystem*, defined as a setting that does not itself contain a developing person but in which events occur that affect the setting containing the person. For example, for a school-age child in America, exosystems might include the parents' workplace, the school attended by an older sibling, the parents' network of friends, a teacher's home life, and activities of the local school board. Exosystems are important in two ways. First, while not containing the developing person, they may involve "significant others" in that person's life. For example, data from one of our pilot studies indicate that, after finances, the area of greatest stress experienced by parents in caring for and bringing up a child is "conditions at work."

But active involvement of people from the child's own world in other settings is not the only source of exosystem influence. Any social institution that makes decisions that ultimately affect conditions of family life can function as an exosystem. In some instances, the causal chain can be quite convoluted. A recent example, brought to my attention by colleagues, involved an unintended consequence of lowering the maximum income level for family eligibility to enroll a child in federally sponsored day care. The immediate result was that many mothers who could no longer get free day care for their children had to quit work in order to stay home and care for the child themselves. At a recent conference, staff members from agencies monitoring child abuse reported that placing mothers in this situation had led them to mistreat their children. While the evidence remains anecdotal, the possibility of such a ricochet effect cannot be ruled out.

Finally, the outermost ring of the ecological environment is represented by the *macrosystem*, which encompasses the overarching patterns of stability, at the level of the subculture or the culture as a whole, in forms of social organization and associated belief systems and lifestyles. Such patterns result in similarities among the lower-order systems to which particular groups of persons are exposed. For example, within a given culture, one school classroom looks and functions much like another. It is as if all had been constructed from the same blueprint. Similarly, from city to city within a given society, one urban slum resembles another, as do neighborhoods where young executives live or the Italian section of town. And associated with each of these subcultures are characteristic patterns of ideology and lifestyles that are reflected in goals and practices of socialization. As a result, the everyday experiences of children from a given socioeconomic, ethnic, or religious group tend to be similar.

Thus one reason why children from one or another subcultural group may develop in a particular way is to be found in the character of the micro-, meso-, and exosystems that are operative for that particular subculture. Such a formulation carries with it important implications for both research and public policy. On the first count, it argues against the scientific utility of the prevailing pattern of studying ethnic and cultural differences by comparing developmental outcomes, with little or no attention to the nature of the ecological context in which these outcomes occur or the processes through which they are achieved. Instead, we should be focusing our scientific work on a systematic effort to describe the ecological environment in which a given cultural group finds itself—in particular, the way in which exo- and mesosystem influences direct and delimit the kinds of activities and relations that are possible to children and those responsible for their care. Once such analyses are carried out, instead of regarding social class, ethnicity, and religion as attributes of the person, we shall come to see them for what they are, namely, structured aspects of the environment that function to enhance or inhibit the processes of making human beings human.

The foregoing considerations point to a second and even more powerful scientific strategy that, borrowing a term from Soviet psychologists, I have referred to as a *transforming experiment*. A transforming experiment is one that calls into question, or actively alters, practices or beliefs that are part of the prevailing macrosystem in which the research subjects live. Experiments of this kind are essential for two purposes: first, to understand the nature, strengths, and weaknesses of existing structures and strategies of socialization; second, and far more important, to modify these forms and practices in ways that will enhance cognitive developmental processes.

Those of you who may know Kurt Lewin's work will recognize in this formulation his own, much misunderstood concept of "action research." There are those who have looked upon action research as a betrayal of the true scientific faith, a renunciation of research in favor of reform. But in doing so, the critics have misjudged the scientific power of Lewin's dynamic theory. As my first mentor in graduate school, Walter F. Dearborn, once put it: "Bronfenbrenner, if you want to understand something, try to change it." Or, to reverse the classical Lewinian maxim: "There is nothing like the practical to build a good theory."[3]

Notes

1. There is yet another and, for me, more compelling ground for acquainting you with Kurt Lewin's early formulation. Kurt Lewin's unprecedented formulations provided both the inspiration and foundation for what was to become the bioecological theory of human development (see Bronfenbrenner, 2001).

2. Freeman's book on individual differences (1934) was also ahead of its time, anticipating by almost 40 years today's socioculturally sophisticated rebuttals to the simplistic hereditarian arguments of Jensen and his academic compatriots.

3. These remarkably insightful early theoretical formulations bearing directly on this subject were published first in Germany (Lewin, 1917) and then in subsequent English translations (Lewin, 1931, 1935). Their content is summarized, justifiably at some length, in Article 8 of this book ("Interacting Systems of Human Development. Research Paradigms: Present and Future").

References

Bronfenbrenner, U. (1951). Toward an integrated theory of personality. In R. R. Blake & G. V. Ramsey (Eds.), *Perception: An approach to personality* (pp. 206–257). New York: Ronald.

Bronfenbrenner, U. (2001). The bioecological theory of human development. In N. J. Smelser & P. B. Baltes (Eds.), *International encyclopedia of the social and behavioral sciences* (Vol. 10, pp. 6963–6970). St. Louis, MO: Elsevier Science.

Freeman, F. S. (1934). *Individual differences.* New York: Holt.

Lewin, K. L. (1917). Kriegslandschaft. *Zeitschrift für Angewandte Psychologie, 12*, 440–447.

Lewin, K. L. (1931). Environmental forces in child behavior and development. In C. Murchison (Ed.), *A handbook of child psychology* (94–127). Worcester, MA: Clark University Press.

Lewin, K. L. (1935). *A dynamic theory of personality.* New York: McGraw-Hill.

Piaget, J. (1931). Children philosophies. In C. Murchison (Ed.), *A handbook of child psychology* (377–391). Worcester, MA: Clark University Press.

Article 6

A Future Perspective

Although the material that follows was published in 1979, almost a decade before the article "Interacting Systems in Human Development" (Article 8), much of its content deals with research designs more complex than those presented in Article 8. The excerpts that follow illustrate the purposes, structures, and applications of these research designs and the findings that they generate.

I n this volume, I offer a new theoretical perspective for research in human development. The perspective is new in its conception of the developing person, of the environment, and especially of the evolving interaction between the two. Thus development is defined in this work as a lasting change in the way in which a person perceives and deals with his or her environment. [For this reason, it is necessary at the outset to give an indication of the somewhat unorthodox concept of the environment presented in this volume.] Rather than begin with a formal exposition, I shall first introduce this concept by some concrete examples.

The ecological environment is conceived as a set of nested structures, each inside the next like a set of Russian dolls. At the innermost level is the immediate setting containing the developing person. This can be the home, the classroom, or—as often happens for research purposes—the

Source: Bronfenbrenner, U. (1979). *The ecology of human development: Experiments by nature and design* (pp. 3–13). Cambridge, MA: Harvard University Press. Copyright © 1979 by the President and Fellows of Harvard College. Reprinted by permission of the publishers.

laboratory or the testing room. So far we appear to be on familiar ground. The next step, however, already leads us off the beaten track, for it requires looking beyond single settings to the relations between them. I shall argue that such interconnections can be as decisive for development as events taking place within a given setting. A child's ability to learn to read in the primary grades may depend no less on how the child is taught than on the existence and nature of the ties between the school and the home.

The third level of the ecological environment takes us yet farther afield and evokes a hypothesis that the person's development is profoundly affected by events occurring in settings in which the person is not even present. I shall examine data suggesting that among the most powerful influences affecting the development of young children in modern industrialized societies are the conditions of parental employment.

Finally, there is a striking phenomenon pertaining to settings at all three levels of the ecological environment outlined above: within any culture or subculture, settings of a given kind—such as homes, streets, or offices—tend to be very much alike, whereas between cultures they are distinctly different. It is as if within each society or subculture there existed a blueprint for the organization of every type of setting. Furthermore, the blueprint can be changed, with the result that the structure of the settings in a society can become markedly altered and produce corresponding changes in behavior and development. In another case, a severe economic crisis occurring in a society is seen to have positive or negative impact on the subsequent development of children throughout the life span, depending on the age of the child at the time that the family suffered financial duress (Elder, 1974).

The detection of such wide-ranging developmental influences becomes possible only if one employs a theoretical model that permits them to be observed. Moreover, because such findings can have important implications both for science and for public policy, it is especially important that the theoretical model be methodologically rigorous, providing checks for validity and permitting the emergence of results contrary to the investigator's original hypotheses. The present volume represents an attempt to define the basic parameters of a theoretical model that meets these substantive and methodological requirements. The work also seeks to demonstrate the scientific utility of the ecological model for illuminating the findings of previous studies and for formulating new research problems and designs.

The environment as conceived in the proposed schema differs from earlier formulations not only in scope but also in content and structure. On the first count, the ecological orientation takes seriously and translates into operational terms a theoretical position often lauded in the literature of social science but seldom put into practice in research. This is the thesis, expounded by psychologists and sociologists alike, that what matters for behavior and development is the environment as it is perceived rather than as it may exist in "objective" reality. Evidence exists, however, of consistent differences in the behavior of children and adults observed in the laboratory and in the actual settings of life. These differences in turn illuminate the various meanings of these types of settings to the participants, as partly a function of their social background and experience.

Different kinds of settings are also analyzed in terms of their structure. Here the approach departs in yet another respect from that of conventional research models: environments *are analyzed in systems terms*. Beginning at the innermost level of the ecological schema, one of the basic units of analysis is the dyad, or two-person system. Although the literature of developmental psychology makes frequent reference to dyads as structures characterized by *reciprocal relations*, we shall see that, in practice, this principle is often disregarded. In keeping with the traditional focus of the laboratory procedure on a single experimental subject, data are typically collected about only one person at a time—for instance, about either the mother or the child but rarely both simultaneously. In the few instances in which the latter does occur, the emerging picture reveals new and more dynamic possibilities for both parties. For instance, from dyadic data it appears that if one member of the pair undergoes a process of development, the other does also. Recognition of this relationship provides a key to understanding developmental changes not only in children but also in adults who serve as primary caregivers—mothers, fathers, grandparents, teachers, and so on. The same consideration applies to dyads involving husband and wife, brother and sister, boss and employee, friends, or fellow workers.

In addition, a systems model of the immediate situation extends beyond the dyad and accords equal developmental importance to what are called $N + 2$ systems—triads, tetrads, and larger interpersonal structures. Several findings indicate that the capacity of a dyad to serve as an effective context for human development is crucially dependent on the presence and participation of third parties, such as spouses, relatives, friends, and neighbors. If such third parties are absent, or if they play a disruptive rather than a supportive role, the developmental process, considered as a system, breaks down; like a three-legged stool, it is more easily upset if one leg is broken, or shorter than the other.

The same triadic principle applies to relations between settings. Thus the capacity of a setting—such as the home, school, or workplace—to function effectively as a context for development is seen to depend on the existence and nature of social connections between settings, including joint participation, communication, and the existence of information in each setting about the other. This principle accords importance to questions like the following: Does a young person enter a new situation such as school, camp, or college alone or in the company of familiar peers or adults? Are the person and his or her family provided with any information about or experience in the new setting before actual entry is made? How does such prior knowledge affect the subsequent course of behavior and development in the new setting?

Questions like these highlight the developmental significance and untapped research potential of what are called ecological transitions—shifts in role or setting, which occur throughout the life span. Examples of ecological transitions include the arrival of a younger sibling, entry into preschool or school, being promoted, graduating, finding a job, marrying, having a child, changing jobs, moving, and retiring.

The developmental importance of ecological transitions derives from the fact that they almost invariably involve a change in role—that is, in the expectations for behavior associated with particular positions in society. Roles have a magic-like power to alter how people are treated, how they act, what they do, and thereby even what they think and feel. The principle applies not only to the developing person but to the others in his or her world.

The environmental events that are the most immediate and potent in affecting a person's development are activities that are engaged in by others with that person or in his or her presence. Active engagement in, or even more exposure to, what others are doing often inspires the person to undertake similar activities on his or her own. A three-year-old is more likely to learn to talk if others are talking and especially if they speak directly to the child. Once the child begins to talk, it constitutes evidence that *development* has actually taken place in the form of a newly acquired molar activity (as opposed to behavior, which is momentary and typically devoid of meaning or intent). Finally, the molar activities engaged in by a person constitute both the internal mechanisms and the external manifestations of psychological growth.

The sequence of nested ecological structures and their developmental significance can be illustrated with reference to the above example. Thus we can hypothesize that a child is more likely to learn to talk in a setting containing *roles* that obligate adults to talk to children or that encourage or enable other persons to do so (such as when one parent does the chores so that the other can read the child a story).

But whether parents can perform effectively in their child-rearing *roles* within the family depends on role demands, stresses, and supports emanating from other settings. As we shall see, parents' evaluations of their own capacity to function, as well as their view of their child, are related to such external factors as flexibility of job schedules, adequacy of child care arrangements, the presence of friends and neighbors who can help out in large and small emergencies, the quality of health and social services, and neighborhood safety. The availability of supportive settings is, in turn, a function of their existence and frequency in a given culture or subculture. This frequency can be enhanced by the adoption of public policies and practices that create additional settings and societal roles conducive to family life.

The structure of the ecological environment may also be defined in more abstract terms. As we have seen, the ecological environment is conceived as extending far beyond the immediate situation directly affecting the developing person—the objects to which he or she responds or the people with whom he or she interacts on a face-to-face basis. Of equal importance are connections between others present in the setting, the nature of these links, and their indirect influence on the developing person through their effect on those who deal with him or her firsthand. This complex of interrelations within the immediate setting is referred to as the *microsystem*.

The principle of *interconnectedness* is seen as applying not only within settings but with equal force and consequence to linkages between settings, both those in which the developing person actually participates and those he or she may never enter but in which events occur that affect what happens in the person's immediate environment. The former constitute what I shall call *mesosystems*, and the latter *exosystems*.

Finally, the complex of nested, interconnected systems is viewed as a manifestation of overarching patterns of ideology and organization of the social institutions common to a particular culture or subculture. Such generalized patterns are referred to as *macrosystems*. Thus, *within a given society or social group*, the structure and substance of micro-, meso-, and exosystems tend to be similar, as if they were constructed from the same master model, and the systems function in similar ways. Conversely, between different social groups, the constituent systems may vary markedly. Hence by analyzing and comparing the micro-, meso-, and exosystems characterizing different social classes, ethnic and religious groups, or entire societies, it becomes possible to describe systematically and to distinguish the ecological properties of these larger social contexts as *environments for human development*.

Most of the building blocks in the environmental structures are familiar concepts in the behavioral and social sciences. What is new is the way in which these entities are related to each other and to the course of human development. In short, as far as the external world is concerned, what is presented here is a theory of environmental interconnections and their impact on the forces directly affecting psychological development.

Furthermore, an ecological approach to the study of human development requires a reorientation of the conventional view of the proper relation between science and public policy. The traditional position, at least among social scientists, is that *whenever possible social policy should be based on scientific knowledge.* The line of thought in this volume leads to a contrary thesis: in the interests of advancing fundamental research on human development, basic science needs public policy even more than public policy needs basic science. Moreover, what is required is not merely a complementary relation between these two domains but their functional integration. Knowledge and analysis of social policy are essential for progress in developmental science because they alert the investigator to those aspects of the environment, both immediate and more remote, that are most critical for the cognitive, emotional, and social development of the person. Such knowledge and analysis can also lay bare ideological assumptions underlying, and sometimes profoundly limiting, the formulation of research problems and designs, and thus the range of possible findings. A functional integration between science and social policy of course does not mean that the two should be confused. In examining the impact of public policy issues for basic research in human development, it is all the more essential to distinguish between interpretations founded on empirical evidence and those rooted in ideological preference.

Especially in its formal aspects, the conception of the environment as a set of regions each contained within the next draws heavily on the theories of Kurt Lewin (1917, 1931, 1935, 1948). Indeed this [1979 volume] may be viewed as an attempt to provide psychological and sociological substance to Lewin's brilliantly conceived topological territories.

Perhaps the most unorthodox feature of Lewin's proposed theory is its conception of development. Here the emphasis is not on the traditional psychological processes of perception, motivation, thinking, and learning but on their contents—what is perceived, desired, feared, thought about, or acquired as belief and how the nature of this psychological material changes as a function of a person's exposure to and interaction with the environment. Development is defined as the person's evolving conception of the ecological environment, and his or her relation to it, as well as the person's growing capacity to discover, sustain, or alter its properties.

Once again, this formulation shows the influence of Lewin, especially of his emphasis on a close connection and isomorphism between the structure of the person and of the situation (Lewin, 1935). The proposed conception also leans heavily on the ideas of Piaget, particularly as set forth in *The Construction of Reality in the Child* (1954). The present thesis, however, goes considerably further. By contrast with Piaget's essentially "decontextualized" organism, it emphasizes the evolving nature and scope of perceived reality as it emerges and expands in the child's awareness and in his or her active involvement with the physical and social environment. Thus the infant at first becomes conscious only of events in its immediate surroundings, in what I have called the *microsystem*. Within this proximal domain, the focus of attention and of developing activity tends initially to be limited even more narrowly to events, persons, and objects that directly impinge on the infant. Only later does the young child become aware of relations between events and persons in the settings that do not from the outset involve his or her active participation. In the beginning the infant is also conscious of only one setting at a time, the one that it occupies at the moment. My own treatment of development not only includes the infant's awareness of the continuity of persons across settings, as implied by Piaget's concept of perceptual constancy, but also encompasses its dawning realization of the relations between events in different settings. In this way the developing child begins to recognize the existence and to develop an emerging sense of the *mesosystem*. The recognition of the possibility of relations between settings, coupled with the capacity to understand spoken and written language, enables the child to comprehend the occurrence and nature of events in settings that he or she has not yet entered, like school, or those that he or she may never enter at all, such as the parents' workplace, a location in a foreign land, or the world of someone else's fantasy as expressed in a story, play, or film.

As Piaget emphasized, the child also becomes capable of creating and imagining a world of his or her own that likewise reflects the child's psychological growth. Again, an ecological perspective accords to this fantasy world both a structure and a developmental trajectory, for the realm of the child's imagination also expands along a continuum from the micro- to the meso-, exo-, and even macro-level.

The development of the child's fantasy world underscores the fact that his or her emerging perceptions and activities are not merely a reflection of what he or she sees but have an active, creative aspect. To use Piaget's apt term, the child's evolving phenomenological world is truly a "construction of reality" rather than a mere representation of it. As both Lewin and Piaget point out, young children at first confuse the subjective and objective features of the environment and as a result can experience frustration, or even bodily harm, as they attempt the physically impossible. But gradually they become capable of adapting their imagination to the constraints of objective reality and even of refashioning the environment so that it is more compatible with their abilities, needs, and desires. It is this growing capacity to remold reality in accordance with human requirements and aspirations that, from an ecological perspective, represents the highest expression of development.

In terms of research method, the child's evolving construction of reality cannot be observed directly; it can only be inferred from patterns of activity as these are expressed in both verbal and nonverbal behavior, particularly in the *activities, roles,* and *relations* in which the person engages. These three factors also constitute what are designated as *elements of the microsystem.*

In sum, this volume represents an attempt at theoretical integration. It seeks to provide a unified but highly differentiated conceptual scheme for describing and interrelating structures and processes in both the immediate and the more remote environment as it shapes the course of human development throughout the life span. This integrative effort is regarded as the necessary first step in the systematic study of human development in its human context.

Throughout the volume, theoretical ideas are presented in the form of definitions of basic concepts, propositions which, in effect, constitute the axioms of the theory, and hypotheses that posit processes and relationships subject to empirical investigation. Although some of the hypotheses to be proposed are purely deductive, following logically from defined concepts and stated propositions, the great majority derive from the application of the proposed theoretical framework to concrete empirical investigations. Thus I have by no means limited myself to theoretical exposition. I have made an effort throughout to translate ideas into operational terms. First, I have tried to find studies that illustrate the issues in question either by demonstration or, failing that, by default—by pointing out what investigators *might have done.* Second, I have used investigations already published or reported to show in what way the results can be illuminated by applying concepts and propositions from the proposed theoretical framework. Third, where no appropriate research could be found, I have concocted hypothetical studies that, to my knowledge, have never been carried out but are capable of execution. The investigations cited have been drawn from diverse disciplines and reflect a range of theoretical orientations. In addition, I have tried to select research conducted in, or connected with, varied settings (such as homes, hospitals, day care centers, preschools, camps, institutions, offices, and factories), contrasting broader social contexts (social classes, ethnic and religious groups, and total societies), and different age levels from early infancy through the life span. Unhappily, these attempts at achieving some representativeness across the spectra of ecology and age have met with only partial success. To the extent that they exist, ecologically oriented investigations of development in real-life settings have most often been conducted with infants and preschoolers studied in homes or centers. Acceptable research designs involving school-age children, adolescents, or adults observed in extrafamilial settings are few.

One may well ask how an ecology of human development differs from social psychology on the one hand and sociology or anthropology on the other. In general the answer lies in the focus of the present undertaking on the phenomenon of development in context. Not only are the above three social science disciplines considerably broader, but none has the phenomenon of development as its primary concern. To describe the ecology of human development as the social psychology, sociology, or anthropology of human development is to overlook the crucial part played in psychological growth by biological factors, such as physical characteristics and in particular the impact of genetic propensities. Indeed the present work does not give such biological influences their due, once again because this cannot be done satisfactorily until an adequate framework for analyzing the environmental side of the equation has been developed, so that the interaction of biological and social forces can be specified.

Finally, lying at the very core of an ecological orientation and distinguishing it most sharply from prevailing approaches to the study of human development is the concern with the progressive accommodation between a growing human organism and its immediate environment and the way in which this relation is mediated by forces emanating from more remote regions in the larger physical and social milieu. The ecology of human development lies at a point of convergence among the disciplines of the biological, psychological, and social sciences as they bear on the evolution of the individual in society.

References

Elder, G. H., Jr. (1974). *Children of the Great Depression*. Chicago: University of Chicago Press.

Elder, G. H., Jr. (1979). Historical change in life patterns and personality. In P. Baltes & O. Brim (Eds.), *Lifespan development and behavior* (Vol. 2, pp. 117–159). New York: Academic Press.

Elder, G. H., Jr., & Rockwell, R. C. (1978). Economic depression and post-war opportunity in men's lives: A study of life patterns and health. In R. A. Simmons (Ed.), *Research in community and mental health* (pp. 240–303). Greenwich, CT: JAI.

Lewin, K. (1917). Kriegslandschaft. *Zeitschrift für Angewandte Psychologie, 12,* 440–447.

Lewin, K. (1931). Environmental forces in child behavior and development. In C. Murchison (Ed.), *A handbook of child psychology* (pp. 94–127). Worcester, MA: Clark University Press.

Lewin, K. (1935). *A dynamic theory of personality.* New York: McGraw-Hill.

Lewin, K. (1943). Defining the "field at a given time." *Psychological Review, 50,* 292–310.

Lewin K. (1948). *Resolving social conflicts: Selected papers on group dynamics.* New York: Harper.

Lewin K. (1951). *Field theory in social science: Selected theoretical papers.* New York: Harper.

Lewin, K., Lippitt, R., & White, R. K. (1939). Patterns of aggressive behavior in experimentally created "social climates." *Journal of Social Psychology, 10,* 271–299.

Piaget, J. (1954). *The construction of reality in the child.* New York: Basic Books.

Article 7

Toward a Critical History of Development

A Propaedeutic Discussion

This article contains excerpts of my contributions to a discussion session with Frank Kessel, William Kessen, and Sheldon White at the 1983 biennial meeting of the Society for Research in Child Development. The discussion sought to address the social, cultural, and historical contexts of developmental psychology and issues of the necessity and function of critical and social history; the problematic notion of progressive development vis-à-vis both ontogenesis and scientific knowledge itself; the fragmentation of the field of developmental psychology; and the relations between scientific theory and research and sociopolitical circumstance. I began my comments by reassessing a chapter written with Nan Crouter for the then newly published *Handbook of Child Psychology* (Bronfenbrenner & Crouter, 1983) in which we traced the evolution of research models used in our field over the past 100 years or more. The text remains faithful to the colloquial tone of the session.

I undertook to derive my theses by rereading the manuscript of a chapter published in the new 1983 *Handbook of Child Psychology*, specifically in Volume 1, edited by P. H. Mussen and Bill Kessen (Bronfenbrenner &

Source: Bronfenbrenner, U., Kessel, F., Kessen, W., & White, S. (1986, November). Toward a critical history of development: A propaedeutic discussion. *American Psychologist, 41*(11), 1218–1230.

Crouter, 1983). In this chapter, Nan Crouter and I trace the evolution of research models used in our field over the past 100 years or more. I discovered on rereading that there were some developmental trends in this history that I had missed.

I am reminded in this connection of a well-known fable by the great Russian fabulist Krilov, in which a man is speaking of his visit to the zoo and all the creatures that he saw there: "The tiny flies and beetles, and ladybirds, jewel-like butterflies, and insects with a head no bigger than a pin. What marvels!"

"And did you see the elephant?" asked his friend.

"Oh, do they have one there? I guess I must have missed the elephant."

Well, I missed two of them, and here they are. The first vision that emerged as I reread our analysis was one that Bill noted. Given that the discussion was an overview of research in human development over the past 100 years, one could discern a process of progressive fragmentation of our field—progressive precisely in the direction of Krilov's fable, that is, looking more and more at less and less.

The second trend of which I became aware was not progressive but persistent: "recurring scientific bias." I don't mean that the biases have remained the same, for the objects of predilection and prejudice do keep changing, but the degree of bias remains unabated.

The bias was manifested not in the distortion of data but in their selective omission. Such omission occurred at two stages. The first took the form of selection, or nonselection, of the particular problems to be investigated; here, preferences changed from decade to decade. A second and somewhat more serious manifestation of bias operated on the research actually done, through the selection or nonselection, in successive historical periods, of the findings to be included in the corpus of our knowledge—that is, in the definitive reviews of progress in the field. This "in again, out again" phenomenon shows up especially clearly in Volumes 1 and 2 of the *Handbook of Child Psychology* (Mussen & Kessen, 1983; Mussen, Haith, & Campos, 1983).

In terms of empirical work, our most sophisticated models, reflecting the greatest degree of integration that we possess, appear in the volumes on infancy. Here we are dealing with the organism as a whole, possessed of genetic, physiological, emotional, cognitive, and social characteristics that function differentially in diverse settings and larger contexts. But once we get beyond early childhood, genetics and biology are forgotten; indeed, the notion of a complex, integrated organism is forgotten. After infancy, developmental psychology becomes the study of variables, not of human beings.

It is a curious segmentation. Indeed, an instructive lesson could be learned were one to ask: What would happen if you took the models of infancy and applied them in research on childhood or adolescence? If you consider that prospect, you will find that it is perfectly feasible to carry out. But no one has done it. Apparently, there is no felt need for the new concepts, the new methods, or new research models when one extends the study of human development beyond the age of three. The more complex paradigms employed in research on organism-environment interaction in infancy are missing in studies of later stages of development. For example, the key notion of reciprocal interaction seldom appears in socialization research on school-age children; by and large, child-rearing patterns at this age level are still being presented as one-way streets (Bronfenbrenner, 1986). For another, the study of genetic influences on development in early childhood, where it occurs at all, remains isolated from investigations of parent-child interaction. The exciting research questions that emerge upon simply taking the models of one age period and applying them to the next are quite provocative and potentially productive for developmental science.

Then there are the strange shifts in scientific attention and priority that our field has exhibited throughout its history. Sex differences come and go. We seem to have them in the first decade; they disappear in the second, only to reappear in the third. What happened? Are sex differences cyclical in the human species? Clearly not. Consider one other domain: the role of parents in the lives of children. I am referring, not to the facts that we have, but to those we have *not* gathered. It would seem from our research literature today [1986] that parents have little significance for our lives and our development once we become adolescents, and surely after the age of 20.

I trust I have given enough illustrations of what one might call our fickleness as a scientific discipline—shifting our research attention across the years from one sphere to another without either theoretical or empirical justification. Why do we act in such capricious fashion? One reason occurred to me as I reread the historical review that Nan Crouter and I had written. It is the almost pointed avoidance among developmental researchers across the decades of speaking to the question: What distinguishes *development* from *behavioral change*, and in which direction does development go?

It is a curious historical circumstance that new paradigms in our field tend to come primarily from disciplines other than our own and from scholars outside the mainstream of American developmental psychology. Going back one step further, the insights of the paradigm makers were stimulated by historical events in their own lives. We have, then, a picture of "hybridism" enforced by changes in conceptions of what children and families and schools become as a function of historical events and by the changes induced by these same events in the minds of the theorists as they seek to understand phenomena in their own lives.

A third manifestation of this same dialectic process is represented, in my view, by a phenomenon Nan Crouter and I referred to as the operation of "latent paradigms." We argued that the new models that have been developing since the period of the great paradigm makers (Freud, Piaget, Lewin, Vygotsky, and others) in the 1930s and 1940s have also served to redefine our conceptions of what a child is, what an environment is, what the nature of interaction is, and what development is—except that we have resisted any effort to think through and be explicit about exactly what these new conceptions are.

It is characteristic of us Americans to prefer to carry out our science operationally and to shy away from defining conceptually what the operation is. It was for this reason that, in the *Handbook* chapter, Nan Crouter and I sought to trace and make explicit the research paradigms lying latent in the operational models that developmentalists have been employing in pursuit of their science across the decades. What we discovered was a countertrend to the manifest movement toward specialization in contents. In contrast, the latent models implied in research designs were becoming ever more differentiated, interactive, and systemlike, with smaller subsystems being interlinked to form higher-order systems of organism-environment interaction.

Although our subject matter has become more fragmented, the research models we have been using in our effort to understand reality have become increasingly more complex in order to allow for the operation of concomitant interacting forces functioning at various levels of hierarchically organized systems.

All this has come about so gradually that only now are we beginning to recognize the scope of the process and the changes it has wrought in our ways of thinking. In the beginning, our researches were indeed modular. But then, one investigator after another—perhaps accidentally, but more likely "accidentally on purpose"—began to include more than one module in the design. Once this happened, it became necessary to investigate the relations between modules, and the recognition of higher-order systems became inescapable. For example, a perusal of Volume 2 of the new *Handbook* (Mussen, Haith, & Campos, 1983) reveals that, from a biological point of view, the creature whose development we are studying is now seen as a highly complex system in which biological, cognitive, emotional, and social elements are powerfully intertwined. As additional evidence for this view, I call attention to a number of the papers presented at this meeting, including the interesting synthesis we heard from Michael Rutter (1983), in which he spelled out the subtle interplay between forces emanating from the developing organism, from the immediate environment, and from the larger contexts in which both the person and the setting are embedded.

In sum, I am suggesting corresponding integrated empirical systems for research in human development. I am suggesting further that when the specifications of these empirical systems are not met, the living systems can fall apart. I have in mind two kinds of systems—the biopsychological system that a human being is and the socioeconomic-political system that an environment is. I am proposing that for human development to flourish, there must be a complementarity between these two systems. I am also suggesting that, at the present moment in history, we are experiencing a progressive disorganization and fragmentation in both of these domains. Paradoxically, our science may profit as a consequence, for we stand to learn most about the directional and value options of developmental science in those periods in our history that are most destructive to the development of human beings.

I have in my earlier remarks emphasized the dangers of the fragmentation of our field. But I would emphasize that Volume 1 of the Handbook—History, Theory, and Method (Mussen & Kessen, 1983)—still stands. We have not totally fallen apart yet. In any event, I regard our present awareness of our fragmentation as the beginning of a reintegration of what our field is about. Today we are beginning to see complementarities between the affective, intellectual, and social aspects of developmental processes. Similarly, we are seeing complementarities in what a family is, what a classroom is, and what a workplace is, and the relations that must obtain between these contexts if each of them is to sustain and enhance the development of human beings. These are insights that we did not have before. As I view our present situation, we are at the bottom of a parabola in which the disorganization of systems that foster human development has proceeded so far that we are in a position to understand what the nature of that disintegration is and, thereby, the nature of the systems themselves.

The new knowledge also offers hope. For example, among the papers presented at these meetings on the effects of the current economic scene on children's development was a series of ingeniously designed studies of the effects of federal programs that are now being cut. For example, Milton Kotelchuck (1983) reported on the long-range effects of the Women, Infants, and Children Program. This program had been set up without any provision for research. But by working with the birth certificates of children born to the women who enrolled in this program, Kotelchuck was able to set up matched index and control groups and to demonstrate fairly persuasively that the WIC Program was having precisely the effects that it had been designed to achieve: namely, to reduce prematurity and enhance the quality of the offspring born to teenage mothers.

We were not in a position to carry out such studies until a few years ago. And the reason that we now are in that position is, I think, *that we have finally taken as our laboratory the society in which children grow.* The reason why I emphasize the term *laboratory* is to make clear that, in doing such studies, we are imposing *the rules of evidence* that we learned in the actual laboratory setting, but we have now developed both the motivation and the skill for applying these rules with reasonable success in the more complex situations of everyday life. To cite another example, we now have evidence of the long-range consequences of the Great Depression for children. This evidence (Elder, 1974) consists not merely of journalistic reports but also of findings from carefully crafted objective procedures and designs capable of contradicting the expectations of investigators.

So I see our field as having reached an important turning point. The issue is whether we will have the resolve and the wisdom to confront the newly discovered complexities of the phenomena we are committed to study. Our science can *regress* if we continue to allow it to move toward fragmentation, toward a greater division between the various segments of our population. I believe that both of these regressions can be avoided because we are now beginning to get sufficient grasp of some of the reintegrative processes that can counteract the prevailing disruptive trend and move us forward. In this sense, I concur with the position that we are in an experimental situation that is conducting experiments and that we are now better placed to have some understanding of how to evaluate the experimental results. We are also in a better position to report back to the participants—in the first instance, to ourselves; in the second, to the society of which we are a part. It is only a glimmer of wisdom, but it's more than we were capable of only a decade ago.

As I look at the history of our field, and our society, I do detect some inroads of concepts and ideas that have come out of our field and have affected the way in which our society functions in relation to children. We are now experiencing "an experiment of nature," where many of the ways in which we as scientists have thought about and dealt with families, children, and schools are undergoing radical change. So we may have a test whether what we contributed to a somewhat richer conception of human beings, how they grow and how they deal with each other, has any significance. I do not expect that there is going to be a rapid *major* improvement in developmental processes as the result of our contributions. But I do think that there has been a marked reconceptualization in the minds of people in our country, and in modern industrial societies generally, as a result of the kinds of redefinitions that have been introduced of what a child is, what parents do, and how parents' and children's lives are affected by the circumstances in which they live. These are reconceptualizations to which we have contributed. And at the present time [1986], we are seeing precisely those new conceptions being treated as if they did not matter. Therefore, we shall soon be able to see whether we have, in fact, made any difference in the lives of children and families in our time. Alas, I wish we were not in that position. Given the choice, I would rather have the product than the proof of its importance by default.

References

Bronfenbrenner, U. (1986). Ecology of the family as a context for human development: Research perspectives. *Developmental Psychology, 22*, 723–742.

Bronfenbrenner, U., & Crouter, A. C. (1983). The evolution of environmental models in developmental psychology. In P. H. Mussen (Series Ed.) & W. Kessen (Vol. Ed.), *Handbook of child psychology: Vol. 1. History, theory and methods* (4th ed., pp. 357–414). New York: John Wiley.

Elder, G. J., Jr. (1974). *Children of the Great Depression.* Chicago: University of Chicago Press.

Kotelchuck, M. (1983, April). *Research on fathers and public policy.* Paper presented at the meeting of the Society for Research in Child Development, Detroit, MI.

Mussen, P. H. (Series Ed.), & Haith, M. M., & Campos, J. J. (Vol. Eds.). (1983). *Handbook of child psychology: Vol. 2. Infancy and developmental psychobiology* (4th ed.). New York: John Wiley.

Mussen, P. H. (Series Ed.), & Kessen, W. (Vol. Ed.). (1983). *Handbook of child psychology: Vol. 1. History, theory and methods* (4th ed.). New York: John Wiley.

Rutter, M. (1983, April). *Influences from family and school.* Paper presented at the meeting of the Society for Research in Child Development, Detroit, MI.

Article 8

Interacting Systems in Human Development

Research Paradigms: Present and Future

The original text of this article was written for a study group organized by the editors, then PhD students at Cornell, under the auspices of the Society for Research in Child Development. Participants were asked to write papers summarizing their approaches to understanding the processes linking persons and contexts in the course of development. For my part, I analyzed the interacting systems that were involved—implicitly or explicitly—in existing research paradigms for the study of human development.

M y purpose in this article is threefold: first, to describe systematically the nature and scope of the models currently employed [as of 1988]; second, to identify the strengths and shortcomings of each; and third, to explore possibilities for improving on existing paradigms by combining their constructive elements in more comprehensive conceptual and operational designs.

Especially, given the third objective, it seems appropriate to examine existing paradigms by proceeding from the more simple and segmental to the more complex and developed. But in order to carry out this task, one must establish the criteria for complexity and completeness. Even before that, however, one must ask, and answer, a more basic question: Along what parameters do research paradigms of development in context vary?

The first domain of variation is the nature of possible *developmental outcomes*. Within a given paradigm, what characteristics of the person are regarded by researchers as susceptible to development? How are these characteristics conceptualized, explicitly or implicitly, and how do various paradigms differ in this respect?

The second sphere of variability also deals with characteristics of the individual, but from a different perspective: namely, how do the characteristics of the *person* at Time 1 influence the development of subsequent characteristics at Time 2?

The third area of potential variability lies in the conceptualization of the *environment*. What properties of the external world incorporated in the model are envisioned as capable of affecting the course and consequence of human development?

Within each of these three domains, variation may occur not only with respect to *content*, the kinds of characteristics that are distinguished within the domain, but also in *structure*, the way in which these characteristics are organized and related to each other. As might be expected, this structural aspect of a given domain represents one determinant of the degree of complexity of a given paradigm.

Since that equation defines development as a *joint* function of person and environment, the question arises about what forms such joint influence can take. As we shall see, many developmental investigations today [1988] employ analytic models that assume only *additive* effects: that is, the influences emanating from the person and the environment are treated as operating independently of each other, with the net effect estimated from an algebraic sum of the various factors included in the model. Yet, in those instances in which more complex schemas have been applied, they have typically revealed important interactive effects. That is, particular environmental conditions have been shown to produce different developmental consequences, depending on the personal biological and psychological characteristics of individuals living in that environment; conversely, the same personal qualities at Time 1 may lead to different psychological consequences at Time 2, depending on the environmental conditions to which the individual has been exposed.

Finally, yet another domain of positive variation deriving from the relation of *development* to variously combined characteristics of the *person* and the *environment* is not one of mere statistical association but involves a set of *processes* through which the course and consequences of development are determined. Not only do some of the processes turn out to be quite convoluted—involving feedback mechanisms, sequential stages, and alternative paths of direct and indirect influence—but some paradigms fail to provide any indication whatsoever of what the processes might be. In other words, the mechanisms through which development is brought about are not yet fully understood and therefore must receive priority status on the scientific agenda of the future.

Lewin (1931, 1935) had a term for models of this kind. He referred to them as "Aristotelian" or "class-theoretical." In such formulations, phenomena are "explained" by the categories to which they are assigned, as with Aristotle's four elements (earth, air, fire, and water). In opposition to such static concepts, Lewin argued for "field-theoretical" or "Galileian" paradigms that specify the particular *processes* through which the observed phenomenon is brought about. Typically in the historical development of a given science, class-theoretical categories precede field-theoretical formulations but are gradually replaced by the latter. Lewin wished to accelerate the process. However, although half a century has gone by since the publication of Lewin's seminal formulations, Aristotelian concepts and research models today [1988] still abound in the scientific study of human development. Moreover, I suggest that, given the incomplete state of our knowledge, such paradigms may often be the strategies of choice for exploring uncharted domains. Like the surveyor's grid, they provide a useful frame for describing the new terrain. I also contend, however, that today [1988], when much research is conducted in areas for which usable maps have already been constructed, the continued widespread use of class-theoretical models yields results that are likely to be not only redundant but also highly susceptible to misleading interpretations. This risk arises when class-theoretical paradigms are employed, as they frequently are, for field-theoretical purposes: that is, when the investigator goes beyond purely descriptive information to draw conclusions about causal processes that are not specifically assessed in the research design. Some illustrations of such unwarranted inferences are offered below.

I now turn to a systematic analysis of the existing and research paradigms in terms of the five domains cited above.

Class-Theoretical Models
in Research on Human Development

In some contemporary designs, only a single element is included; others introduce still more. The following are those now most often employed.

The Social Address Model

This class-theoretical model is an all-time favorite. Today, to an even greater extent than when it first appeared more than a century ago (Schwabe & Bartholomai, 1870), it is the paradigm most frequently employed for the study of human development in context. It is also an appropriate first choice on our dimension of simple to complex. Indeed, from this perspective, it verges on the simplistic, since it involves little more than the comparison of children or adults growing up in different geographical or social locations. Accordingly, in their historical review, Bronfenbrenner and Crouter (1983) have referred to this type of research design as a *social address model*. Among the most common social "addresses" appearing in the research literature are the following: social class, rural versus urban, different nationalities or ethnic groups, and, more recently, what Bronfenbrenner and Crouter have called the "new demography"—one-versus two-parent families, home care versus day care, mother's employment status, how many times remarried, or—perhaps soon—hours father spends in child care and household tasks, or homes with and without computers.

As already indicated, the structure of the social address is rudimentary in several respects. First, not only is it limited to the environment, but even that environment is little more than a name. "One looks only at the *social address*—that is, the environmental label—with no attention to what the environment is like, what people are living there, what they are doing, or how the activities taking place could affect the child" (Bronfenbrenner & Crouter, 1983, pp. 382–383). In other words, as far as process is concerned, some feature of the environment existing at the social address, a feature that remains *unspecified and uninvestigated,* is presumed to bring about the observed developmental outcome *through a mechanism that remains unidentified and unexamined.*

Second, this model carries an often unrecognized assumption: namely, the developmental impact of a given social address is presumed to be the same for all persons living at that address, *irrespective of their biological or psychological characteristics.*

The Personal Attributes Model

What kinds of paradigms do incorporate characteristics of the developing organism? Again we begin with the most rudimentary case, the analogue of the social address model in the personal domain. Like its counterpart, it involves the comparison of psychological characteristics in later life among individuals or groups, this time distinguished by *particular personal characteristics present earlier in life*. Since it is convenient to be able to refer to designs of this type by name, I call them *personal attribute models*. Thus far, the prior characteristics studied in this kind of paradigm have been primarily those identified by a biological or physical feature, such as age, sex, or—less frequently—the physiological state of the organism, such as premature birth, or, later on in life, pubertal changes and menarche, and physical body type.

What about studies of the sequelae of such prior *psychological* characteristics? There have been many investigations of this kind, but almost all have been limited in scope, confined to examining continuity and change in the *same* characteristic over time, for example, constancy in IQ, temperament, or other personality trait. Like their environmental counterparts, personal attribute models neither specify nor investigate the processes through which characteristics observed early in life can affect the course of later development. Whenever some predictability is found, it is typically assumed, consistent with the truncated research paradigm being applied, that the observed relationship reflects the influence of biological factors. For example, changes with age are interpreted as products of maturation, the constancy of the IQ is viewed as an entirely genetic phenomenon, and the predictability of subsequent psychological development as resulting from prematurity or other physical characteristics of the newborn.

At a more general level, the principal shortcoming of the *personal attributes* model repeats in reverse the overgeneralizing error of its environmental counterpart. Like the *social address* paradigm, it is based on a broad and often unexamined assumption, in this instance the tacit presupposition that particular personal characteristics present early in life will have the same consequences for later development *irrespective of the environments in which such later development takes place*.

It is clear that, like its environmental counterpart, the personal attributes model can be criticized for being incomplete and even simplistic. It may therefore seem paradoxical, if not outright dim-witted, for any researcher to assert, as I do now, that the model has been underused and deserves a brighter scientific future. I hasten to add that what I have in mind is the application of the design not in its isolated form but as an essential constituent in a more complex and comprehensive paradigm. Specifically, I suggest that underlying the personal attributes model is a valid and powerful principle of psychological development, well known in clinical practice but all too seldom subjected to systematic scientific investigation: namely, that *particular psychological characteristics of the person at Time 1 can be extremely important in influencing the development of subsequent psychological characteristics at Time 2.* Moreover, these subsequent characteristics may be quite different and thereby unrelated to those manifested by the same person in the earlier period.

Before we can discuss these possibilities in more concrete terms, we need to consider a set of research paradigms still in the class-theoretical mode but at a somewhat higher level of structural complexity.

Sociological Niche Model

In the first six decades of their application, social address models were limited to the study of the developmental "effects" of various types of social addresses taken one at a time. Then, an advance not in developmental theory but in purely statistical design led to a new analytic schema. R. A. Fisher's (1925) development of analysis of variance permitted the assessment of the joint effects of two or more factors simultaneously in the form of interaction effects. This meant that one could analyze statistically the psychological characteristics of persons living at the intersection of two or more social addresses. In more concrete, substantive terms, it was now possible to identify certain social locations particularly favorable, or unfavorable, for psychological development (e.g., single-parent mothers of low income and low education, with two or more children). I refer to such locations of differential risk as *sociological niches.*

Person-Context Model

Our next paradigm introduces a new element that involves no change in its formal (still class-theoretical) design but is of key importance for developmental theory: namely, in addition to multiple social addresses, the design also includes groups differing in their personal characteristics (e.g., male versus female, age before versus after puberty). In other words, categories of social address and personal attribute are crisscrossed with each other. Moving from the operational to the conceptual level, this means that the paradigm now incorporates a distinctive feature of Lewin's original equation, the possibility, indeed the likelihood, that various combinations of environmental and personal characteristics can produce developmental effects that cannot be predicted from knowledge about each of these domains examined independently of the influence of the others.

Despite the fact that the paradigm is hardly too complex from a theoretical or methodological perspective, it has all too seldom been applied in developmental research. As a result, very little is known about the extent to which the same environments can have *different effects* on human beings with differing personal characteristics. A striking finding demonstrates the paucity of our knowledge in this sphere. The modest but significant association between family background factors in childhood and subsequent educational and occupational achievement in adulthood has been documented many times. Yet it is only recently that Scarr and McAvay (1984) reported an important qualification with respect to this often-cited relationship. Exploiting the methodological leverage provided by a longitudinal study of brothers and sisters brought up by adoptive versus biological parents, the investigators demonstrated that, within biological families, such family background characteristics are much more predictive for sons than for daughters.

This sex or gender difference appears to have some generality across both temporal and social dimensions. In two independent longitudinal studies completed more than two decades ago (Kagan & Moss, 1962; Schaefer & Bayley, 1963), the investigators found that parental treatment in early childhood predicted subsequent behavior in adolescence significantly better for boys than for girls.

The reason for this asymmetry is as yet unknown. Nor can it be determined from the kinds of research paradigms we have discussed thus far. For neither the *social address* model, the *personal attributes* model, the *sociological niche* model, nor their combination in the *person-context model* includes within the paradigm itself any explicit definition of the *processes* through which properties of the person or the environment, alone or in combination, function to produce a particular developmental outcome. As noted at the outset, all of these research designs reflect a *class-theoretical* mode of thought in which the process is left unspecified.

Before examining paradigms that fill the gap, I wish, once again, to emphasize the scientific utility and unexploited potential of the class-theoretical designs we have just discussed, in particular, the more comprehensive *person-context* model. Such designs are especially useful in exploratory studies for the purpose of identifying aspects of the person, environment, or their combination that offer the most promise for more theoretically oriented investigations of process. Some especially promising possibilities in this regard are discussed below in the context of more complex process paradigms that also incorporate a person-context interface.

Process Paradigms in Research on Human Development

What processes do researchers assume to be operating in producing developmental change? Applying our empirical criterion, we find operational definitions for mechanisms of different types functioning at different levels. The first, and most common, pertain to the effects of *proximal* environmental and organismic influences on human development. Such proximal influences emanate either from within the person or from physical features, objects, and persons in the immediate face-to-face setting. Bronfenbrenner (1976, 1979) has used the term *microsystem* to refer to this innermost region of person-environment interaction.

Microsystem Process Models

Up to the present time [1988], four types of proximal influences on human development have received major research attention:

1. *Studies of the genetic transmission of psychological characteristics.* The research models here are extensions of Galton's (1876) classic nature-nurture paradigm involving the comparison of groups differing in the degree of consanguineous relationship.

2. *Investigations of the subsequent effects of the physical and physiological state of the organism in early childhood.* The most common examples include prematurity, birth complications, temperament, and physical handicaps. Curiously, the influence of childhood illnesses on later development has seldom been investigated.

3. *Analyses of interpersonal interactions, relations, and attitudes, especially within the family.* It is of some interest, and considerable consequence, that developmental research on family interaction using techniques of direct observation has by and large been limited to the periods of infancy and early childhood. By contrast, studies at older age levels have relied overwhelmingly on verbal reports by the subjects themselves or their acquaintances. As will become apparent from what follows, this separation by method has had the unfortunate consequence of delaying the development and application of several especially promising theoretical and operational paradigms for investigating psychological growth at all stages of the life course.

4. *Research on the developmental effects of the immediate physical environment.*
   These investigations have focused on two types of variables: the availability of objects that enable and invite particular types of activity, such as toys or reading materials; and the structure of the setting with respect to barriers and pathways restricting or directing movement and activity.

The first two of these four microsystem models clearly envisage a causal process emanating primarily from characteristics of the organism itself. The remaining two designs focus mainly on events in the child's immediate surroundings. Until the late 1960s and early 1970s, each type of process was assumed to be entirely unidirectional, with *either* the organism *or* the environment seen as determining the behavior and development of the child. But, especially after the publication of Bell's influential paper "A Reinterpretation of the Direction of Effects in Studies of Socialization" (1968), the research paradigms were modified to allow for and to analyze the possibility in each case of influences operating in both directions. It is of interest that the more recent studies in this domain, employing more rigorous designs, reveal that, despite the prominent role of child-initiated developmental trajectories in early infancy, the balance of power and developmental influence in exchanges between parent and child appears to lie more with the former than the latter, primarily as a function of the parent's greater knowledge and ability to structure the nature of the child's experience, even in the parent's absence (Bronfenbrenner & Crouter, 1983).

As already mentioned, all four of these process models are limited to what I have referred to as the *microsystem,* the immediate environment of the developing person, within which direct manipulation and face-to-face communication are possible.

What about causal processes originating far afield?

Process-Context Models

Research paradigms for investigating causal processes affecting psychological development from outside the microsystem have been slow to emerge in the behavioral sciences. One reason for this delayed growth may lie in the history of psychology as a discipline. The systematic empirical study of psychological processes began in the laboratory. Moreover, the basic prototype was not the laboratory of the biological sciences but that of physics, in which the processes sought for and analyzed were viewed as universal: for example, the law of gravity was assumed to be everywhere the same (at least before Einstein). Given this provenience, developmental psychologists, especially the more "scientific" among them, have not come easily to the thought that the processes they were observing under controlled conditions might operate differently for people in different situations. To be sure, it was both obvious and understandable that individuals and groups differed in *levels* of psychological functioning. But the mechanisms through which these varying levels were attained were presumed to be the same and to operate with equal effectiveness, wherever applied.

The possibility that this might not actually be the case was difficult to recognize, mainly because it was not provided for in the operational models traditionally employed in developmental research. One of the earliest and, in my judgment, theoretically most significant set of innovations appeared in a doctoral dissertation conducted at Harvard by Tulkin in 1970. His aim was to study the influence of socioeconomic status on socialization processes and outcomes in a sample of 10-month-old female infants and their mothers. The most noteworthy feature of the investigation, from the perspective of the present analysis, was the research design that evolved over the course of the investigation. In the end, it both provided for and demonstrated the influence of the environment not only on developmental outcomes but also on the nature and effectiveness of the processes producing these outcomes. For example, Tulkin (1970, 1977) began by demonstrating that *middle-class mothers* engaged in more reciprocal interaction with their infants and regarded both infants and themselves as more capable. He then went on to show that the correlation between these behaviors and attitudes was appreciably higher for the middle-class group. Moreover, *the mother's involvement in reciprocal interaction when her infant was 10 months old predicted her child's performance in school six years later* on tests of mental ability and language skill. As before, these correlations were stronger for the middle-class families, ranging in the high .50s to lower .60s. Perhaps even more important from a developmental perspective, the relationships of early maternal behavior to the child's development at age six were greater than the contemporaneous relationships between both types of variables in the first year of life.

As the foregoing findings illustrate, Tulkin's implicit paradigm not only specifies some proximal processes through which developmental change is brought about but also makes it possible to investigate whether and how these processes vary as a function of the broader context in which the process takes place (in this instance, the family's social class position). Hence the name *process-context model*.

Tulkin's implicit paradigm is noteworthy in yet another respect. His conceptions of process include not only objective behaviors (e.g., patterns of mother-infant interaction) but also subjective psychological states (e.g., maternal belief systems about child rearing) and, what turns out to be even more critical, the relationship between these two process domains. Such simultaneous consideration of subjective and objective factors, in both developmental processes and outcomes, constitutes a dual component for designing more effective research models.

Although Tulkin's study reflects a significant advance in scientific strategy, the addition of yet another element can produce an even more revealing analytic system.

Process-Person-Context Models

The nature and scope of these paradigms is perhaps best conveyed by a concrete example drawn from an analysis of data from a study of the developmental impact on children of the transition from home to school (Bronfenbrenner & Cochran, 1979; Cochran & Woolever, 1982). This research provided an index of the frequency of joint activities engaged in by the mother with her infant when the latter was three years old. This measure was positively related to teacher evaluations, obtained several years later, of the child's performance and behavior in school. Thus far, we have an example of a simple process paradigm. The next analysis revealed that, consistent with a pattern of findings reported earlier in this chapter, the relationship between joint mother-child activity and subsequent school outcomes was significantly stronger for boys than for girls. The paradigm has now been expanded to what might be called a "person-process" model. In the next phase, a contextual variable was added to the regression equation, specifically, the number of years the mother had gone to school. Although maternal education and the mother's joint activity with the child were correlated with each other, each was found to exert an independent effect on school outcomes, and both of these effects were stronger for boys than for girls. Finally, to assess the joint influence of the mother's schooling and her joint activity, the product of these two variables was also added to the regression equation.

Solutions for points of maximum and minimum value yielded an intriguing result. It turned out that the mother's joint activity facilitated the child's performance in elementary school *only* if the mother herself had some education *beyond high school,* and the more higher education she had, the greater the effect of her joint activity on the child's achievement at school. By contrast, for mothers with a high school education or less, the relationship was nonsignificant and negative in sign.

Here we see the *process-person-context model* in its entirety. The power and, in this instance, even the direction of the process was shown to vary as a *joint* function of the context (the mother's educational background) and of characteristics of the person (the gender of the child). Moreover, the effects of person and context were not merely additive but interactive, since the joint impact of education and activity was significantly greater for boys than for girls.

We are now in a position to specify the defining properties of a *process-person-context model*. The first requirement is that the design provide for systematic information in at least three separable domains: (a) the *context* in which development is taking place; (b) the *personal characteristics* (biological or psychological) of the persons present in that context; and (c) the *process* through which their development is brought about. But the mere presence of information in these three spheres is not enough. A second sine qua non of the paradigm is analysis of the possibility that the potency and even the direction of the process may vary as a joint function both of the properties of the context and of the characteristics of the developing person. In short, the process is subject to the *interactive moderating effects* of both person and context.

As I have indicated elsewhere (Bronfenbrenner, 1984b), the nature and range of such moderating effects can be depicted in formal terms as segments of a geometric surface known as a *hyperbolic paraboloid*. The surface defines moderating effects of two general types—positive and negative. If we consider the minimal possible case of two moderating factors (e.g., one varying attribute of the person, the other of the context), a *positive moderating effect* is one in which each factor *enhances* any positive moderating influence of the other but *buffers* any negative influence the latter may have. Thus, in the example cited from the school transition study, each additional year of schooling tended to increase the positive influence of the mother's joint activity on the child in the case of mothers with some education beyond high school but to reduce the negative impact of such activity from mothers with no education beyond high school.

The condition of *poverty* is also useful for highlighting the distinction between moderating factors and those that represent *links in a direct or indirect causal chain*. I refer to the latter as *mediating* factors. The same environmental condition can often function in both modes simultaneously, poverty being a case in point. For example, Elder (Elder, 1974; Elder, Caspi, & Downey, 1986; Elder, Caspi, & van Nguyen, 1986) showed that loss of income through the father's unemployment increased the likelihood of family conflict, with resulting ill effects on the development of the children. Moreover, this disorganizing process was most severe in those families in which the father had been described as a difficult and irascible person. Finally, the destructive effects of this overall pattern were most pronounced in those families that had a low income to start with. In other words, poverty not only set the vicious circle in motion (a mediating effect) but also accelerated its downward course (a moderating effect).

It is also possible, under certain ecological conditions, for moderating effects to change direction: that is, to transform negative forces into positive ones, or vice versa. An example of such a reversal is documented in Crockenberg's research on the effects of support networks on the mother-infant relationship. In her initial study (Crockenberg, 1981), she had demonstrated that such networks foster the development of maternal responsiveness, particularly if the infant is irritable. In a subsequent investigation, however, Crockenberg (1987) showed that, for mothers living under highly stressful environmental conditions, social networks not only cease to exert a positive influence but become a source of stress.

A similar result is reported in a recent paper by Riley and Eckenrode (1986). In a study of stresses and supports in mothers' lives, the investigators found that the influence of social networks on psychological well-being shifted direction from positive to negative as a function of three kinds of factors: (a) reduced socioeconomic status; (b) the occurrence of misfortune in the lives of significant others (e.g., a close relative suffering an accident); or (c) low levels of belief either in one's capacity to influence one's own life (i.e., locus of control) or in the probable success versus failure of one's own help-seeking efforts.

Processes and outcomes of social support are set within a still broader social context in Crockenberg's (1985) study of English teenage mothers and a matched sample of their American counterparts. She found that "English mothers engaged in more smiling and eye contact, less frequent routine contact, and responded more quickly to their babies' crying than did American mothers" (pp. 413–414). Control of possibly confounding variables through regression analysis pointed to the amount and type of social support as a key factor accounting for the difference. Crockenberg elaborates:

> In the United States most mothers rely on private doctors to serve their own and their children's health needs. . . . Public health nurses or social workers may be assigned to families in need of special assistance, but there is no comprehensive system designed to provide health-related and child care advice to parents. In contrast, England incorporates community-based social support for parents in a comprehensive program of health care. This care begins before the child's birth and continues through the school years. . . . Midwives provide postnatal care for mothers and babies after they leave the hospital following delivery, and home health visitors see new mothers on a regular basis. . . . In England, mothers had only to be home and open their doors. (pp. 414–415)

The foregoing examples illustrate the double-edged scientific power of the process-person-context model, for it is at once both more rigorous and more revealing. On the one hand, it operates conservatively to guard against unwarranted doubts about generalizability across different types of people or environments. On the other hand, the paradigm can illuminate the ways in which particular characteristics of the person or the context can influence such processes as mediating factors, moderating factors, or both.

This last feature bears further examination since, in effect, it extends the analysis of process beyond the immediate setting to more remote regions of both the person and the environment. Thus, in the latter, personal domain, it highlights the conceptual structures and strategies typically employed by the individual in interpreting and manipulating the outside world. This process of interpretation and manipulation in turn influences the ways in which the environment can affect the course of subsequent development. In sum, the use of a process-person-context model permits assessment of the individual's contribution to his or her own development.

On the environmental side, the paradigm's primary focus on process forces the investigator to confront the issue not only of the *proximal mechanisms* through which features of the immediate setting bring about developmental change (or stability) in the individual but also of the *distal mechanisms* through which features of the environment beyond the immediate setting can influence the power and direction of the proximal processes that affect development directly. To be more specific, in previous publications (Bronfenbrenner, 1976, 1977, 1979; Bronfenbrenner & Crouter, 1983), I have proposed a conceptualization of contexts of development in terms of a hierarchy of systems at four progressively more comprehensive levels:

1. The *microsystem,* which involves the structures and processes taking place in an immediate setting containing the developing person (e.g., home, classroom, playground).

2. The *mesosystem,* which comprises the linkages and processes taking place between two or more settings containing the developing person (e.g., the relations between home and school, school and workplace). In other words, a mesosystem is a system of microsystems.

3. The *exosystem,* which encompasses the linkages and processes taking place between two or more settings, at least one of which does *not* ordinarily contain the developing person, but in which events occur that influence processes within the immediate setting that does contain that person. (e.g., for a child, the relation between the home and the parent's workplace; for

a parent, the relation between the school and the neighborhood peer group).

4. The *macrosystem*, which is defined as an overarching pattern of ideology and organization of the social institutions common to a particular culture or subculture. In other words, the *macrosystem* comprises the pattern of micro-, meso-, and exosystems characteristic of a given society or segment thereof. It may be thought of as a societal blueprint for a particular culture or subculture.

The relevance of this more differentiated conceptualization of the environment for the present discussion lies in the fact that the process-person-context design provides for its operationalization: that is, it makes possible the analysis of the mediating and moderating processes that constitute the linkages between and within these four environmental systems shaping the course of human development. In addition, the paradigm incorporates as a key domain, having equal status within the environment, a set of factors all too frequently omitted in studies of development in context—the contribution to development of the biological and psychological characteristics of the persons involved in the process.

These scientific virtues notwithstanding, full-fledged process-person-context models are still comparatively rare in developmental research. Somewhat more common are truncated designs in which one of the principal moderating elements, either the person or the context, is missing. Paradoxically, given the fact that most developmental research is conducted by psychologists, it is the differentiating characteristics of the individual that are most often left unspecified. There are more process-context models to be found in the literature than process-person paradigms. As a result, we are typically left, by default, with the usually unacknowledged assumption that the processes operating in the given context affect the development of all persons in that context in the same way.

Such recognition of missing elements and unstated but challengeable assumptions can also be viewed in a more positive light; for, also by default, it defines a promising, and as yet little explored, terrain for future research. The prospect is scientifically promising because, to judge from the limited evidence generated thus far through the still infrequent use of more complex models, it would appear that prevailing research paradigms considerably underestimate the role of the person's own psychological characteristics in affecting the course of his or her future development, be it for better or for worse.

If we now broaden the perspective further to add as yet uncharted domains in the environment, the prospects for extending scientific knowledge appear even brighter. At the present time, studies of process in developmental research are limited almost entirely to the family. The extension of process-person-context models beyond this core microsystem should enable us to look beyond the superficial labels of place and person; to identify the human realities that lie behind such uninformative categories as class, gender, race, or residence; and to discover the processes through which these realities shape the kinds of human beings that we progressively become.

Having sought to persuade the reader of the superiority of the process-person-context model over most of its contemporaries, I shall now, perversely, point to a major lacuna in this powerful design, the omission of an entire domain that is critical for the study of development. Not only is the dimension is missing from all of the paradigms we have examined thus far; it is absent even from the revised Lewinian equation that has served as the conceptual framework for our analysis.

The missing parameter is the very dimension along which development occurs—the dimension of *time*. Lewin's failure to include this parameter in his formula was not accidental but deliberate. In his view (Lewin, 1931), the Galileian mode of thought was by its very nature ahistorical. He argued that in psychology as in physics, present events can be influenced only by forces operative in the present situation. It was perhaps Lewin's predilection for the paradigms of physics, and their ahistorical orientation, that led him, and many other psychologists as well, to be far more interested in the study of behavior than of development.

The fact remains, however, that, as mentioned above, the process of human development cannot be defined except in relation to time, since the central concern of developmental study is the nature of continuity and change in the biological and psychological structures of individual human beings throughout their life course. Moreover, it is along this same temporal dimension that another major advance has recently taken place in the design of research paradigms for investigating psychological development.

Chronosystem Paradigms

Traditionally in developmental science, the passage of time has been treated as being synonymous with chronological age: that is, as a scale for ordering individuals in terms of how long they have lived. Moreover, age has been viewed as a purely personological construct: that is, one presumed to reflect developmental changes *within the individual* and thus not directly related to external conditions or events. Especially during the past decade, however, research on human development has projected the factor of time along a new axis. Since the mid-1970s, an increasing number of investigators have formulated research designs in which time is employed not only for ordering individuals according to age but also for ordering events in their historical sequence and context. I have referred to designs of this kind as *chronosystem models* (Bronfenbrenner, 1984a).

True to their nature and name, such models have a history that ante-dates their present popularity. Thus the first formal, systematic critique of chronological age as a purely personological construct appeared in the work of Baltes and Schaie in the late 1960s and early 1970s (Baltes, 1968; Baltes & Schaie, 1973; Schaie, 1970). The sophisticated analyses conducted by these investigators demonstrated the confounding effects of age and cohort. At a substantive level, Baltes and Schaie argued that cohort differences reflect the influence of diverse historical contexts. Not only do persons in the same age group share a life history of common experience, but those of a given age in different generations could have quite diverse experiences, depending on the period in which they live.

The research paradigms that these investigators employed to unravel the confounding were primarily statistical in nature. Little effort was made to identify the particular experiences that influenced the person's development or the specific effects that these experiences produced. Studies of the latter kind, however, were already present in the research literature, although, at the time, their scientific significance and power generally remained unrecognized. For instance, in the late 1940s, Baldwin (1947) reported dramatic changes in the mother's behavior toward the first child before, during, and after the mother's pregnancy with a second child. A decade earlier Stone and Barker (1937, 1939) described the marked shifts in interests and preferences exhibited by adolescent girls before and after menarche, even after control for chronological age.

Both of these early examples illustrate the defining property of a *chronosystem model: its design permits one to identify the impact of prior life events and experiences, singly or sequentially, on subsequent development.* These experiences may have their origins either in the external environment (e.g., the birth of a sibling) or within the organism (e.g., the first menstruation). A further distinction, introduced by Baltes and his colleagues (Baltes, 1979; Baltes, Reese, & Lipsett, 1980), differentiates between *normative* experiences (school entry, puberty, entering the labor force, marriage, retirement) and *non-normative* events (a death or severe illness in the family, divorce, moving, winning the sweepstakes). Experiences of both types occur throughout the life span and may often serve as the impetus for developmental change.

At least three types of research strategies have been used in *chronosystem designs.*

1. The most common is a *cross-sectional design* in which developmental outcomes are compared between different groups of subjects who have and have not been previously exposed to a particular life experience, with appropriate controls for possibly confounding factors. Stone and Barker's (1937) study of the impact of menarche in altering patterns of motivation and interest among adolescent girls provides an early example. The groups were matched to rule out possible effects of both chronological age and socioeconomic status. While profiting from the advantages of a chronosystem design, this pioneering study lacked a number of key elements found in other paradigms that we have examined. These were features that considerably enhance their scientific power. For example, although Stone and Barker (1937, 1939) speculated that the psychological changes provoked by menarche may involve an interaction between biological and social factors, their model did not provide for any investigation of such joint effects (e.g., the possible moderating influence of social class or personal belief systems on the psychological impact of first menstruation). In short, Stone and Barker did not incorporate a process-person-context model in their chronosystem design. As we shall see, such incorporation offers special promise for future research on human development.

2. A second strategy for implementing a chronosystem model involves a *short-term longitudinal design* in which data are obtained for the same group of subjects both before and after a particular life experience or *life transition.* This strategy is particularly applicable to normative events, since their occurrence can be anticipated. A case in point is Baldwin's study of changes in parent-child interaction induced by the impending arrival of a sibling. As has been argued elsewhere (Bronfenbrenner & Crouter, 1983), a design of this kind has special advantages from the viewpoint of scientific method, since it represents a ready-made experiment of nature in which the usual sources of confounding are eliminated, since each subject serves as his or her own control. Moreover, the fact that life transitions occur throughout the life course provides opportunities for studying development during the stage that is both the longest and the one about which we have the least knowledge—adulthood between the ages of 25 and 60.

3. This same consideration applies with even greater force to the most powerful form of chronosystem design, a long-term longitudinal investigation of the often cumulative effects of what Elder (1974) has referred to as the *life course.* Elder's systematic studies of the different developmental paths set in motion by the Great Depression of the 1930s represent both a prototype and, in a number of respects, a paragon for this type of research design.

I use the term *paragon* advisedly because Elder manages to avoid two major pitfalls that characterize most of the research designs currently being employed in the study of life-course development. Both pitfalls involve a typically unrecognized theoretical oversimplification.

The first danger derives from the uncritical use of an especially powerful methodological tool—*causal modeling*—especially in the highly sophisticated form in which it has been developed and adapted for computer use by the Swedish statisticians Joreskog and Sorbom (1976). Although path analysis as a statistical tool for analyzing causal processes was conceived and applied in the field of genetics by Sewell Wright (1934) half a century ago, its application in developmental research has been relatively recent. Structural models, typically being purely abstract and mathematical in nature, do not in themselves constitute theoretical conceptions of development in context. They have nevertheless made a significant conceptual contribution by highlighting the importance of, and providing a method for analyzing, two types of phenomena that have turned out to be frequent and often critical features of developmental processes: bidirectional influences on the one hand and direct versus indirect effects on the other. However, the increasing use of structural equations for exploring these important phenomena has often led investigators to overlook other process possibilities not allowed for in the orthodox path-analytic paradigm.

The omission derives from the fact that, with all their mathematical and statistical complexity, structural equations, as typically employed, are essentially main-effect models, with no allowance made for possible interactions. To state the issue in substantive and theoretical terms, if an investigator relies exclusively on a conventional causal model, developmental sequences are implicitly conceptualized and explicitly analyzed as if they were invariant across both person and situation. No matter how many pathways through life are found, or how convoluted each course may be, once travelers embark on a particular route, they are seen as proceeding at the same pace to the same place, irrespective of who they are, whence they came, or the nature of the terrain they may be traversing.

To move from metaphor to concrete cases, it is a common practice in applying path-analytic models in developmental research to introduce as either exogenous or control variables such factors as socioeconomic status, age, family size, or even sex of child. Such a procedure assumes that any developmental processes or effects under investigation are invariant across these parameters. As has been demonstrated in the preceding discussion, such invariance can hardly be taken for granted.

The preceding discussion also points the way to a more powerful paradigm that preserves the advantages of a path-analytic model while avoiding its questionable universalistic assumptions. The preferred alternative is to *incorporate structural equations within the larger framework of a process-person-context model.* In effect, this means calculating separate path diagrams for each of the potential moderator factors included in the design: for example, whether and how path diagrams may differ for males versus females, lower-class versus middle-class families, single-parent versus two-parent households, and so on.[1] This was the strategy employed by Elder. It can yield new knowledge of considerable theoretical and practical significance. For instance, more than a decade ago, Scarr-Salapatek (1971) showed that middle-class children were more likely to realize their genetic potential than the offspring of lower-class families. In a different domain, research teams working independently both in West Germany (Schneewind, Beckmann, & Engfer, 1983) and in the United States (Elder, Caspi, & Downey, 1986) have found that economic hardship exerts its impact on family processes and the child's subsequent development primarily as a function of personality characteristics of the parent of the same sex.

What Is a Developmental Outcome?

The second pitfall besetting contemporary studies of the life course forces us to confront, at long last, the first and most definitive term in the original Lewinian equation—the D that stands for Development. If development is the product of interaction between person and environment, how are we to distinguish it from its prototypic predecessor—the B that stands for Behavior? And are there other outcomes of the conjoint process that further complicate the task of identifying the true object of study—namely, *the impact of continuity and change over time on the evolving psychological characteristics of the developing person?*

The answers to these questions are by no means obvious. This fact becomes readily apparent when we examine some of the variables that have been taken as measures of developmental outcome in studies of life-course development. They have included, among other elements, the number of years of schooling ultimately completed, achieved occupational status, and whether the person is on welfare. To be sure, these are clearly waystations on the life course, and often also ends of the line, but are they also appropriate measures of human development?

Implicit in this question is a basic theoretical issue: What is the conceptual definition of a developmental outcome? Somewhat to my surprise, I have not been able to find a formal definition of this construct in the research literature. Operational definitions of course abound in great variety. They include everything from indices of life-course status of the type mentioned above to highly specific responses in laboratory experiments, results of psychological tests, clinical assessments, descriptions and ratings by personal acquaintances, and systematic appraisals based on coded interviews or observations conducted in real-life situations. Clearly, such a diverse array precludes a quick and easy calculation of a theoretically lowest common denominator.

Under these circumstances, to pursue the issue to a critical point, I am faced with two alternatives, neither of which is pleasant to contemplate. The first is to resort to the hackneyed device of declaring the problem a priority for further study, clearly a case of passing the buck. The second option is to go out on a limb by proposing a presumably more adequate conceptual formulation of my own. If the proposal is to have any theoretical coherence, it must of necessity rule out one or more operational definitions that are currently regarded as quite acceptable by one or another group of established researchers in the field. Since the first alternative risks criticism from all sides, whereas the second may be somewhat more selective in provoking objections, I shall opt for the latter. The proposed conceptual definition of a developmental outcome takes the form of a series of propositions as follows:

1. Psychological development is a process that, in the last analysis, takes place within the mind; it involves the evolution, through the life course, of established patterns of mental organization and content that are characteristic of the particular person. Such established patterns are referred to as *developmental outcomes*.

2. Patterns of mental organization and content cannot be observed directly in the brain (at least not yet); they can only be inferred from the characteristic ways in which the person subjectively experiences and objectively deals with the world in which he or she lives (including perceptions of the behaviors of others toward the self).

3. The term *evolution* refers to change over time, yet the expression *established pattern* similarly implies some degree of stability in the emergent product of change. Hence the demonstration of a developmental outcome requires evidence of patterns of subjective experience and objective behavior that exhibit some degree of continuity across space and time but have their origins in conditions, events, and processes taking place at an earlier period in the life of the person.

4. Moreover, since psychological development has been defined as a process, a full demonstration of its occurrence must also identify one or more mechanisms through which particular prior conditions or events affect subsequent patterns of subjective experience and behavior.

5. The expression *patterns of subjective experience and objective behavior* also implies a functional relationship between these two domains. Therefore, a full description of developmental processes should encompass both subjective and objective aspects of human activity and document the functional relationship between them.

Operational definitions of developmental outcomes typically address one or the other of the several elements outlined in the foregoing propositions, but rarely, as they were in Tulkin's work, have more than one or two of them been integrated in the same research design. For this reason, it is useful to distinguish between a narrow, or minimal, definition of a developmental outcome and one that is more comprehensive.

A. Under a *narrow* operational definition, a developmental outcome is considered established if it can be shown that observed patterns of subjective experience *or* of objective behavior can be predicted from conditions or events taking place at an earlier period in the life of the person. Implicit in this minimal formulation is the dual assumption that, if past circumstances predict present patterns, then the former must have had some role in producing the latter, and the latter, in turn, must have exhibited some kind of functional continuity over time.

B. Two important elements are missing from the above definition and are therefore added in the broader formulation:
   1. The first is the requirement to specify one or more *processes* through which past conditions or events bring about the evolution of established patterns of psychological functioning. As the reader will have observed, the narrow operational definition does not call for such specification. Hence a social address model, a personal attributes model, or a combination of the two in a person-context model can be adequate to the task. By contrast, the broader operational definition requires the addition of process terms to the equation.
   2. The second additional requirement calls for the specification of developmental patterns in both the subjective and the objective domains, as well as an analysis of the functional relationship between them. In the narrow definition, the identification of patterns in only one or the other of these domains is deemed sufficient. When a dual-domain model is employed, it is also essential, again as illustrated in Tulkin's research, that the subjective and objective elements included be selected on a theoretical rather than an ad hoc basis, so that there must be some

possibility of demonstrating a functional relationship between the particular beliefs and behaviors under investigation.

Up to the present time, only a few studies have undertaken to follow the broader operational definition, but these few have been especially valuable scientifically. In addition to the work by Tulkin and his colleagues referred to earlier in the chapter, another outstanding example is Elder's demonstration in a series of studies extending over a decade (Elder, 1974; Elder, Caspi, & Downey, 1986; Elder, Caspi, & van Nguyen, 1986) of the impact of the Great Depression in shaping both the behavior systems and belief systems of his subjects in later life. A third investigation that approximates the broader criteria is Mortimer's longitudinal investigation of life-course patterns leading to professional and managerial success (Mortimer & Kumka, 1982; Mortimer & Lorence, 1979; Mortimer, Lorence, & Kumka, 1982). Specifically, Mortimer and her colleagues have shown that occupational attainment in American men is the product, in part, of value orientations fostered by processes beginning in the family of origin but ultimately encompassing experiences and linkages in educational and work settings, as well as in the men's marital relationships. The research falls short of the broader operational definition only in the fact that measures of occupational achievement are limited to indices of career progress and income and do not extend to actual performance on the job, but it remains an outstanding achievement nonetheless.

Retrospect and Prospect

Despite the diversity of models and materials reviewed, it is not difficult to suggest a combination of paradigm properties, and their constituent interacting systems, that may be especially likely to lead to scientific progress in future research on human development in context. It will be no easy task, however, to integrate and implement these properties and systems within an integrated theoretical formulation and corresponding research design.

To begin with the easier task, in the light of the ideas and evidence we have examined, a productive design for research on development in context might well incorporate the following system elements:

1. The design should use a process-person-context model involving a contrast between at least two settings and between two groups of subjects distinguished by differing personal characteristics.

2. Observations in all three domains of the above model, as well as data on developmental status, should be obtained at *two or more* points in time.

3. The measures of developmental status should include assessments of behavioral and experiential functioning, as well as assessments of the inter-relations between these two domains.

It will be observed that the above elements encompass not only key features of a "person-process-context" model but also properties of a number of other system paradigms examined in this chapter, in particular, the chronosystem, the meso- or exo-system, and a developmental outcomes model. It is even more obvious that few researchers will have the time, resources, or, for that matter, the scientific "nerve" to undertake so ambitious an endeavor. To be sure, as we have seen, a number of investigators have already come fairly close to bringing off such an awesome enterprise quite successfully; only one or two of the specified elements were missing.

The ideas and models presented here are offered as an aid to that endeavor. Their purpose is not to establish a set of criteria that every researcher should strive to meet but rather to provide an array of promising systems paradigms from which the investigator can choose the most suitable theoretical and practical alternatives and, at the same time, be able to recognize and to specify the ambiguities of interpretation created by the omission of important elements in the selected design so that others can fill in the gaps. If this discussion contributes to the achievement of this modest goal, it will have served its highest hope.

Note

1. To be sure, no method exists as yet for testing the significance of differences between two formally analogous structural models. It is possible, however, to test differences between corresponding regression coefficients. Moreover, purely technical considerations should not deter investigators from looking at relevant data from any perspective that can reduce the danger of unwarranted generalization by calling attention to possible variations in process as a function of context, personal characteristics, or some combination of the two.

References

Baldwin, A. L. (1947). Changes in parent behavior during pregnancy. *Child Development, 18,* 29–39.

Baltes, P. B. (1968). Longitudinal and cross-sectional sequences in the study of age and generation effects. *Human Development, 2,* 145–171.

Baltes, P. B. (1979). Life-span developmental psychology: Some converging observations on history and theory. In P. B. Baltes & O. G. Brim (Eds.), *Life-span development and behavior* (Vol. 2, pp. 256–279). New York: Academic Press.

Baltes, P. B., Reese, H. W., & Lipsett, L. P. (1980). Life-span developmental psychology. *Annual Review of Psychology, 31,* 65–110.

Baltes, P. B., & Schaie, K. W. (1973). *Life-span developmental psychology: Personality and socialization.* New York: Academic Press.

Bell, R. Q. (1968). A reinterpretation of the direction of effects in studies of socialization. *Psychological Review, 75,* 81–95.

Bronfenbrenner, U. (1976). The experimental ecology of education. *Teachers College Record, 78,* 157–204.

Bronfenbrenner, U. (1977). Toward an experimental ecology of human development. *American Psychologist, 32,* 513–531.

Bronfenbrenner, U. (1979). *The ecology of human development: Experiments by nature and design.* Cambridge, MA: Harvard University Press.

Bronfenbrenner, U. (1984a). *The ecology of the family as a context for human development: Research perspectives.* Position paper prepared at the request of the Human Learning and Behavior Branch of the National Institute of Child Health and Human Development as a contribution to the preparation of its Five-Year Plan.

Bronfenbrenner, U. (1984b). *The graphic analysis of moderating effects.* Ithaca, NY: Cornell University, Department of Human Development and Family Studies.

Bronfenbrenner, U., & Cochran, M. (1979). *The comparative ecology of human development: Research methods and designs.* Ithaca, NY: Cornell University, Department of Human Development and Family Studies.

Bronfenbrenner, U., & Crouter, A. C. (1983). The evolution of environmental models in developmental research. In P. H. Mussen (Series Ed.) & W. Kessen (Vol. Ed.), *Handbook of child psychology: Vol. 1. History, theories, and methods* (4th ed., pp. 357–414). New York: John Wiley.

Cochran, M., & Woolever, F. (1982). *Beyond the deficit model: The empowerment of families with information and informal supports.* Ithaca, NY: Cornell University, Department of Human Development and Family Studies.

Crockenberg, S. B. (1981). Infant irritability, mother responsiveness, and social support influences on the security of infant-mother attachment. *Child Development, 52,* 857–865.

Crockenberg, S. B. (1985). Professional support and care of infants by adolescent mothers in England and the United States. *Journal of Pediatric Psychology, 10,* 413–428.

Crockenberg, S. B. (1987). Support for adolescent mothers during the postnatal period: Theory and research. In C. F. Z. Boukydis (Ed.), *Research on support for parents and infants in the postnatal period* (pp. 3–34). Westport, CT: Ablex.

Elder, G. H., Jr. (1974). *Children of the Great Depression.* Chicago: University of Chicago Press.

Elder, G. H., Jr., Caspi, A., & Downey, G. (1986). Problem behavior and family relations: Life course and intergenerational themes. In A. Sorensen, F. Weinert, & L. Sherrod (Eds.), *Human development and the life course: Multidisciplinary perspectives* (pp. 293–340). Hillsdale, NJ: Lawrence Erlbaum.

Elder, G. H., Jr., Caspi, A., & van Nguyen, T. V. (1986). Resourceful and vulnerable children: Family influences in hard times. In R. K. Silbereisen, K. Eyferth, & G. Rudinger (Eds.), *Development as action in context: Problem behavior and normal youth development* (pp. 167–186). New York: Springer.

Fisher, R. A. (1925). *Statistical methods for research workers.* Edinburgh: Oliver & Boyd.

Galton, F. (1876). The history of twins as a criterion of the relative power of nature. *Anthropological Institute Journal, 5,* 391–406.

Jöreskog, K. G., & Sörbom, D. (1976). Statistical models and methods for analysis of longitudinal data. In D. J. Aigner & A. S. Goldberg (Eds.), *Latent variables in socioeconomic models* (pp. 285–326). Amsterdam: North Holland.

Kagan, J., & Moss, H. A. (1962). *Birth to maturity: A study in psychological development.* New York: John Wiley.

Lewin, K. (1931). The conflict between Aristotelian and Galilean modes of thought in contemporary psychology. *Journal of Genetic Psychology, 5,* 141–177.

Lewin, K. (1935). *A dynamic theory of personality.* New York: McGraw-Hill.

Mortimer, J. T., & Kumka, D. (1982). A further examination of the "occupational linkage hypothesis." *Sociological Quarterly, 23,* 3–16.

Mortimer, J. T., & Lorence, J. (1979). Work experience and occupational value socialization: A longitudinal study. *American Journal of Sociology, 84,* 1361–1385.

Mortimer, J. T., Lorence, J., & Kumka, D. (1982). Work and family linkages in the transition to adulthood: A panel study of highly educated men. *Western Sociological Review, 13,* 50–68.

Riley, D., & Eckenrode, J. (1986). Social ties: Subgroup differences in costs and benefits. *Journal of Personality and Social Psychology, 22,* 770–778.

Scarr, S., & McAvay, G. (1984). *Predicting the occupational status of young adults: A longitudinal study of brothers and sisters in adoptive and biologically-related families.* Unpublished manuscript, Department of Psychology, University of Virginia.

Scarr-Salapatek, S. (1971). Race, social class, and IQ. *Science, 74,* 1285–1295.

Schaefer, W. S., & Bayley, N. (1963). Maternal behavior, child behavior and their intercorrelations from infancy through adolescence. *Monographs of the Society for Research in Child Development, 28,* 1–27.

Schaie, K. W. (1970). A reinterpretation of age-related changes in cognitive structure and functioning. In L. R. Goulet & P. H. Baltes (Eds.), *Life span developmental psychology: Research and theory* (pp. 486–507). New York: Academic Press.

Schneewind, K. A., Beckmann, M., & Engfer, A. (1983). *Eltern und Kinder.* Stuttgart, West Germany: Kohlhammer.

Schwabe, B., & Bartholomai, F. (1870). Der Vorstellungskreis der Berliner Kinder beim Eintritt in die Schule. In *Berlin und seine Emwickelung: Städtisches Jahrbuch für Volkswirtschaft und Statistik: Vierter Jahrgang.* Berlin: Guttentag.

Stone, C. P., & Barker, R. G. (1937). Aspects of personality and intelligence in postmenarcheal and premenarcheal girls of the same chronological ages. *Journal of Comparative Psychology, 23,* 439–455.

Stone, C. P., & Barker, R. G. (1939). The attitudes and interests of premenarcheal and postmenarcheal girls. *Journal of Genetic Psychology, 54,* 27–71.

Tulkin, S. R. (1970). *Mother-infant interaction in the first year of life: An inquiry into the influences of social class.* Unpublished doctoral dissertation, Harvard University.

Tulkin, S. R. (1977). Social class differences in maternal and infant behavior. In P. H. Leiderman, A. Rosenfeld, & S. R. Tulkin (Eds.), *Culture and infancy.* New York: Academic Press.

Wright, S. (1934). The method of path coefficients. *Annals of Mathematical Statistics, 5,* 161–215.

Article 9

The Developing Ecology of Human Development:

Paradigm Lost or Paradigm Regained

This oral presentation, which draws from the text of "Ecological Systems Theory" (Article 10), raises the question whether, in the 1980s, the ecology of human development was evolving or declining as a scientific discipline. It focuses on developmentally instigative characteristics— characteristics of the person likely to be most powerful in affecting the course and outcome of subsequent development—and reformulates conceptualizations of the micro- and macrosystem to include them. It also proposes research designs that combine in the same research model measures of developmentally instigative characteristics with measures of cognitive ability, temperament, or personality in order to assess their joint synergistic effects.

The paradigm is unlikely to be regained today, for this morning I am faced with the challenge of condensing a 60-page chapter (Bronfenbrenner, 1989) into a talk of less than 20 minutes. In response to the challenge, I propose to offer you some selected excerpts from the text. To hazard a risky metaphor, rather than read you a menu, I shall offer

Source: Bronfenbrenner, U. (1989). *The developing ecology of human development: Paradigm lost or paradigm regained.* Paper presented at the Biennial Meeting of the Society for Research in Child Development, Kansas City, Missouri, April 27–30, 1989.

a foretaste of some of the courses you could choose should you care to partake of the whole.

I begin with an appetizer, at once sweet and bitter. It is a report of the failure of success. But I trust, as the title of my presentation suggests, that there is still some hope for the future. To turn briefly to the past, it was more than a decade ago that, being somewhat younger, I presumed to challenge the then-prevailing conventions in our field by describing the developmental research of the day as "the study of the strange behavior of children in strange situations with strange adults for the briefest possible period of time." Instead, I argued, as if it were simply a matter of choice, that we should be studying *development in context*: that is, in the actual environments in which human beings live and grow. I then proceeded, in a series of articles culminating in a book, to lay out a theoretical framework for what I called the "ecology of human development," succinctly defined as "the scientific study of development as a function of the progressive, reciprocal interplay, through the life course, between an active, growing human organism and the changing properties of its environment, both immediate, and more remote" (Bronfenbrenner, 1979).

Today, more than 10 years later, one might think that I have good reason to rest content. Studies of children and adults in real-life settings are now commonplace in the research literature on human development both in the United States and abroad, and a substantial number of these investigations explicitly acknowledge an ecological model.

But there is a problem. As evidenced by the definition I have just cited, lying at the core of the ecological paradigm is a view of development as a *joint* function of *person* and *context*. However, as I have documented in a series of articles and reviews published over the past several years, existing developmental studies subscribing to an ecological orientation have provided far more knowledge about *the nature of developmentally relevant environments, near and far, than about the characteristics of developing individuals, then or now.* As I have written elsewhere:

> It is an instance of what might be called "the failure of success." For some years I harangued my colleagues for avoiding the study of development in real-life settings. No longer able to complain on that score, I have found a new bête noir. In place of too much research on development "out of context," we now have a surfeit of studies on "context without development." (Bronfenbrenner, 1986, p. 288)

What's more, ironically enough, I must acknowledge some responsibility for this state of affairs, for the criticism I have just made also applies to my own writings. For example, *The Ecology of Human Development* (Bronfenbrenner, 1979) offers a differentiated conception of the environment as a system of nested structures, ranging from the *microsystem*—at the level of the immediate, face-to-face setting—on through the *meso-* and *exosystems* to overarching *macrosystems*. My point at the moment [1989] is that nowhere in the 1979 monograph, or elsewhere in my writings thus far, will the reader find these three terms for distinguishing the environments in which human beings develop. Moreover, this omission is the result not of an oversight but of a deliberate decision. In the preface to the 1979 volume, I expressed the conviction that further advance in the scientific understanding of the basic processes of human development must wait upon the formulation and implementation of a more differentiated and dynamic conception of the environment. I then undertook what I regarded as the necessary prior task, postponing—for the time being— my primary interest in the psychological development of the individual. A dream deferred.

Deferred far too long. The chapter on which today's talk is based represents a beginning and belated effort to make up for past sins of omission. It offers, at long last, a first approximation of the theoretical framework for the second half of the scientific task that I undertook more than a decade ago: formulating a differentiated conception of the *person* as both the product and partial producer in the process of his or her own development.

That undertaking, in turn, has had an unanticipated result. It has led to a *reformulation* and elaboration of my earlier conceptions regarding the structure of the environment and its role in the developmental process. Finally, the necessity of integrating these two newly reconstructed domains has had the further serendipitous effect of generating some new, and I believe promising, perspectives for future research in our field.

But the proof of the pudding is in the eating. So here is a first taste. The initial task I set for myself was to identify, and define conceptually, those characteristics of the person that were likely to be most powerful in affecting the course and outcome of subsequent development. Where to begin on such a task? I reasoned as follows. If development was indeed a function of reciprocal interplay between person and the environment, then, in the last analysis, this interplay had to be manifested at the level of the microsystem—that is, in processes of interaction between particular characteristics of the person and specific features of the immediate setting. Clearly, in order to be able to identify such personal characteristics, it would be helpful to know something about the nature of the interactive processes taking place. Upon reviewing the research literature on this subject, I was somewhat surprised to discover that such processes are relatively few, at least in terms of existing knowledge. Essentially, they are of two general kinds. First, there are processes of social interaction between the developing person and one or more others, usually older, occasionally of the same age, and rarely younger. In the chapter, I call attention to some unwarranted restrictions, and thereby unexploited opportunities in this regard, but I must omit such discussion now. A second family of developmental processes has a rich theoretical base but, as yet, is less grounded in systematic empirical work. I refer to the thesis, originally set forth by Lev Vygotsky (1978, 1979), and subsequently further developed both by Soviet scientists (Leontiev, 1932, 1978, 1981) and, more recently, American scientists (Rogoff & Wertsch, 1983; Wertsch, 1981, 1985), that the principal engine of development is engagement in progressively more complex activities and tasks.

Given these two broad classes of proximal developmental processes, it appears plausible that, among the personal characteristics likely to be most potent in affecting the course of subsequent psychological growth, are those that set in motion, sustain, and encourage processes of interaction between the developing person and two aspects of the proximal environment: first, the people present in the setting; and second, the physical and symbolic features of the setting that, in both cases, invite, permit, or inhibit engagement in sustained, progressively more complex interaction with and activity in the immediate environment. For great want of a better term, I refer to such qualities as *developmentally instigative characteristics*.

Before discussing such attributes, I need to forestall a possible misinterpretation in advocating scientific attention to what I have called developmentally instigative characteristics. I do not mean to imply that this should be done to the neglect of more familiar measures of cognitive and socioemotional functioning. Quite the contrary, among the research paradigms I recommend for application in future research are those that combine both types of personal characteristics in the same design in such a way as to permit assessing their possible synergistic effect.

Four types of developmentally instigative characteristics are usefully distinguished. The first, and the one most often to be found in the research literature, consists of personal qualities that invite or discourage reactions from the environment of a kind that can disrupt or foster processes of psychological growth. Examples include a fussy versus a happy baby; attractive versus unattractive physical appearance; and hyperactivity versus passivity. Half a century ago, Gordon Allport (1937), borrowing a term originally introduced by Mark A. May (1932), spoke of such characteristics as constituting "personality" defined in terms of its "social stimulus value." Accordingly, I shall refer to personal features of this kind as *personal stimulus* qualities. The developmental importance of such characteristics lies in the fact that they can set in motion reciprocal processes of interpersonal interaction, often escalating over time, that, in turn, can influence the course of development. Although a number of studies of the developmental effects of such characteristics have been conducted, almost all of them are restricted to looking for evidence for their constancy over the years, while neglecting to investigate the complex of environmental forces and personal characteristics that shape the course of future development.

The remaining three forms of developmentally instigative characteristics are probably even more powerful in their developmental impact but have seldom been examined from this point of view. Attributes of this kind differ from social stimulus characteristics in the following respect: rather than merely evoking a reaction from others, they share a differential responsiveness to, and active, selective orientation toward, the environment—both social and physical. The three are distinguished from each other primarily by their tendency to emerge sequentially during childhood and to exhibit progressively more complex levels of psychological functioning.

The first and earliest forms of such active orientation produce individual differences in reaction to, attraction by, and exploration of particular aspects of the environment, both physical and social.

The transition from one to another of these dynamic forms of psychological orientation during early childhood is illustrated in successive publications from a longitudinal study of infants being carried out by Leila Beckwith, Sarale Cohen, Claire Kopp, and Arthur Parmelee at UCLA (Beckwith & Cohen, 1985; Beckwith, Cohen, Kopp, Parmelee, & Marcy, 1976; Cohen & Beckwith, 1979; Cohen, Beckwith, & Parmelee, 1978; Cohen & Parmelee, 1983; Cohen, Parmelee, Beckwith, & Sigman, 1986). Their imaginative and careful work reveals a progressive sequence of such environmentally oriented orientations from birth through seven years of age. The results reveal that immediately after birth, infants are especially responsive to vestibular stimulation (being picked up and held in a vertical position close to the body), which has the effect of soothing the baby so that it begins to engage in mutual gazing; by three months, visual exploration extends beyond proximal objects, and it is the mother's voice that is most likely to elicit responses, especially in the form of reciprocal vocalizations.

From about six months on, the infant begins actively to manipulate objects spontaneously in a purposeful way and to rearrange the physical environment. By this time, both vocalization and gesture are being used to attract the parents' attention and to influence their behavior. In addition, there is a growing readiness, across modalities, to initiate and sustain reciprocal interaction with a widening circle of persons in the child's immediate environment. Here we see the emergence of what I have called "structuring proclivities." As I shall illustrate in a moment, they can take other forms as well.

But first, I should like to underscore what I regard as most significant about the foregoing developmental trajectory revealed in the work of the California group: namely, at each successive stage, there is evidence of substantial individual differences that exhibit considerable consistency with persons and in situations with which the infant has become familiar. Moreover, these differences, in turn, predict (rs between .30 and .50) the level of responsiveness and interactive involvement *in other domains* in succeeding years, at least up to age seven, *subject, however, to the degree of appropriately gauged initiatives and reciprocal responses by the mother.*

A number of other investigations have yielded comparable findings and have extended them to still other activity domains: for example, individual differences in children's creativity in play and fantasy behavior (Connolly & Doyle, 1984; MacDonald & Parke, 1984); longitudinal studies of "ego resiliency" and "ego control" (Block & Block, 1980; Block, Block, & Keyes, 1988); and, especially, the as yet largely speculative ideas emerging from the field of behavioral genetics. Here, for example, other colleagues (Scarr & McCartney,1983; Plomin & Daniels, 1987; Plomin & Nesselroade, in press [1990]) have proposed models emphasizing the emergence of genetically based dispositions to select, explore, conceptualize, elaborate, reorganize, and construct social and physical environments both for the self and for others. The possibility of developing reliable and valid measures of such dispositions does not seem to lie beyond the scope of present knowledge and know-how.

The nature of the fourth and final class of developmentally instigative characteristics reflects the growing capacity and active propensity of children as they grow older to conceptualize their experience. It deals with what I have called *directive belief systems about the relation of the self to the environment*, or, for short, *directive beliefs*. If these expressions bring to mind such familiar concepts as "locus of control," and "goal orientation," then we are on the same track. My intent is indeed to focus attention on the growing child's realization of his or her own power to progress toward concrete goals in everyday life. Why, then, introduce a new terminology? The reason for doing so derives from the present state of research in this domain. I have explored the now voluminous literature on *locus of control, self-esteem, efficacy,* and related concepts but, as yet, have been able to find only one study in which such orientations were treated not as developmental outcomes but as possible developmental determinants. I still continue to hope, and even to believe, that somewhere, sometime, somebody has carried out studies of this kind. In the meantime, I am operating on the chance that giving the concept a new name for a new purpose will stimulate further concerted work in this domain.

These, then are the four types of developmentally instigative characteristics that I propose for priority entry as "person" terms in ecological models for the study of human development. In the analysis and interpretation of the findings generated by such models, it should be kept in mind that developmentally instigative characteristics do not *determine* the course of development; rather, they may be thought of as "putting a spin" on a body in motion. The effect of that spin depends on the other forces, and resources, in the total ecological system.

In that connection, I should like to return to my earlier comment pointing to the potential advantage of combining in the same research model measures of developmentally instigative characteristics with measures of cognitive ability, temperament, or personality. Such measures can be thought of as indexing psychological resources and socioemotional states. By combining these with the dynamic element inherent in the former, and then employing a design that can assess their joint synergistic effect, one can obtain a fuller appreciation of the contribution of the individual to his or her own development.

As I noted at the outset, this further effort to identify and to conceptualize developmentally relevant characteristics of the person has led to a reformulation of earlier conceptualizations of the environment. Specifically, and not surprisingly, it has suggested the notion of conceptualizing analogous developmentally instigative elements at each environmental level from the proximal to the distal.

For example, the definition of the *microsystem* has been expanded to include reference to social, physical, and symbolic aspects of the immediate setting that invite, permit, or inhibit, engagement in sustained, progressively more complex interaction with and activity in the immediate environment. With respect to the *macrosystem*, once again it was a Vygotskian concept that paved the way. In his theory of the "sociohistorical evolution of the mind" (Vygotsky, 1978; Vygotsky & Luria, 1956 [English version in Lloyd & Fernyhough, 1999]), Vygotsky had set forth the thesis that the potential options for individual development are defined and delimited by the possibilities available in a given culture at a given point in its history. This means, for example, that, in a particular microsystem setting, such as the home or the classroom, the structure and content of the setting, and the forms of developmental process that can take place within it, are to a large extent defined and delimited by the culture, subculture, or other macrosystem structure in which the microsystem is embedded. It follows that the definition of the macrosystem should include provision for recognizing the developmentally instigative properties that it incorporates. Accordingly, the original definition of the macrosystem has been expanded as follows:

> The *macrosystem* consists of the overarching pattern of micro-, meso-, and exosystems characteristic of a given culture, subculture, or other extended social structure, *with particular reference to the developmentally instigative belief systems, resources, hazards, lifestyles, opportunity structures, life course options, and patterns of social interchange that are embedded in such overarching systems.*

This expanded definition has powerful implications at two levels, first in the realm of developmental theory, second with respect to research design. On the former count, the reformulation implies that developmental processes are likely to differ significantly—not just statistically, but substantively—from one macrosystem to the next. Evidence for the validity of this proposition has been documented recently in a series of reports from two programs of research, one directed by Sanford Dornbusch at Stanford University (Dornbusch, 1987; Dornbusch, Ritter, Leiderman, Roberts, & Fraleigh, 1987) and the other by Laurence Steinberg, now at Temple University (Steinberg, 1989; Mounts, Lamborn, & Steinberg, 1989). In addition, taking as their point of departure the classic work of Diana Baumrind (Baumrind, 1971, 1973; Baumrind & Black, 1967) on the superiority of authoritative parental styles over either permissiveness or authoritarianism, both groups of investigators have demonstrated that these parental patterns have reliably and dramatically different, and even contradictory, effects when separately examined in the four principal ethnic groups in the United States—whites, blacks, Hispanics, and Asians. These findings, in turn, are generating new and promising hypotheses relating the observed variation in process to the differences in resources, belief systems, opportunity structures, and other developmentally instigative conditions characterizing the lives of each of these groups in American society. Studies by other investigators have revealed similarly pronounced variation in developmental processes and outcomes associated with other macrosystem contrasts: for instance, social class (Bee et al., 1982), family structure (Hetherington, 1989), and mother's employment status (Bronfenbrenner, Alvarez, & Henderson, 1983).[1]

The demonstration of such differences is of little scientific value, however, if the research designs employed do not go beyond the conventional labels used to distinguish various social groups in a society. It is necessary, in addition, to gather specific information about one or more of the substantive domains specified in the revised definition of the macrosystem. In the words of my colleague Stephen Ceci, who has made signal contributions to our understanding of the role of context in cognitive development: "The context in which cognition takes place is not simply an adjunct to the cognition, but constituent of it" (Ceci, Bronfenbrenner, & Baker, 1988, p. 243). Ceci's elegant aphorism applies to all spheres of psychological development.

This presentation ends with the following statement, introduced as a possible preposterous proposal: To the extent that it is practically possible, every program of research on human development should include, at an early state, a contrast between at least two macrosystems most relevant to the developmental phenomenon under investigation.

Why should such a provision be desirable? I offer what I hope are two compelling reasons. First, the recommended procedure provides one of the most effective checks against arriving at and publishing a false conclusion. Second, and even more important for scientific advance, the strategy constitutes one of the most powerful tools we have for illuminating our understanding of how developmental processes function in species *Homo sapiens*. In the words of a leading British neuropsychologist, "We are a species wired for culture." Short of trying to change human beings, an effort for which the chances of success are not high, our next best hope as scientists is to try to understand how human nature does that very job. And macrosystems are where we humans do it on the grandest scale, the better or the worse for our own development.

Note

1. The foregoing principle and associated findings call into serious question the widespread practice of controlling for environmental and personal factors (e.g., social class, family structure, maternal employment, gender, age) by entering them as covariates in a conventional regression equation. This practice assumes that the processes or relationships under investigation operate in the same way and to the same degree in all categories and levels of the control factor. When this assumption is violated, as is often the case, the use of this technique can produce distorted results, even to the point of indicating the opposite of what is in fact the case. Under such circumstances no adjustment for the control variable is possible, just as one cannot control for the effect of differences between animal species.

References

Allport, G. W. (1937). *Personality: A psychosocial interpretation*. New York: Holt.
Beckwith, L., & Cohen, S. E. (1985). Home environment and cognitive competence in preterm children during the first 5 years. In A. W. Gottfried (Ed.), *Home environment and early cognitive development: Longitudinal research* (pp. 235–271). Orlando, FL: Academic Press.
Beckwith, L., Cohen, S. E., Kopp, C. B., Parmelee, A. H., & Marcy, T. G. (1976). Caregiver-infant interaction and early cognitive development in pre-term infants. *Child Development, 47*, 579–587.
Bee, H. L., Barnard, K. E., Eyres, S. J., Gray, C. A., Hammond, M. A., Spietz, A. L., Snyder, C., & Clark, B. C. (1982). Prediction of IQ and language skill from perinatal status, child performance, family characteristics, and mother-infant interaction. *Child Development, 53*, 1134–1156.
Baumrind, D. (1971). Current patterns of parental authority. *Developmental Psychology, 4*(1, Pt. 2), 1–103.
Baumrind, D. (1973). The development of instrumental competence through socialization. In A. D. Pick (Ed.), *Minnesota symposia on child psychology* (Vol. 7, pp. 3–46). Minneapolis: University of Minnesota Press.
Baumrind, D., & Black, A. E. (1967). Socialization practices associated with dimensions of competence in preschool boys and girls. *Child Development, 38*(2), 291–327.
Block, J. H., & Block, J. (1980). The role of ego-control and ego-resiliency in the organization of behavior. In W. A. Collins (Ed.), *Minnesota symposia on child psychology* (Vol. 13, pp. 39–101). Hillsdale, NJ: Lawrence Erlbaum.
Block, J., Block, J. H., & Keyes, S. (1988). Longitudinally foretelling drug usage in adolescence: Early childhood personality and environmental precursors. *Child Development, 59*, 336–355.
Bronfenbrenner, U. (1979). *The ecology of human development: Experiments by nature and design*. Cambridge, MA: Harvard University Press.
Bronfenbrenner U. (1986). Recent advances in research on human development. In R. K. Silbereisen, K. Eyferth, & G. Rudinger (Eds.), *Development as action in context: Problem behavior and normal youth development* (pp. 287–309). New York: Springer-Verlag.
Bronfenbrenner, U. (1989). Ecological systems theory. In R. Vasta (Ed.), *Six theories of child development* (pp. 185–246). Greenwich, CT: JAI.
Bronfenbrenner, U., Alvarez, W., & Henderson, C. R. (1983). Working and watching: Maternal employment status and parents' perceptions of their three-year-old children. *Child Development, 55*, 1362–1378.
Ceci, S. J., Bronfenbrenner, U., & Baker, J. G. (1988). Memory in context: The case of prospective memory. In F. Weinert & M. Perlmutter (Eds.), *Universals and changes in memory development* (pp. 243–256). Hillsdale, NJ: Lawrence Erlbaum.
Cohen, S. E., & Beckwith, L. (1979). Preterm infant interaction with the caregiver in the first year of life and competence at age two. *Child Development, 50*, 767–776.

Cohen, S. E., Beckwith, L., & Parmelee, A. H. (1978). Receptive language development in preterm children as related to caregiver-child interaction. *Pediatrics, 61,* 16–20.

Cohen, S. E., & Parmelee, A. H. (1983). Prediction of five-year Stanford-Binet scores in preterm infants. *Child Development, 54,* 1242–1253.

Cohen, S. E., Parmelee, A. H., Beckwith, L., & Sigman, M. (1986). *Developmental and Behavioral Pediatrics, 7,* 102–110.

Connolly, J. A., & Doyle, A. (1984). Relation of social fantasy play to social competence in preschoolers. *Developmental Psychology, 20,* 797–806.

Dornbusch, S. (1987, April). *Adolescent behavior and school problems: The importance of context.* Paper presented at the biennial meeting of the Society for Research in Child Development, Baltimore.

Dornbusch, S. M., Ritter, P. L., Leiderman, P. H., Roberts, D. F., & Fraleigh, M. J. (1987). The relation of parenting style to adolescent school performance. *Child Development, 58,* 1244–1257.

Hetherington, E. (1989). Coping with family transitions: Winners, losers, and survivors. *Child Development, 60,* 1–14.

Leontiev, A. N. (1932). Studies on the cultural development of the child. *Journal of Genetic Psychology,* 52–83.

Leontiev, A. N. (1978). *Activity, consciousness, and personality* (M. J. Hall, Trans.). Englewood Cliffs, NJ: Prentice Hall.

Leontiev, A. N. (1981). *Problemy razvitiia psikhiki* [Problems of the development of mind]. Moscow: Moscow State University.

Lloyd, P., & Fernyhough, C. (Eds.). (1999). *Lev Vygotsky: Critical assessments: Vol. 1. Vygotsky's theory* (pp. 56–88). Florence, KY: Taylor & Francis/Routledge.

MacDonald, K,. & Parke, R. D. (1984). Bridging the gap: Parent-child play interaction and peer interactive competence. *Child Development, 55,* 1265–1277.

May, M. A. (1932). The foundations of personality. In P. S. Achilles (Ed.), *Psychology at work* (pp. 81–101). New York: McGraw-Hill.

Mounts, N., Lamborn, S. D., & Steinberg, L. (1989, April). *Relations between family processes and school achievement in different ethnic contexts.* Paper presented at the biennial meeting of the Society for Research in Child Development, Kansas City, MO.

Plomin, R,. & Daniels, S. (1987). Why are children in the same family so different from one another? *Behavioral and Brain Sciences, 10*(1), 1–16.

Plomin, R., & Nesselroade, J. R. (In press [1990]). Behavioral genetics and personality change. *Journal of Personality, 58*(1), 191–220.

Rogoff, B., & Wertsch, J. (Eds.). (1983). *Children's learning in the "zone of proximal development."* San Francisco: Jossey–Bass.

Scarr, S., & McCartney, K. (1983). How people make their own environments: A theory of genotype-environment effects. *Child Development, 54,* 424–435.

Steinberg, L. (1989, March). *Parenting academic achievers: When families make a difference (and when they don't).* Paper presented at the annual meeting of the American Educational Research Association, San Francisco.

Vygotsky, L. S. (1978). *Mind in society*. Cambridge, MA: Harvard University Press.

Vygotsky, L. S. (1979). Consciousness as a problem of psychology of behavior. *Soviet Psychology, 17*, 5–35. (Original work published 1925)

Vygotsky, L. S., & Luria, A. R. (1956). Psikhoilogicheskie vozzreniia Vygotskogo [Vygotsky's views on psychology]. In L. Vygotsky, *Izbrannye psikhologicheskie issledovaniia* [Selected psychological investigations]. Moscow: Academy of Pedagogical Sciences.

Wertsch, J. (Ed.). (1981). *The concept of activity in Soviet psychology*. New York: M. E. Sharpe.

Wertsch, J. (1985). *Vygotsky and the social formation of mind*. Cambridge, MA: Harvard University Press.

Article 10

Ecological Systems Theory

In this article I undertake a difficult task: to be at once the critic and the creator of my own work. The inherent conflict of interest is obvious, but I have been so long and so deeply involved in it that I can no longer escape it.

Ever since the publication of *The Ecology of Human Development* (Bronfenbrenner, 1979), now almost a decade ago, I have been engaging in a smuggling operation. In a series of articles written ostensibly for other purposes,[1] I have been pursuing a hidden agenda: that of reassessing, revising, extending—as well as regretting and even renouncing—some of the conceptions set forth in my 1979 monograph. The original invitation to write this article therefore presented me with an opportunity, indeed an obligation, to perform this task explicitly and systematically.

Source: Bronfenbrenner, U. (1992). Ecological systems theory. In R. Vasta (Ed.), *Six theories of child development: Revised formulations and current issues* (pp. 187–249). London: Jessica Kingsley. Reprinted with permission from Jessica Kingsley Pub., Ltd.

Author's Note: The author is indebted to a number of his colleagues at Cornell and elsewhere for their constructive criticisms and suggestions on earlier drafts of this chapter. Particular appreciation is expressed to Stephen Ceci, who, in the course of our collaboration in research and many conversations in between, has contributed more than I can any longer distinguish from the ideas developed here, especially in Section IV.

I begin with a warning and a reaffirmation. Any readers who might have welcomed the words *regret* and *renounce* in the preceding paragraph should note the absence of *recant*. Those who choose to disregard the warning and to read on will discover that the basic elements and imperatives of the ecological paradigm not only still stand but are further strengthened and extended by both scientific evidence and scientific argument. In the pages that follow, additions, subtractions, and revisions, albeit substantial, apply almost exclusively to corollaries, not to fundamental theorems of an ecological paradigm for research on human development.

In evidence of that fact, I begin with what I regard as the cornerstone of the theoretical structure—then, as now, appropriately introduced as "Definition 1." It reappears below unaltered, except for the addition of a clarifying phrase, identified by italics.

> *Definition 1.* The ecology of human development is the scientific study of the progressive, mutual accommodation, *throughout the life course,* between an active, growing human being and the changing properties of the immediate settings in which the developing person lives, as this process is affected by the relations between these settings, and by the larger contexts in which the settings are embedded.

I. Context Without Development

Alas, no sooner had I reaffirmed a first principle than I found myself obliged to acknowledge a first infirmity of equal magnitude. It weakens not the principle but its implementation. The principle defines as the ultimate aim of the scientific endeavor the systematic understanding of the processes and outcomes of human development as a joint function of the *person* and the *environment.* Yet an examination of the now substantial body of research conducted within an ecological perspective over the past decade reveals a striking imbalance. As I have documented in the series of articles and reviews, existing studies in the ecology of human development have provided more knowledge about the nature of developmentally relevant environments, near and far, than about the characteristics of developing individuals, then or now.[2] As I have written elsewhere:

> It is an instance of what might be called "the failure of success." For some years, I harangued my colleagues for avoiding the study of development in real-life settings. No longer able to complain on that score, I have found a new bête-noir. In place of too much research on development "out of

context," we now have a surfeit of studies on "context without development." (Bronfenbrenner, 1986d, p. 288)

Ironically, having made the criticism, I must now also acknowledge that it applies to my own writings. Anyone who takes the trouble to examine my book *The Ecology of Human Development* (Bronfenbrenner, 1979) will discover that it has much more to say about the nature and developmental contribution of the environment than about the organism itself.

II. An Ecological Paradigm for Development in Context

The paradigm is derived from, and hence most appropriately introduced as, a transformed and extended version of Kurt Lewin's (1935) classical formula:[3]

B = f(PE) [Behavior is a joint function of person and environment]

The first transformation involves a provocative substitution:

D = f(PE) [Development is a joint function of person and environment]

The substitution is provocative because it focuses attention on the conceptual difference between "behavior" and "development." The key distinction lies in the fact that development involves a parameter not present in Lewin's original equation—the dimension of time.[4] Thus, at a purely descriptive level, human development may be defined as *the phenomenon of constancy and change in the characteristics of the person over the life course.* In light of this definition, careful consideration of the reformulated formula reveals that the "D" term refers not to the phenomenon of development but to its outcome at a particular point in time. What the revised Lewinian equation does accomplish, however, is to move the formulation from description to process (or, in Lewin's terms, from phenotype to genotype); it does so by stipulating the existence of two types of forces that interact to generate constancy and change in development. By incorporating the implied dimensions of time, and substituting words for symbols, we may translate the formula as follows: *The characteristics of the person at a given time in his or her life are a joint function of the characteristics of the person and of the environment over the course of that person's life up to that time.* Thus science defines development as *the set of processes through which properties of the person and the environment interact to produce constancy and change in the biopsychological characteristics of the person over the life course.*

The primacy of our interest, however, should not limit the scope of our concern; for, clearly, an ill-considered conceptualization and choice of developmental *outcomes* can trivialize the most scientifically elegant demonstration of the *processes* actually capable of producing the predicted effects.

But there is one other element in the equation that demands consideration because of its profound significance for both theory and research. *Lewin explicitly ruled out the possibility that the combination was one of simple addition. Consistent with the Gestalt tradition in which Lewin's theory was developed, the whole was presumed to be different from the sum of its parts.* The issue takes on added importance because, as of 1989, despite occasional theoretical assertions to the contrary, most developmental investigations in fact employ analytic models that assume only *additive* effects: that is, the influences emanating from the person and the environment are treated as operating independently of each other, with the net effect estimated from an algebraic sum of the various factors included in the model. Yet in those instances in which more complex models have been applied, they have typically revealed important *interactive* effects: that is, particular environmental conditions have been shown to produce different developmental consequences depending on the personal characteristics of individuals living in that environment. It was this kind of person-environment interaction that Lewin envisioned in his original formulation. Its investigation in the sphere of human development constitutes one of the most promising, but at the same time theoretically and methodologically most challenging, directions for future research.

Lewin's concept of function had yet another implication of even greater significance for theory and research design. In his writings, he drew what he regarded as a fundamental distinction between two kinds of research paradigms (Lewin, 1931, 1935, 1951). The first he referred to as Aristotelian or *class theoretical*. In such formulations, phenomena are "explained" by the categories to which they are assigned, as with Aristotle's four elements (earth, air, fire, and water). In opposition to such static concepts, Lewin argued for "field-theoretical" or "Galilean" paradigms that specify the particular *processes* through which the observed phenomenon is brought about. Typically in the historical development of a given science, class-theoretical concepts precede field-theoretical ideas and are gradually replaced by the latter. Lewin wished to accelerate the process. As we shall see, however, although half a century has gone by since the publication of Lewin's seminal essay, Aristotelian concepts and research models still abound in the scientific study of human development. Moreover, I shall argue below that, given the incomplete stage of our knowledge, such paradigms may often be the strategies of choice for exploring uncharted domains. Like the surveyor's grid, they provide a useful frame for describing the new terrain.

Nevertheless, purely class-theoretical models, while often suggestive, do not reveal the mechanisms that account for observed relationships. As is the rule in all science, what is required for this purpose is a conceptualization of a particular process (or set of processes) expected to produce a special effect either in enhancing constructive development or in undermining the process.

Lewin's distinction between class-theoretical and field-theoretical models provides a point of departure for a less complex task. Having formulated a general theoretical paradigm, we are now faced with the problem of its operational definition. For possible solutions of this problem, we turn to an analysis of research designs currently employed for the study of development in context to determine the extent to which they can be used or adapted to fit the requirements of our revised theoretical paradigm. In accord with Lewin's dichotomy, these designs are usefully distinguished in terms of those that do, versus do not, include in the model a consideration of the *processes* through which characteristics of person, environment, or both together can influence human development. The principal variants of each type are discussed below in order of their increasing complexity and completeness of the elements composing our general paradigm.[5]

III. Additional Research Models in the Study of Development in Context

Because these designs are more simple in structure, we begin with a consideration of these. Models in which the "r" term is omitted can take a variety of forms. The most common is one in which only the "E" term is present: that is, development is viewed solely as a product of environmental factors but through some process or processes that remain unspecified. I have referred to this type of research design as a *social address model*[6] (Bronfenbrenner & Crouter, 1983, pp. 361–362). Among the most common "social addresses" appearing in the research literature are social class, family size and ordinal position, rural versus urban residence, and differences by nationality or ethnic group. More recently, I have referred to a "new demography" (Bronfenbrenner & Crouter, 1983, p. 373): one- versus two-parent families, home care versus day care, children in private versus public schools, mother's employment status, how many times remarried, or—perhaps soon—the number of hours the father spends in child care and household tasks, or presence or absence of computers in the home.

The principal limitation of the social address model is readily apparent.[7] Like all class-theoretical concepts, it is little more than a name. As I have written elsewhere, "One looks only at the *social address*—that is, the environmental label—with no attention to what the environment is like, what people are living there, what they are doing, or how the activities taking place could affect the child" (Bronfenbrenner & Crouter, 1983, pp. 382–383).

Albeit less frequent, an analogous form of class-theoretical design is available on the side of the person. I have referred to this type of design as a *personal attributes model.*[8]

Finally, there are designs that combine the two domains—the *person context model.* Here characteristics *both* of the person and of the environment are taken into account *jointly.* Although this model suffers from the same limitations as the two preceding, from an ecological perspective it possesses a structural feature that makes it useful in the study of development in context. The particular strength of person-context designs lies in their capacity to identify what I call *ecological niches.* These are particular *regions in the environment that are especially favorable or unfavorable to the development of individuals with particular personal characteristics.* Operationally, occupational niches are defined by the intersection between one or more social addresses and one more personal attributes of individuals or groups who live at these addresses. For example, an analysis (Bronfenbrenner, 1988c) of data published annually by the National Center for Health Statistics reveals that a pregnant mother is more likely to have a low-birth-weight baby (under 2,500 grams or 5.5 pounds) if she comes from an environmental background distinguished by two or more of the following features: the mother has had less than a high school education, lives in the central section of a large metropolitan city, or is unmarried. This risk almost doubles, however, if she is 19 or under. Another group at special risk, albeit to a somewhat lesser degree, are mothers in the same environmental contexts who do not have their first child until they are 35 or over.

Although such findings are typically interpreted in terms of increased risk, the very same facts can be viewed from the perspective of positive growth (in this instance judged on a criterion of physical health). To wit, pregnant mothers least likely to have a low-birth-weight baby are white, college-educated women living in middle-class neighborhoods who are married and have their first child when they are in their middle or late 20s.

Informative as such findings are, they do not tell us what it is about mothers' education, place of residence, marital status, or age and race that affects the weight of the babies they bear. In other words, how does a given combination of environmental and personal features characterizing a particular ecological niche operate to influence human development? To answer that question, we must move from what Lewin called a class-theoretical model to one that is field theoretical by postulating some *process* associated with the above characteristics that could account for the observed variation.

Fortunately, the annual report on the vital statistics of the United States includes data relevant to one such process. Since 1969, the annual volume on natality data has carried several tables documenting the distribution of live births by birth weight and by the month of pregnancy that prenatal care began. Among the facts revealed by analysis of these data (Bronfenbrenner, 1988a) are the following:

- In general, the percentage of low-birth-weight babies decreases, the earlier prenatal care is begun.
- By far the highest frequency of premature births occurs among mothers who received no prenatal care at all—20%, as against 6% among those who received some prenatal care, even if only in the last month of pregnancy.
- Nearly a quarter of all babies born in 1985 were born to mothers who received no medical care during the critical first three months of pregnancy.
- The percentage of newborns whose mothers received prenatal care during the first trimester rose from 65% in 1969 to almost 75% in 1979, at which point the trend leveled off until 1985, when, for the first time since annual statistics have been published, the figure showed a drop from the previous year.
- The preceding turnabout is mirrored in the 1985 figures on the frequency of low birth weight. For the first time in two decades, the percentage of newborns weighing under 2,500 grams increased. The increase of 1% in one year is equal to a preceding 1% decrease that had taken more than three decades to achieve.
- A further analysis of the above data with the effects of education and maternal age taken into account revealed that the availability of prenatal care was associated with a reduction in the occurrence of low birth weight. This relationship was stronger among black families than among white.

Although the above analysis suffers from the well-known limitation of aggregate data (i.e., relationships at the individual level remain unknown), it nicely illustrates the distinction between class-theoretical and field-theoretical models and also serves as an introduction to more comprehensive process designs to be discussed in the next section. Before proceeding to that discussion, however, it is important to provide an example of a more complex person-context model in which the developmental outcomes go beyond physical characteristics into the domain of psychological functioning.

Most of the studies in this sphere are concerned with identifying groups at psychological risk, probably because of the greater concern, on the part of both professionals and the general public, with problem behavior. Hence, the question arises: What ecological niches are favorable to psychological growth, and what is to be understood by such a concept? One of the few studies that explicitly sought to identify some of the elements that define a "good ecology," which, in turn, fosters "good" psychological development, is Werner and Smith's (1982) monograph provocatively entitled *Vulnerable but Invincible*. The work involves a longitudinal study of a group of Hawaiian children who, despite having been "born and reared in chronic poverty, exposed to higher than average rates of prematurity and perinatal stress, and reared by mothers with little formal education . . . managed to develop into competent and autonomous young adults who 'worked well, played well, loved well, and expected well'" (Werner & Smith, 1982, p. 153). With respect to the topic at hand, the authors identified a number of characteristics early in life that appeared to differentiate these children from their matched controls, who had grown up in the same deprived environment and exhibited the types and degrees of developmental impairment often observed in such settings. On the environmental side, the distinguishing characteristics of those who "escaped" included smaller family size; greater spacing between the index child and the next-born sibling; the number and type of alternate caregivers available to the mother within the household (in the Hawaiian context, these were all family members); steady employment of the mother outside the household; and the presence of a multigenerational network of kin and friends in adolescence. But the structure of the children's environment did not tell the whole story. From their earliest years onward, the youngsters themselves also exhibited a number of distinctive characteristics:

The resilient high-risk boys and girls had fewer serious illnesses in the first two decades of life and tended to recuperate more quickly. Their mothers perceived them to be "very active" and "socially responsible" when they were infants, and independent observers noted their pronounced autonomy and social orientation when they were toddlers. Developmental examinations in the second year of life showed advanced self-help skills and adequate sensorimotor and language development for most of these children. (p. 154)

We shall have occasion to examine such characteristics more systematically below, particularly in Section IV. For the moment, I would only point out that the attributes mentioned are those that are valued in Western—and especially American—white, middle-class culture.

Not only did the characteristics of both the person and the environment play a significant role in the subsequent developmental progress achieved by the Hawaiian children, but, through the use of a *person-context design,* the investigators were able to show that youngsters growing up in similar environmental circumstances developed differently as a function of their particular personal characteristics. One of the most striking examples of this phenomenon was *the contrasting pattern of development observed for boys versus girls.* A distinctive feature of the pattern was the fact that it reversed itself over the first two decades of life.

> At birth, and throughout the first decade of life, more boys than girls were exposed to serious physical defects or illness requiring medical care, and more boys than girls had learning and behavior problems in the classroom and at home. . . .
>
> Trends were reversed in the second decade of life: the total number of boys with serious learning problems dropped, while the number of girls with serious disorders rose. Boys seemed now more prepared for the demands of school and work, although they were still more often involved in antisocial and delinquent behavior. Girls were now confronted with social pressures and role expectations that produced a higher rate of mental health problems in late adolescence and serious coping problems associated with teenage pregnancies and marriages.
>
> While control of aggression appeared to be one of the major problems for the boys in childhood, dependency became a major problem for the girls in adolescence. . . .
>
> Related to this trend was the cumulative number of stressful life situations reported by each sex. Boys with serious coping problems experienced more adversities than girls in *childhood*; girls with serious coping problems reported more stressful life events in *adolescence*. In spite of the biological and social pressures, which in this culture appear to make each sex more vulnerable at different times, more high-risk girls than high-risk boys grew into resilient young adults. (Werner & Smith, 1982, pp. 153–154)

Note that, despite the richness of information obtained in this study about the environmental and personal characteristics of a group of highly vulnerable children who ultimately exhibited contrasting developmental outcomes, the specific processes and pathways that enabled some of them to "escape" remain unclear. The principal reason for this seeming contradiction is that the analysis of processes requires a more differentiated research design, to be described below.

A. The Process-Person-Context Model

As its name implies, this design permits analysis of variations in developmental processes and outcomes as a *joint function of the characteristics of the environment and of the person*. The nature and power of the model are perhaps best conveyed by a concrete example. For this purpose, I select a study that addresses a scientific question made more urgent by the recent increase in the already high rate of babies born under 5.5 pounds in the United States.[9] What are the consequences of low birth weight for subsequent psychological development, and what are the processes involved?

Perhaps the best demonstration of the scope of possible effects and the processes that underlie them is still to be found in a classic study conducted in Scotland a quarter of a century ago. In the 1950s and 1960s, Cecil Mary Drillien (1957, 1964), a physician and professor of child life and health at the University of Edinburgh, carried out a seven-year longitudinal investigation of psychological development in two groups: 360 children of low birth weight (under 2,500 grams, or 5.5 pounds) and a control group selected "by taking the next mature birth from the hospital admission list" (Drillien, 1957, p. 29). In her follow-up assessments, the investigator found that the children of low birth weight were more likely to exhibit problems in physical growth, susceptibility to illness, impaired intellectual development, and poorer classroom performance, with all of these tendencies being more pronounced in boys (Drillien, 1964). With respect to school achievement, a special analysis revealed that those with low birth weight were especially likely to be working below their mental capacity.[10] In relation to this finding, the author comments as follows: "In most cases, failure to attain a standard commensurate with ability was associated with problems of behaviour, which were found to increase with decreasing birth weight [and] to be more common in males" (Drillien, 1964, p. 209).

Drillien's research is replete with far more explicit evidence of the interplay between biological and environmental forces, including some findings that, when fully examined, reveal implications for preventive strategies. Of particular significance in this regard are data on what she refers to as "maternal efficiency," a composite rating based on observations during successive home visits throughout the preschool years. Items considered included mother-child relationships, management of the home, and family health practices. In general, ratings of maternal efficiency (by observers who had no information about the children's classification by birth weight) were appreciably lower for mothers of low-weight new-borns than for those of the normal controls. The same relationship held for physical growth. In addition, "those males who were smallest at birth appear to be affected rather more by poor maternal care than females" (Drillien, 1964).

Although research findings on low-birth-weight babies are typically interpreted in terms of increased developmental risk, the very same data can also be viewed from the perspective of positive growth. To wit, *the more effective the maternal care, the better the development of the young child, particularly for low-birth-weight children. In other words, where the mother is willing and able to make the effort, she can do much to reduce the developmental risk that this handicap entails.*

It would be a mistake to assume, however, that the environment does the job all by itself, independent of the organism. Living organisms have the capacity, and indeed the active disposition, to heal themselves over time. We are all familiar with this phenomenon in the sphere of physical injury and illness, but we may not be as conscious of its operation in the psychological realm as well. An example appears in another of Drillien's analyses. Having demonstrated that children with low birth weight tended to be somewhat retarded in intellectual development, Drillien went on to show that, in successive assessments from six months up to seven years of age, this difference tended to decrease. The improvement was especially marked during the period up to age two. After that time, it declined slightly for infants with the lowest birth weight (under 3.5 pounds) but continued to increase for less handicapped cases so that, by school age, these youngsters were well within the normal range of intellectual functioning. In sum, *significant resources for counteracting effects of prenatal handicaps exist on the side of both the environment and the organism itself.*

Unfortunately, on the environmental side, these resources are not equally available to all. Drillien was one of the first to document the substantially higher proportion of low-birth-weight babies born to lower-class families. But she also went a significant step farther by identifying and investigating processes that could account for this difference. Drillien began by showing that the quality of maternal behavior (as classified and then rated by the home visitor) also varied systematically by the family's socioeconomic status, with care in lower-class homes being less consistent and responsive. Drillien then went on to analyze the relationship between quality of care and developmental outcomes, *separately* within each combination of three levels of social class and of weight at birth, during each of two age periods: from birth to two years and from two to five years. Thus the effectiveness of the mother-infant process was being examined as a joint function of characteristics of the broader environment (social class) and of the individual child (birth weight and age).[11]

The principal developmental outcome examined by Drillien was the frequency and severity of reported behavior disturbances, such as hyperactivity, overdependence, timidity, and negativism. The results revealed a general effect of maternal responsiveness in reducing both the incidence and the severity of problem behavior, particularly as the children got older. With respect to social class, however, the pattern of relationships was more complex. The effect of maternal care in reducing the *number of* children exhibiting one or more forms of disturbed behavior was strongest in the two highest social class groups. In other words, it would appear that these mothers got a bigger return on their investment. Whereas this is the finding emphasized by Drillien, further examination of the data reveals another, equally pronounced trend with respect to the *severity* of the reported problem behavior. Here it was the children from families at the bottom of the socioeconomic scale whose behavioral problems, while still present, were most relieved by maternal attention and care. Finally, while there was an increase in both incidence and severity of problems as birth weight decreased, this effect was not as great as that associated with social class and quality of maternal care.

In sum, responsive maternal care can substantially reduce the severity of psychological problems associated with low birth weight among socioeconomically deprived families and can subsequently reduce the number of low-birth-weight children experiencing any serious difficulty.

At a broader level, Drillien's research findings illustrate an important characteristic of the process of human development that is revealed through the application of process-person-context models: namely, the frequent occurrence of vicious or benign circles. The term *synergism* is used to describe a phenomenon of this kind, in which *the joint operation of two or more forces produces an effect that is greater than the sum of the individual effects.* In this instance, the combination of low birth weight and disadvantaged socioeconomic status still had greater negative impact than would have been expected from the separate effects of each. With respect to research design, Drillien's analyses, taken as a whole, illustrate the two key defining properties of a process-person-context model:

1. The design permits assessment not only of developmental outcomes but also of the effectiveness of the processes producing these outcomes.

2. The design reveals how both developmental outcomes and processes vary as a joint function of the characteristics of the person and of the environment, thus permitting the detection of synergistic effects.

Stated more succinctly, the model identifies *any differences in developmental processes and outcomes associated with different ecological niches.* What is the special scientific utility and importance of a model of this kind? The results of Drillien's analysis also provide an illustration of the answer to this question. Prior to the 1960s, the generally accepted explanation for the observed correlation between low birth weight and subsequent psychological impairment assumed minimal brain damage as the intervening mechanism; indeed, this was the heading under which Drillien presented her discussion. Her finding, however, that this correlation varied systematically by social class clearly implies a more complex set of processes. Drillien's speculations on this score focused mainly on a variety of physiological deficits (including minimal brain damage) associated with low birth weight that, in turn, could lower the resistance level to socioenvironmental stress in later life (Drillien, 1964). In her view, there was little possibility of separating out these factors, given the limitations of the then-available data.

Today [1989], as the result of the earlier work of Drillien and others, the range of possible processes has broadened in both variety and complexity, and the prospect of sorting them out is now considerably brighter, again through the use of process-person-context models. Two scientific advances, in particular, have contributed to this changed situation. First, the development of modern imaging techniques, such as ultrasound, now permit the detection of a variety of physiological brain malfunctions (Catto-Smith, Yu, Bajusk, Orgill, & Astbuty, 1985; Stewart, 1983). The availability of such a measure makes it possible to assess both the independent and joint effects of a number of possibly handicapping organic factors often existing together at the time of birth, such as minimal brain damage, congenital malformations (minor anatomical abnormalities), complications in the birth process, low birth weight, and early gestation age (age at birth calculated from estimated date of conception). Second, the recognition that conventional indices of social class are but a weak reflection of the quality of the environment affecting family life has led to the design of more powerful measures of the family's ecology: for example, indices that incorporate characteristics not only of the child's own family but those of families living in the same neighborhood or involved in the same social network. Such more differentiated process-person-context designs, however, are still to be applied specifically in the study of long-term effects of perinatal influences.[12]

As the preceding examples illustrate, the principal scientific power of the process-person-context model lies in its capacity not so much to produce definitive answers as to generate new questions by revealing the inadequacies of existing formulations in accounting for observed complexities. As the history of science shows, herein lies one of the principal keys to scientific advance.

A similar purpose is served by process models *that include only two other domains.* Some examine how mechanisms and outcomes vary solely with respect to context (*process-context models*), others only in relation to contrasting characteristics of the individual (*process-person models*). Both of these truncated designs can contribute new knowledge and understanding of development.

B. The Chronosystem Model

Having sought to persuade the reader of the superiority of the process-person-context model over its contemporaries, I shall now, perversely, point to a major lacuna in this powerful design. The missing element is the same one that was omitted in Lewin's original formula—the dimension of *time.* This dimension has been given short shrift in most empirical work as well. For many decades, it was taken into account only as it applied to constancy and change in the characteristics of the person; the environment was treated as a fixed entity, observed only at a single point in time, and presumed to remain constant (e.g., family composition and social class were dealt with as if they were unchanging structures).

Especially in recent years, however, research on human development has projected the factor of time along a new axis. In the mid-1970s, an increasing number of investigators began to employ research designs that took into account constancy and change not only in the person but also in the environment. I have referred to designs of this kind as *chronosystem models*[13] (Bronfenbrenner, 1986c, 1986d). Particular attention was focused on developmental changes triggered by life events or experiences. These experiences may have their origins either in the external environment (e.g., the birth of a sibling, entering school, divorce, winning the sweepstakes) or within the organism (e.g., puberty, severe illness). Whatever their origin, the critical feature of such events is that they alter the existing relation between person and environment, thus creating a dynamic that may instigate developmental change.

Chronosystem models may be either short term or long term. In the former case, data are obtained for the same group of subjects both before and after a particular life experience or *life transition*. An early example is Baldwin's (1947) study of changes in parent-child interaction induced by the impending arrival of a sibling. The results revealed marked changes in the mother's behavior toward the first child before, during, and after the mother's pregnancy with the second child.

A long-term chronosystem design permits examining the often cumulative effects of a sequence of transitions in what sociologists, from as far back as the 1930s, have referred to as the *life course* (Clausen, 1986; Elder, 1985). The degree of scientific sophistication and power that such models have achieved in recent years is well illustrated in the work of Glen Elder and his colleagues (Elder, 1974; Elder & Caspi, 1988; Elder, Caspi, & Downey, 1986). Their studies have revealed the systematically different developmental paths, now extending across three generations, that were set in motion by the Great Depression of the 1930s. Elder's work represents a prototype—indeed, because of its elegance and imaginativeness, almost a paragon—of this type of chronosystem design.[14]

The description of the chronosystem model completes our discussion of formal paradigms and research designs for the study of development in context. We now move from the abstract to the concrete with the consideration of the substantive content of the two major substantive domains in the general paradigm—the developmentally relevant characteristics of *persons* and of *environments*. Although the paradigm emphasizes the necessity for analyzing the interaction between these two spheres, such analysis requires prior understanding of the structure and content of each of the interacting domains.

IV. Properties of the Person
From an Ecological Perspective

In examining scientific conceptions of the developing person from an ecological perspective, one is struck by a curious fact: the overwhelming majority of these conceptions are *context free*: that is, the characteristics of the person are defined, both conceptually and operationally, without any reference to the environment and are presumed to have the same meaning irrespective of the culture, class, or setting in which they are observed or in which the person lives.

There have been, however, some violations of this unstated assumption. Most of them are implicit: that is, they occur at the level of method rather than explicit theory. Any findings that might call the assumption into question are treated as error in the form of method variance and in this way dismissed from further consideration. But in a few instances, the assumption has been explicitly and systematically challenged. Until recently, the challenges have been overlooked, mainly because most of the challengers have been scholars from abroad or from disciplines other than developmental psychology.

In this section, we shall examine these challenges in terms of their implications for the scientific study of human development. Because the most systematic alternative conceptualizations have been formulated in relation to the nature and origin of the *cognitive capacities* of human beings, we shall begin our considerations in that sphere. We shall then cross the illusory and deceptive "great divide" in contemporary developmental psychology to undertake a similar analysis in a second domain—that of *socioemotional and motivational characteristics*, traditionally classified under the rubrics of temperament and personality.

A third and final category introduces a different, as yet untried, frame of reference for conceptualizing properties of the developing person. Consistent with an ecological view of organism-environment interaction, the orientation takes as its point of departure *a conception of the person as an active agent who contributes to his or her own development. Correspondingly, personal characteristics are distinguished in terms of their potential to evoke response from, alter, or create the external environment, thereby influencing the subsequent course of the person's psychological growth.* Because such active potentials simultaneously involve cognitive, socioemotional, and motivational aspects, the traditional separation between cognitive capacities, on the one hand, and qualities of temperament and personality, on the other, is not appropriate for this interactive domain.

A. Cognition in Context

As previously noted, most scientific conceptions and measures of cognitive capacities are characterized by an underlying assumption that the abilities in question (e.g., formal operations in Piaget's sense) are invariant across place and time: that is, they are presumed to have the same psychological significance irrespective of social structure, culture, or historical era. This assumption characterizes a wide range of measures, including objective tests of intelligence, academic achievement, or personality; assessments of Piagetian or neo-Piagetian stages of cognitive[15] or moral[16] development; analyses of cognitive style (Kagan, Moss, & Sigel, 1963; Kogan, 1973, 1983) and personal style (Block & Block, 1980);

characterizations of persons based on their patterns of response in laboratory experiments (Witkin, Dyk, Faterson, Goodenough, & Karp, 1962); and modes of cognitive functioning based on information theory and theories of artificial intelligence (Brown, Bransford, Ferrara, & Campione, 1983).

In progressive degree, the conceptualizations and methods of cognitive functioning that follow call this tacit assumption of contextual irrelevance into question.

1. Competence as an Achieved Status

This first subcategory challenges the above assumption only by implication and default. It does so by defining a person's level of competence solely by that person's achieved status in the environment. Entirely lacking is any specification of psychological qualities that may have enabled the person to attain the given status, but the underlying assumption is that such qualities do in fact exist. The most common examples are the number of years of schooling obtained or the highest occupational status reached. Corresponding indices on the debit side include dropping out of school, ending up on welfare, failing to meet requirements for professional status, and the like. Note that the criteria of "positive" versus "negative" outcomes of development implicit in such operational definitions are socioeconomic and social success versus failure as defined by the society at large.

2. Competence Evaluated Within the Setting

While still focused on achieved status in a real-life setting, this category adds two new elements. First, status is judged by persons within the setting who occupy roles that involve responsibility for evaluation. Second, the evaluation is made not with regard to general levels of ability or competence but with respect to capacity to function effectively in specific kinds of activities and tasks conducted within a particular type of setting in everyday life. The most common examples include teachers' grades given in various school subjects or supervisors' ratings of subordinates' job performance. Here again there is an implicit criterion of positive versus negative development, but this time it is defined operationally in terms of specific competencies deemed essential for success in the context of particular social institutions accorded status in the larger society.

An additional aspect of assessments of this kind is that, to the extent that the judges of performance continue to be participants in the person's life or to influence decisions on future opportunities (e.g., promotion), their judgments not only represent an evaluation of the person's present level of functioning but may also play a role in shaping his or her future career and thereby influence the course of later development.[17] Recognition of this possibility points to the advantage of including both non-contextual and contextual measures of competence within the same research design, a topic to receive further consideration below.

3. Competence as the Mastery of Culturally Defined, Familiar Activities in Everyday Life

In both of the preceding subcategories, the assessment of competence in real-life settings is based mainly on pragmatic considerations rather than on more general theoretical grounds. By contrast, the environmentally oriented attributes described below are derived from a broad, a priori conception requiring the inclusion of context as an element essential to the very definition of competence. Because of the special significance of such formulations for the ecology of human development, I shall describe them in some detail.

Similar formulations have emerged from the work of researchers from rather different disciplines and intellectual perspectives. Perhaps the earliest and most explicit theoretical conception of competence in context is found in the writings and research of the Soviet psychologists Vygotsky (1929, 1978), Luria (1928, 1931, 1976, 1979, 1982), and Leontiev (1932, 1959, 1975). Although the latter two have each made original contributions to a common scientific endeavor, both acknowledge Vygotsky as the primary source of their own ideas. The group's conception of cognitive competence is deeply grounded in Vygotsky's theory of development, which, in turn, is built on a Marxist base. The basic tenets of the theory may be summarized as follows. Central to the formulation is the thesis that development in human beings is fundamentally different from that in other animals. Specifically, the human species, by virtue of its unique capacity to use tools and symbols, continually creates and elaborates its own environment in the form of culture. The evolution of culture, in turn, is seen as a historical process that has taken different forms across both time and place. Moreover, human beings are not only a culture-producing species, they are also culture produced: that is, the psychological characteristics of the species are a joint, interactive function of the biological characteristics and potentials of an active organism, on the one hand, and, on the other, of the forms of psychological functioning and possible courses of development existing in a given culture at a particular point in its history. It follows that the repertoire of mental processes and outcomes available as possibilities for individual development can vary from one culture or sub-culture to the next, both within and across time. Taken as a whole, this conceptualization constitutes what Luria (1978) referred to as Vygotsky's theory of "the sociohistorical evolution of the mind" (p. 5).[18]

So sweeping a theory may appear to elude any possibility of an empir-ical test. The protagonists of the theory, however, thought otherwise and acted accordingly. Luria (1976) tells the story in his autobiography.[19] The time was the early 1930s.

> We conceived the idea of carrying out the first far-reaching study of intellec-tual functions. . . . By taking advantage of the rapid cultural changes that were then in progress in remote parts of our country, we hoped to trace the changes in thought processes that are brought about by technological change. . . . At that time, many of our rural areas were undergoing rapid change with the advent of collectivization and mechanization of agriculture. (p. 60)

The basic research design took advantage of the fact that the process of modernization had not been introduced in all areas of the region at the same time. As a result, it became possible to carry out a comparison of cognitive functioning in communities differing in their degree of expo-sure to social change. Vygotsky died of tuberculosis before this extraordi-nary investigation was completed. The following is Luria's succinct summary of the findings:[20]

> Our data indicate that decisive changes can occur in going from graphic and functional-concrete and practical methods of thinking to much more theoret-ical modes of thought brought about by changes in social conditions, in this instance by the socialist transformation of an entire culture. (Luria, 1976, p. iv)

In the Vygotskian framework, this same principle applies to intracul-tural contexts as well. For example, in what appears to be his first paper published in the United States, Luria (1928) delineates analogous devel-opmental differences in the contrasts between preschool and school, and village and town.

> We consider [that] the development of the child's conduct can be reduced to a series of transformations, that these transformations are due to the growing influence of cultural environment, the constant appearance of new cultural inventions and habits, and that each invention of a new "artificial" habit involves the change of the structure of the child's conduct. Compare the

conduct of a pupil in the first year at school with that of a preschool pupil. Compare the mental processes of these two and you will note two structures essentially different in principle. Compare the village boy with another boy of the same age who lives in town and you will be struck by the huge difference in the mentality of both, the difference being not so much in the development of natural psychical functions (absolute memory, the quickness of reactions, etc.) *as in the subject-matter of their cultural experience and those methods which are used by those two children in realizing their natural abilities.* (p. 494)

What is the relation of such formulations to the cognitive characteristics of the child? A clue to the answer appears in the opening paragraph of the first and only journal article by Vygotsky published in the United States. In 1929, he wrote:

In the process of development the child not only masters the items of cultural experience, but the habits and forms of cultural behavior and cultural methods of reasoning. We must, therefore, distinguish the main lines in the development of the child's behavior. First, there is the line of natural development of behavior which is closely bound up with the processes of general organic growth and maturation of the child. Secondly, there is the line of cultural improvement of the psychological functions, the working out of new methods of reasoning, the mastering of the cultural methods of behavior. (p. 415)

The same point is made by Luria (1979):

The "cultural" aspect of Vygotsky's theory involved the socially structured ways in which society organizes the kind of tasks that the growing child faces and the kinds of tools, both mental and physical, that the young child is provided with to master those tasks. (p. 44)

It is this *mastery of culturally defined and experienced tasks* that defines the basis of cognitive competence in the Vygotskian framework.

For specific examples, we turn to another perspective that led to a similar conclusion but in a more concrete form. In his autobiography, Luria identifies as one of the significant influences on Vygotsky's thought the ideas of the English anthropologist W. H. R. Rivers (1926). Rivers was the forerunner of a number of contemporary ethnologists (Lancy & Strathern, 1981; Lave, 1977; Lave, Murtaugh, & de la Roche, 1984; Murtaugh, 1985; Super, 1980) who, on the basis of their field observations, argued that different environmental demands lead to the development of different patterns of ability. For example, the anthropologist Charles Super (1980) has documented the highly complex cognitive processes employed by the

!Kung San people, a hunting-gathering society of West Africa. Yet, !Kung San adult men perform only at the level of Western children on IQ tests, Piagetian tasks, and information-processing problems, even when such measures are adapted for the local culture.

Other cultural anthropologists have reported analogous "cognitive dissonances" within American society. For example, Jean Lave and her colleagues (Lave et al., 1984; Murtaugh, 1985) have shown that shoppers, upon being confronted with multiple brand items of unequal size and price, could make highly complex, rapid, and accurate estimates of actual per-unit cost. But again, when these same shoppers were administered standardized tests of mental arithmetic, allegedly requiring the same mental operations, no relation was found between test performance and the subject's shopping accuracy.

A similar contrast for children has been demonstrated in a study entitled "Mathematics in the Streets and in Schools," with a sample of street urchins in Recife, Brazil, who were engaged in commercial transactions (Carraher, Carraher, & Schliemann, 1985). "Performance on mathematical problems embedded in real-life contexts was superior to that on school-type word problems and context-free computational problems involving the same numbers and operations" (p. 21).

The two contextual approaches to cognitive development—Vygotskian on the one hand, anthropological on the other—have been brought together and impressively applied in the work of Michael Cole and his colleagues (Cole, Gay, Glick, & Sharp, 1971; Cole & Scribner, 1974; Laboratory of Comparative Human Cognition, 1983; Scribner & Cole, 1981).

Finally, in the most recent concerted effort to assess cognition in context, the experimental psychologist Stephen Ceci (1996) has turned anthropologist but then returned to his root discipline by putting the laboratory itself in context. In a series of experimental studies, Ceci and his colleagues demonstrated that the same cognitive processes, in both children and adults, varied appreciably in both complexity and efficiency as a function of the context in which they were embedded. For example, processes supporting prospective memory progressively increased in efficiency as the same experiment was conducted with samples of children in a physics laboratory, in a laboratory in a home economics building, and in the children's own homes (Ceci & Bronfenbrenner, 1985). In a second experiment (Ceci, 1996), the ability to educe complex visual patterns showed a quantum gain when the same stimulus patterns were depicted as small pictures of familiar objects embedded in a video game instead of by abstract geometrical figures embedded within a laboratory task. In a third study, appropriately titled "A Day at the Races" (Ceci & Liker, 1986), highly successful racetrack bettors were asked to handicap a total of 60 actual and experimentally contrived races. "The analysis revealed that expert handicapping was a cognitively sophisticated enterprise, with experts using a mental model that contained multiple interaction effects and nonlinearity . . . involving as many as seven variables" (pertaining to the characteristics of the horse, the jockey, the other horses in the field, the weather, etc.) (Ceci & Liker, 1986, p. 255). Measures of expertise, however, were not correlated with the subjects' IQs, and four of the top handicappers had IQ scores in the lower to mid-80s. On the basis of their findings, Ceci and his colleagues (Ceci, Bronfenbrenner, & Baker, 1988) conclude that "the context in which cognition takes place is not simply an adjunct to the cognition, but a constituent of it" (p. 243).

Viewed in a Vygotskian perspective, Ceci's study of successful gamblers raises an issue of both theoretical and practical significance. In effect, what Ceci is arguing is that complex cognitive functioning can take a wide variety of forms, all of them equally valid, in terms of the particular culture or subculture in which they evolved. But what if the modes of complex cognitive functioning available and acquired in the particular subculture in which a person has developed do not correspond to the equally complex modes of cognitive functioning expected in the broader culture in which one lives, or in another culture into which one has moved? Does this kind of situation, which exists for so many human beings in modern times, require a new process of enculturation extending over time; or are there more rapid developmental trajectories for achieving new levels of psychological integration across both worlds? The question constitutes one of the principal challenges to the ecology of human development, both as a science and as a context for evolving humane and constructive social policies.[21]

B. Implications for Theory and Research Design

We have now completed a tentative taxonomy of measures of cognitive competence and are in a position to consider its implications for the study of development in context. Such implications are most obvious, indeed they are made quite explicit, in the last group of conceptions outlined above: those that define cognitive competence in terms of processes and outcomes inextricably rooted in a cultural or subcultural context. It is useful for our purposes to summarize these implications, and others to follow, in a series of principles basic to an ecology of human development.

Principle 1. Differences in cognitive performance between groups from different cultures or subcultures are a function of experience, in the course of growing up, with the types of cognitive processes existing in a given culture or subculture at a particular period in its history.

This principle leads to a further implication in the realm of research design and interpretation. We shall use the term *corollary* to denote design-relevant implications of this kind.

Corollary 1.1. Any assessment of the cognitive competence of an individual or group must be interpreted in the light of the culture or subculture in which the person was brought up.

The next important point to be noted is less an implication than a descriptive fact. If we use the taxonomy we have constructed as a map on which to locate the areas in which scientific explorations have been conducted, it becomes clear that the overwhelming majority of empirical investigations have employed *acontextual* assessments of cognitive capacity—that is, on types of cognitive functioning assumed to be invariant across place, social structure, culture, and historical time. Specifically, scientists studying mental ability and task performance have relied primarily (in order of decreasing frequency) on objective tests of intellectual capacity and achievement, assessments of Piagetian-type stages, and measures of cognitive style. By comparison, investigations of cognition as it takes place in the real-life contexts of culture, subculture, or immediate setting have to date been comparatively rare. Thus, what might be called *the ecology of cognition and competence* remains largely an uncharted domain.

From the perspective of research, this descriptive fact has an obvious implication.

Corollary 1.2. Scientific progress in the study of development in context requires the increased use of contextually based measures of cognitive ability and performance of the types described above.

This corollary, however, must immediately be followed by a caveat. *By no means should this recommendation be interpreted as arguing for the abandonment of acontextual measures.* Quite the contrary. As Vygotsky, Luria, and their colleagues demonstrated in their studies of the cognitive effects of social change in Soviet Asia, one of the most productive scientific strategies for revealing the role of culture or subculture in the genesis of cognitive processes and outcomes is to employ measures that are, in varying degree, alien to the culture or subculture in question. In accord with the above-stated corollary, it then becomes not only possible but essential to interpret the obtained results in the light of the culture or subculture in which the person was raised.

This injunction applies not only to groups but also to individuals—especially to persons who have been brought up in a subculture in which patterns of activity and modes of thought differ from those of the broader culture in which the subculture is embedded. Particularly instructive in this regard are research designs that permit the assessment of developmental outcomes at two points in time differentiated by duration of the developing person's exposure to the prevailing social reality: for example, before and after school entry.

The juxtaposition of principle and practice points to yet another implication for research design. An ecologically valid definition of cognitive competence emphasizes the *cultural significance* of the processes and tasks in which mastery can be achieved: that is, how these processes and their outcomes are perceived by members of the prevailing culture. Recognition of this precept leads to the following corollary for scientific strategy.

> *Corollary 1.3.* Evaluations of a person's cognitive competence by members of that person's culture or subculture, judging from their own perspective, becomes a key element for understanding the developmental status achieved by particular individuals or groups.

With respect to research practice, the corollary accords greater scientific legitimacy and importance than has traditionally been granted to descriptions and judgments provided by persons within the society occupying social roles that include responsibility for evaluation, such as teachers and supervisors, as well as by colleagues and peers. Once again, this does not imply the abandonment of more commonly used acontextual measures of cognitive status and style by means of standardized tests or analyses of Piagetian processes and stages. Quite the contrary, the use of both types of measures can illuminate, by similarity and contrast, the nature and social significance of cognitive processes and outcomes existing for a particular cultural or subcultural group. Hence, the next corollary:

> *Corollary 1.4.* The scientific understanding of development in context is enhanced through the use of research designs that incorporate both contextual and acontextual assessments of cognitive processes and outcomes. Specifically, an analysis of their interrelationships in particular cultural and subcultural groups sheds light in two directions. First, it illuminates the

differing meanings and roles of particular types of cognitive ability or skill in different cultural contexts. Second, it indicates the extent to which persons in particular social roles and contexts give weight, in their evaluations of cognitive ability and performance, to intellectual functions that are now commonly assessed acontextually, both in science and in society.

The theoretical and practical importance of both types of information is illustrated in several of the studies cited in the discussion of designs for future research in Section VI below.

Before proceeding to consideration of the next, rather different domain of personal characteristics, it is important to acknowledge major lacunae in each of the foregoing principles and corollaries: namely, in all of them, the terms *culture* and *subculture* remain undefined, and the models and methods to be employed for "interpreting results in the light of the culture or subculture in which the person was raised" remain unspecified. There is a reason for the omission: for a complete formulation must draw on a parallel, complementary analysis of environmental contexts, a topic that is treated below in Section VI. In the interim, it may be helpful to indicate in advance that the two terms *culture* and *subculture* as here used encompass a variety of social structures, each possessing certain defining properties to be specified below. Such structures are typically identified in research operations by phenotypic proxy categories in the form of social addresses, such as nationality, ethnicity, class, religion, region, community, and neighborhood. As the reader will recognize, however, these categories are class theoretical in nature and hence, by themselves, have no explanatory power. The corresponding "field-theoretical" constructs are still to come.

C. Assessment of Temperament and Personality

As one turns from the scientific description of cognitive characteristics of the person to the classification of emotional and social attributes, one is struck by a contrast in perspective. The frame of reference for the former is primarily developmental: that is, researchers have typically used as the basis for their assessment of cognitive processes the changes occurring in this domain as a function of age, particularly at the two extremes of the life span. By contrast, the principal point of orientation for describing socioemotional characteristics is that of psychopathology and deviant behavior. As a result, most of the categories employed, and of the data collected, in the study of human temperament and personality have to do with maladaptive modes of response. Positive features, to the extent that they exist, arise mainly by default, as the opposite poles of negative attributes (e.g., "anxious vs. calm"). But even there one is more likely to find an equally problematic opposite extreme (as in "passive vs. hyperactive"). In the latter circumstance, students of healthy development are left to search on their own for positive markers in an as yet uncharted middle ground.

The concentration on polarities has yet another consequence. Because extreme forms of behavior are most likely to be invariant across place and time, contextually oriented definitions of personality, character, and—especially—temperament are few and far between. In sum, prevailing research definitions of *socioemotional* attributes of the person are neither developmentally nor contextually based. The few departures from this generalization, therefore, especially merit attention.

To begin with, a developmental perspective is clearly implied in the definition and usage of the concept of *temperament*. Both classic (Allport, 1937) and modern (Campos, Caplovitz, Lamb, Goldsmith, & Stenberg, 1983) formulations of this construct emphasize individual differences in arousal, tempo, and intensity of response that are presumed to be biological in origin, remain stable over time, and serve as the substratum for the subsequent development of intrapersonal and interpersonal processes that, in turn, affect future personality structure. Consistent with this view, the term *temperament* is more often employed in research on young infants and children, whereas studies of "personality" are conducted primarily with older children, adolescents, and adults. To this writer's knowledge, the only other developmentally linked descriptors of socioemotional characteristics of the person that have informed empirical work are rooted in Piagetian theories of moral development and find their principal implementation in the work of Kohlberg and his followers.[22]

From an ecological perspective, what is most striking about all of the above formulations is the underlying assumption of the universality of qualities of temperament and personality across time and space: that is, a given socioemotional attribute is presumed to have the same psychological significance irrespective of the cultural and subcultural context in which the person lives or has been raised. That assumption applies as well to the immediate settings and methods employed for measuring individual differences in personality characteristics. For example, studies of temperament in young children rely primarily on three methods for gathering data: (a) parental reports (secured through interviews or questionnaires); (b) observations by trained observers in the laboratory or under controlled experimental conditions; and (c) observations by trained observers in the home or other familiar settings. Any discrepancies in results obtained by these three methods (and such discrepancies are substantial) are treated as errors of measurement in the form of method variance. The justification for this view follows directly from the definition of temperament as an expression "of the individual's emotional nature ... regarded as dependent on constitutional makeup, and therefore largely hereditary in origin" (Allport, 1937, p. 54). Consistent with this formulation, "individual differences in temperamental characteristics are expected to be maintained across time as well as across situations" (Campos et al., 1983, p. 832). Therefore, "the temperament construct should not be method bound. ... Cross-method convergence is to be desired highly" (p. 832).

Yet the cross-method convergence is in fact not very high, ranging from .20 to .40 (Campos et al., 1983, p. 841). How is one to account for this substantial lack of correspondence? One possible explanation calls into question the assumption that temperament, in its basic origin and nature, is in fact context free. Evidence bearing on this issue comes from the contrasting patterns of heritability coefficients, to be described below, that were obtained in twins studies of infant temperament conducted under different ecological conditions (Matheny, Wilson, Dolan, & Krantz, 1981; Plomin & Rowe, 1979).

These ecological conditions also have differential status in psychological science. Reflecting the roots of their discipline in the physical as against the natural sciences, psychologists are prone to attribute greater validity to findings based on laboratory methods. Witness the following statement in the latest edition of the *Handbook of Child Psychology* regarding the growing application of such laboratory-tested techniques in research on infant temperament: "This paradigmatic trend promises to bring temperament research closer to the mainstream of developmental psychology" (Campos et al., 1983, p. 841).

A noteworthy conclusion emerging from such mainstream research is reported in the first of these studies by Plomin and Rowe. These investigators imported the Strange Situation paradigm from the laboratory into the home in order to assess heritability of temperament in a sample of infant twins between two and three years of age. Trained observers noted the infants' responses in such categories as smiling, looking, touching, cuddling, vocalization, and separation distress. The principal finding: "Comparisons between intraclass correlations for identical and fraternal twins yielded significant differences for social behavior directed toward the stranger, but not toward the mother. ... We conclude that in infancy, heredity affects individual differences in social responding more to unfamiliar persons than to familiar persons" (Plomin & Rowe, 1979, p. 62).

Given this conclusion, one would not expect to find in other studies high heritability levels for behaviors directed by infants toward their mothers. Yet two years later, Adam Matheny and his colleagues (Matheny et al., 1981), employing a sample of similar age, reported results hardly consistent with the stated generalization. The strongest differences in concordance rates between identical and fraternal infant twins were found for a behavior cluster (labeled *sociability*) again involving such responses as smiling, cuddling, social responsiveness, and vocalization. The data, however, were based not on observations by a trained observer but on reports by the mother, obtained in an interview, regarding the presence of similarities and differences between the two twins on a wide range of behaviors.

How is one to explain these contrasting findings with respect to basic psychological characteristics that are presumed to be biologically grounded and to remain constant across situations? Note that the phenomenon to be explained is not that genetic effects were found in one study but not in the other; rather, such effects emerged in both settings but in relation to different parties.

Specifically, the question arises: Why, in the first situation, should the genetic component in the infant's attachment to its mother manifest itself only in the behavior of the infant toward a stranger and not to the mother herself? This paradoxical result can hardly be attributed to method variance, since, in the first study, the same measurement techniques were employed in relation to the two parties. And why, in the second situation, should the previously absent genetic component in the infant's response to the mother now emerge as prepotent, the principal difference being that the mother herself, instead of a trained observer, served as the source of information?

There are possible answers to these questions, none of them denying the existence of genetically based differences in temperament but all of them hinging on the meaning of the observed behaviors in the *settings* in which they occurred. To begin with, in the first, more scientifically controlled setting, the context was limited to the experimental situation, whereas in the second investigation the scope covered the full range of the mother's everyday experience with her infant. Moreover, the first study was indeed carried out in a "strange situation." Not only were the observations conducted in the presence of a strange adult, but, as required by the experimental conditions, mothers were asked to limit their responsiveness and, upon instruction, to go out of the room, leaving the infant alone with the stranger. Under such circumstances, it seems quite possible that well-developed patterns of mother-infant interaction, based in part on genetically influenced characteristics of both infant and mother, may be temporarily disrupted and hence not there to be observed. Instead, what comes to the fore is the infant's established pattern of response, again genetically based, to an unfamiliar stressful situation centered in the person of a strange adult.

Whether this particular explanation is in fact correct cannot of course be determined from the available data, nor is the validity central to a broader generalization toward which the findings point: namely, the markedly contrasting results described above are consistent with the interpretation that the observed differences in temperament develop in the context of the early mother-infant relationship and—not despite but because of a high genetic loading—may in fact not be manifested across all situations. To paraphrase and extend Ceci's cognitive thesis to another domain: "The context in which temperament is manifested is not simply an adjunct to the characteristic in question, but a constituent of it" (see Principle 2 below).

Given the above considerations, the widely recommended and applied cross-situational and cross-method criterion as a necessary condition for establishing individual differences in temperament may be inappropriate from the standpoint both of theory and of research operations. Instead, a scientifically more rigorous and productive approach would be one of viewing *temperament in context*: that is, examining the systematic variation across context and method as a defining element of the individual's characteristic pattern of differential response to varying types of environments.

Applying this principle in the study of infant temperament requires prior theoretical consideration of which aspects of temperament are likely to be activated in which types of social contexts. The contrasting findings from the two studies summarized above suggest that a particularly important dimension of context in this regard is familiarity versus unfamiliarity of the situation, especially in terms of the identity of the persons in the infant's immediate environment. Consistency across situations in the expression of a particular temperamental attribute would then be expected only to the extent that the dimension of familiarity was kept constant (or systematically and similarly varied) in each of the situations in which temperament was being assessed.

But, contrary to the prevailing view, it is not in consistency over time that the developmental effects of temperament are most likely to be manifested. From a dynamic ecological perspective, what one should more often expect are synergistic effects set in motion by characteristics of temperament exhibited early in life that then evoke differential patterns of response from the environment. For example, a physically attractive, easily soothed infant may invite affection and attention, leading to reciprocal effects of progressively more complex patterns of interaction that, in turn, facilitate psychological growth, whereas a fussy baby may discourage such interaction. In short, the distinctive characteristics of the person at a given point in time, such as temperament, may be more likely to instigate progressive developmental change in a particular direction, depending on the environmental response, than to ensure unchanging psychological traits throughout life. More extended consideration and illustration of such possibilities are offered below in discussing what are referred to as "developmentally instigative personal characteristics" (see Section D).

Similar considerations apply to prevailing approaches in the scientific study of the broader concept of *personality*. Here too variations across situations and sources of information have typically been dismissed as "method variance" (Campbell & Fiske, 1959), and the recommended strategy of choice, known as the "multitrait-multimethod design," "is simply to appraise the consistency of measurement properties across different observers, conditions, and instruments" (Messick, 1983, p. 490). As before, such a strategy fails to make a distinction between sources of random error and systematic differences in the manifestation and meaning of personality attributes in different contexts. As in the case of temperament, a given socioemotional characteristic is presumed to have the same meaning, be it in science or in life, irrespective of the culture, subculture, or immediate setting in which the characteristic is observed.

This underlying assumption is even more pervasive in the study of temperament and personality than of cognitive capacity and competence. Although, as documented above, Vygotsky's culturally oriented and contextually based definition of the individual characteristics of the person has made some headway in Western studies of cognition, it has yet to make any appreciable impact on contemporary investigations of the social, emotional, or motivational attributes of the person and their development.

There is one notable exception to the foregoing statement, but it lies mostly outside the present borders of psychological science. The approach has its origins, and principal application, in the same discipline from which Vygotsky found his inspiration: cultural anthropology. Beginning with the seminal work of W. H. R. Rivers (1926) more than a half-century ago, the study of "culture and personality" has been an active and valued research domain within the science of anthropology. Indeed, during the late 1930s to the mid-1950s, primarily under the influence of the American anthropologists Edward Sapir and Clyde Kluckhohn, this orientation also captured the imagination, and informed the work, of some influential personality psychologists.[23] Almost all of this effort, however, was focused on the relation between culture and personality in adults in preindustrial societies, with little attention either to younger age levels or to intracultural variation. One outstanding departure from this focus was the study of children in six cultures (including the United States) conducted under the leadership of John and Beatrice Whiting (1973, 1975). The investigation is noteworthy for combining, in complementary fashion, the standardized observational methods of developmental psychology with the ethnographic techniques of the anthropologist. As a result, the investigators were able to interpret their systematic observations and quantitative findings in the context of the culture and community in which the children lived. Unfortunately, few developmentalists have adopted this dual orientation in research on development in context.

The preceding point brings us back to our primary concern with the design of ecological paradigms most appropriate for research on the ecology of human development. *It should now be apparent that Principle 1 and its four corollaries, originally developed and applied in relation to cognitive characteristics of the person, are equally applicable to the socioemotional sphere.* Indeed, given the foregoing evidence and argument, it would appear essential that individual differences in temperament and personality be interpreted from the perspective of the culture and subculture in which the individual was raised. In addition, the prevailing theoretical orientation and associated practice, especially in the socioemotional domain, of treating as error variance differences in descriptions of the developing person obtained in diverse settings by observers differing in their role and relationship to the subject is to be called into question. This is not to imply that the individual personality does not show continuity across place and time. Rather, the continuity is manifested in the consistent way in which the person varies his behavior as a function of the situation. The phenomenon is one of continuity in change. This seeming paradox is sufficiently important theoretically to warrant statement in what becomes a second general principle:

> *Principle 2.* Continuity of temperament and character is expressed primarily not through constancy of behavior across time and place but through consistency over time in the ways in which the person characteristically varies his or her behavior as a function of the different contexts, both proximal and remote, in which that person lives.

The principle finds its precedent in the role theory developed by George Herbert Mead and the Chicago school of sociologists (Mead, 1934; Thomas, 1927; Thomas & Thomas, 1928; Thomas & Znaniecki, 1927). For example, one of Mead's students, L. S. Cottrell (1942), proposed the thesis that in the process of socialization the developing person internalizes both sides of the role of significant others in his or her life. In a characteristically down-to-earth example, Cottrell described the "bicycle rider personality," who "bows down to those above, and beats down on those below" (personal communication, 1943). This kind of phenomenon may explain the emergence later in life, seemingly out of the blue, of personality characteristics that appear to contradict long-existing prior patterns of behavior. From Cottrell's perspective, these would represent the activation, in a new and now appropriate context, of the complementary side of a previously learned role.

Beyond such case study examples, I know of no research evidence bearing directly on Principle 2. The issue, however, would appear to be altogether susceptible to rigorous investigation through the use of research designs focusing on the behavior of the same persons functioning in different social roles, such as superior versus subordinate, spouse versus parent, vendor versus purchaser, or teacher versus student.

Like its predecessor, Principle 2 carries implications for research design in the form of the following corollary:

Corollary 2.1. From an ecological perspective, a scientific understanding of the psychological characteristics of the person and their development is furthered by research designs that permit the systematic comparison and interpretation of assessments made in different contexts by observers who differ in their role and relationship toward that person: for example, parents, peers, teachers, supervisors, trained researchers and—last but not least— the self-perceptions of the subject.

Although the comparative analysis of perception of the same person from the perspective of significant others in various parts of that person's life is a common practice in case studies and clinical work, to date I have not been able to find any instance in which this approach was applied systematically as a scientific strategy in research on human development. While data on children's socioemotional attributes are occasionally obtained in more than one setting from more than one source, the comparison of findings, if it is done at all, is typically limited to methodological issues. Substantive variations by context in the manifestations of temperament and personality of the same child or adult have only begun to be explored (e.g., Hinde & Tobin, 1988; Plomin & Nesselrode, in press [1990]) and thus constitute a terra incognita in contemporary developmental science.

Especially from an ecological perspective, there is good reason to believe that exploration in this terrain will bring significant scientific rewards. Consider, for example, two rather different spheres of considerable research activity in contemporary developmental studies: the first focuses on the effect of day care; the second on the influence of parents versus peers on personality development, particularly in early adolescence. In the former case, data on psychological outcomes are obtained almost exclusively in settings outside the home, in either the day care center, the school, or the psychological laboratory. Information from parents, if collected at all, is treated simply as another, typically secondary source and is accorded no distinctive importance. Yet parents are known to be the most powerful influence on children's development and the persons most sensitive and responsive to their children's behavior. Hence, any changes that parents perceive in their child's characteristics are especially likely to provoke corresponding changes in their own parental behavior toward the child; this altered behavior, in turn, may introduce new forces that affect the child's subsequent psychological growth. A comparative analysis, especially over time, of qualities attributed to the child at home, in school, and in other settings may therefore provide effective vantage points for tracing the dynamics of ongoing developmental change.

An analogous situation occurs with respect to studies of parent-peer influences on adolescent development. Once again, we encounter the phenomenon of primary reliance on a single source of data on psychological outcomes—in this instance, the adolescents' self-reports, obtained through personality inventories. Parents' perceptions of the children are usually not taken into account; nor are those of peers. This comment should not be misinterpreted as implying that descriptions of the young person by significant others from different settings provide a more valid assessment of personality than do self-reports. Rather, the argument is that availability of information from different vantage points in the adolescent's ecology provides a picture of the latter's characteristic modes of adaptation to *differing* life situations. Moreover, because these situations are likely to recur, often across settings with the same participants, each mode of reciprocal adaptation creates a continuing synergistic dynamic that can drive and accelerate the course of future development.

This last consideration suggests a new and different dimension for distinguishing properties of the person: namely, the degree to which a given type of personal characteristic becomes a dynamic force, a vector that both fuels and directs the course of future psychological development. It is this orientation that constitutes the focus of a final, somewhat unconventional point of reference for conceptualizing and analyzing the psychological characteristics of human beings.

D. A Developmental
Conception of the Developing Person

Most developmental research treats the cognitive and socioemotional characteristics of the person solely as dependent variables: that is, as measures of outcome. Much less often are such characteristics examined as precursors of later development, and even more rarely as moderating factors affecting the power or direction of developmental processes. In the latter respects, not all personal attributes have equal potential for influencing subsequent development; some are more likely to be consequential than others. For the researcher, this differential power in affecting subsequent psychological growth provides a useful criterion and conceptual frame for selecting and classifying those human qualities that are especially significant for the person's future development.

Such personal attributes, which I shall refer to collectively as *developmentally instigative characteristics,* are distinguished by either, or both, of two features. The first, and more commonly recognized, are personal qualities that invite or discourage reactions from the environment of a kind that can disrupt or foster processes of psychological growth. Examples include a fussy versus a happy baby; attractive versus unattractive physical appearance; or social responsiveness versus withdrawal. Half a century ago, Allport (1937) spoke of such characteristics as constituting "personality" defined in terms of its "social stimulus value." Accordingly, I shall refer to such personal features as *personal stimulus qualities.*

Probably more potent, but as yet seldom studied, are characteristics that, rather than merely evoking a reaction from others, involve an active orientation toward and interaction with the environment. For example, early in life, such an orientation is seen in an infant's initiation and maintenance of patterns of reciprocal interaction with the mother and other caregivers. A bit later, the dynamic potential becomes manifest in the visual and motoric exploration of the immediate setting, with respect to both its physical and its social content. At older ages, the analogous tendency is expressed in such forms as a readiness to seek out and sustain human relationships; intellectual curiosity; a disposition to manipulate, select, elaborate, reconstruct, and even to create environments for self and others; and a conception of the self as an active agent in a responsive world. I shall use the term *developmentally structuring attributes* to designate active personal orientations of this kind.

Alternatively, to the extent that such an active and responsive personal orientation to the environment exists only in limited degree, the developmental progression may proceed at a slower rate and along fewer developmental pathways. Or, where the impulse to activity is high but not tempered by complementary responsiveness to the surroundings, the resulting expression of diffuse hyperactivity can, in the absence of concerted environmental counterstrategies, set in motion developmental trajectories of progressive incompetence and social disruptiveness.

Both types of developmentally instigative characteristics, when they are manifested over time in particular settings, tend to evoke complementary patterns of continuing environmental feedback, thus creating progressively more complex developmental trajectories that exhibit continuity through time. The result is a person-specific repertoire of evolving context-based and context-differentiated dispositions that continues to be distinguishable over the life course and hence constitutes what we recognize over the years as the person's individual personality.

In recent years, this synergistic process of development has been documented in a number of longitudinal studies. Regrettably, however, all of them thus far are confined to personal characteristics of the first type, what I have called *stimulus attributes*, qualities that evoke developmentally constructive or disruptive reactions from others. For instance, a striking effect of a purely physical feature is documented in one of the follow-up studies of children of the Great Depression by Elder and his colleagues (Elder, van Nguyen, & Caspi, 1985). The investigators found that economic hardship adversely influenced the psychosocial well-being of girls by increasing the rejecting behavior of fathers; the effects of rejection, however, varied inversely as a function of the daughter's physical attractiveness. Indeed, in the authors' words, "Attractive daughters were not likely to be maltreated by their fathers, no matter how severe the economic pressure.... [The results] underscore the importance of viewing economic decline in relation to both the child's characteristics and parenting behavior" (p. 361). Here we have a classic instance of the power of a process-person-context model in revealing the complex interactions between organism and environment that drive the process of development.

The next two examples move from the purely physical into the psychological realm. Caspi and his colleagues (Caspi, Elder, & Bem, 1988) have documented what might be called a "snowballing effect" across both time and space of two contrasting childhood personality characteristics—an explosive temperament on the one hand and a tendency toward social withdrawal on the other. In the first domain, children who, when studied between eight and 10 years of age, had been described as exhibiting frequent or severe temper tantrums were more likely as adults to experience reduced educational attainment, downward occupational mobility, erratic work careers, and disrupted family life. These patterns were further differentiated by characteristics of both person and context. Thus, for women, the effects were greater in the sphere of family life than that of work: females with a history of temper tantrums in childhood were especially likely to become ill-tempered mothers and to experience divorce. By contrast, for men the sequelae of early explosiveness were more apt to be manifested in a delayed and disrupted work history.

The gender contrast across the domains of work and family life emerged as even more pronounced in the life course patterns of shy children. Men who in childhood had been described as socially and emotionally withdrawn married later than matched controls, were more likely to experience divorce, and were slower and less successful in establishing their careers. Women with similar childhood histories, however, showed no particular problems later on (Caspi et al., 1988). In the authors' words:

> Not only did they appear to "float through" early adulthood with little difficulty, they were more likely than other women in their cohort to follow a conventional pattern of marriage, childbearing, and homemaking. Early sex differences in the continuity and consequences of early personality are moderated by cultural and historical prescriptions of gender-appropriate behavior. For this cohort, shy and reserved behavior seemed to be more compatible—if not desirable—for women than for men. It is not clear, however, that sex-role changes in our society have altered the patterns observed here. A recent study of shyness and interpersonal relationships found that correlations were stronger for male than for female respondents, suggesting that the inhibitory effects of shyness on the development of relationships may still be greater for men than women. (Jones & Briggs, 1984, p. 829)

Although "explosiveness" and "shyness" represent rather different styles of childhood behavior that lead to somewhat different outcomes, Caspi and his colleagues propose that "the general mechanisms producing their continuity and consequences appear to be the same: Long-term continuities of personality are to be found in interactional styles that are sustained by the progressive accumulation of their own consequences" (Caspi et al., 1988, p. 830).

The principle is surely both valid and powerful, but, from a dynamic, ecological perspective, it needs to be accompanied by a complementary caveat. If left unqualified, repeated findings of this kind could leave the impression that continuity in psychological development over the life course is the rule. Such a conclusion is, at best, premature. To begin with, most of the longitudinal studies of personality conducted to date, including the work of Caspi and his colleagues, deal with behavioral extremes. And as Clarke and Alan (1988) documented in a recent review, "Greater constancies across time are to be expected in seriously deviant conditions compared with less abnormal development" (p. 3). Moreover, even with respect to the extreme patterns of childhood explosiveness and shyness studied by Caspi et al., an examination of the results suggests that continuity, while clearly present, characterizes only a minority of the cases. For example, the structural model for the sequelae of child-hood temper tantrums—including all analyzed pathways, both direct and indirect—is associated with a total R^2 of .34. This means that, even after allowing for error in measurement, the amount of variance accounted for by continuity is not more than a third. Or, to put the issue more provoca-tively, most youngsters who exhibited patterns of marked explosive behavior in childhood *did not* experience significantly reduced educa-tional attainment, occupational success, or family stability.

What are the forces that counteract the disruptive thrust of early mal-adaptive behaviors? Given our theoretical framework, the answer must be sought in processes set in motion by other characteristics of both per-son and context usually not included in most research designs employed to date. On the context side, an indication of a possible counteractive mechanism comes from a study by Crockenberg (1981). The investigator found that the beneficial impact of maternal social supports on mother-infant interaction varied systematically as a function of the infant's tem-perament. The effect was strongest for the mothers with the most irritable babies and minimal for those whose infants were emotionally calm.

On the person side, the most likely countervailing personal qualities fall into our second class of "developmentally instigative characteristics," those that involve an active, structuring orientation toward the environ-ment. Although the methods and opportunities for investigating these kinds of personal qualities are readily at hand, they have yet to be exploited in research designs that take into account processes of interac-tion between person and context. A tantalizing example of such a missed opportunity is found in the important longitudinal investigations con-ducted over many years by Jack and Jeanne Block (1980). Two well-known measures of children's personality that these investigators have constructed nicely fit the criteria for what I have called *developmentally structuring personal attributes*. "Ego resiliency" refers to the capacity of children actively to cope under environmental stress or uncertainty. "Ego control" involves the ability to regulate impulse expression. The classifi-cations are derived from Q-sorts of personality items made by trained judges familiar with the child, typically by teachers. Both measures have been widely used both as criteria of developmental outcome and as personality predictors of subsequent behavior, but I have been able to find no investigation that examined whether family or peer group processes had a differential effect on the development of children initially exhibiting contrasting levels of ego resilience or control. Particularly intriguing from this perspective is a study by Block, Block, and Keyes (1988) of "early childhood personality and environmental precursors" of drug usage in adolescence. The researchers neatly demonstrated that both children's personality characteristics during the preschool years and early parental patterns of child rearing were related to substance use in adolescence, but, regrettably, the investigators did not examine the interplay between the domains of person and context.

A similar situation exists with respect to another type of developmentally instigative personal characteristic, one that is often subsumed under the general rubric of personality but that, because of its special significance, merits separate consideration here. I refer to the individual's conception of self as an active agent in a responsive environment. The best-known measure of this kind is Rotter's (1966) index of "locus of control," a personality inventory assessing the extent to which the person feels that the sources of failure or success lie within or outside the self. Subsequently, a more sophisticated formulation of the concept, and of its operationalization, was introduced by Bandura (1977, 1982) under the rubric of "self-efficacy." Despite the widespread use of measures of this kind, I am aware of only one study of the impact of self-concept on subsequent development (as distinguished from behavior at the moment). Employing a longitudinal design with a sample of schoolchildren, Newman (1984) was able to show, by causal modeling, that between Grades 2 and 5 mathematics achievement influenced self-ratings of ability but not the reverse; and even this effect diminished in the higher grades.

Although evidence appears to be lacking for any effect of children's own belief systems on their later development, a set of findings emerging from a doctoral dissertation by Tulkin (Tulkin, 1973, 1977; Tulkin & Cohler, 1973; Tulkin & Kagan, 1972) does point to the potency of parental belief systems in this regard. The investigator began by studying social class differences in both the behaviors and the beliefs of mothers of 10-month-old girls. The research was conducted in the home, employing both interviews and observations. Middle-class mothers were distinguished from their working-class counterparts not only by higher levels of reciprocal interaction with their infants but also in their views about what a 10-month-old could do and about their own abilities to influence their baby's development: specifically, the more advantaged mothers attributed greater potentials to both their infants and themselves. In addition, the correlations between maternal behavior and attitudes were substantially greater in middle-class than in lower-class families. Several years later, Tulkin and Covitz (1975) reassessed the same youngsters after they had entered school. The children's performance on tests of mental ability and language skill showed significant relationships to the prior measures of reciprocal mother-infant interaction.

Taken as a whole, the foregoing research findings suggest an additional principle bearing on the role of personal attributes in shaping human development in real-life contexts.

> *Principle 3.* The attributes of the person most likely to shape the course of human development are modes of behavior or belief that reflect an active, selective, structuring orientation toward the environment and/or tend to provoke reactions from the environment. The term *developmentally instigative characteristic* is used to designate personal attributes of this kind. The effect of such characteristics on the person's development depends in significant degree on the corresponding patterns of response that they evoke from the person's environment.

The preceding principle, and especially the impressive research findings marshaled in its support, might lead the reader to conclude that human beings themselves are the primary shapers of their own development, with environment playing only a secondary, essentially reactive role. Such an interpretation would be mistaken. It is true that individuals often can and do modify, select, reconstruct, and even create their environments. But this capacity emerges only to the extent that the person has been *enabled* to engage in self-directed action as a joint function not only of his biological endowment but also of the environment in which he or she developed. There is not one without the other.

To return to the consideration of developmentally instigative characteristics, their potential range goes far beyond the particular attributes of temperament, personality, and beliefs involved in the investigations cited. For instance, they could include customary strength and speed of response, patterns of exploratory behavior, cognitive styles in interpreting and organizing the environment, or expectations and future plans. As this sequence of examples suggests, such characteristics, while exhibiting some continuity over time, evolve progressively in form and complexity as a function of biological and psychological maturation.

A final set of developmentally instigative characteristics that deserve explicit mention involves a variety of purely physical factors that have no psychological substance in themselves but often do lead to psychological sequelae. Three types of such characteristics are usefully distinguished:

1. Forms of organic injury or maldevelopment that threaten subsequent psychological growth. Common examples include low birth weight and other complications of pregnancy, congenital anomalies, physical handicaps, severe illness, and damage to brain function through accident or degenerative processes.

2. Bodily characteristics or changes associated with differing developmental outcomes: for example, body size and type, physical appearance and attractiveness, physical and physiological changes associated with puberty, menopause, or old age.

3. The third set possesses a special distinction: it includes a set of three physical characteristics deemed so potent in influencing the course of future development that they need to be distinguished in every study, irrespective of the particular hypothesis under investigation. These are the familiar demographic factors of *age, sex,* and *race.*

Note that age, sex, and race are all class-theoretical concepts and hence have no explanatory power in themselves. Under these circumstances, the sweeping scientific injunction clearly demands justification. Explanation is also called for on additional grounds: both the reason for and the design implications of the requirement are more complex than the injunction itself conveys. What is involved is not the familiar methodological admonition to control for the possibly confounding effect of these three factors on measures of outcome. The rationale for the requirement is substantive rather than methodological and focuses primarily on possible differences not in outcome but in process. As evidenced by the results of a number of studies described in the preceding pages—and others still to come—processes often operate in different ways, with different effects, in the two sexes; for subjects at different ages; and for persons from different racial groups. The reasons for such differences are themselves highly complex. For example, while obviously rooted in physical characteristics, their dynamics are also driven by the social response to these characteristics in a particular culture or subculture. But whatever their origin, the differences in process associated with these three factors occur so frequently that failure to provide for this possibility in study design entails significant scientific cost.

The cost is of two kinds. First, there is the risk of overgeneralization, arising from the possibility that the reported phenomenon may in fact differ substantially as a function of the gender, age, and race of the subjects. Equally if not more important, however, is the missed scientific opportunity of discovering variations in human development that can stimulate the revision and further explication of existing theory and knowledge. *It is the very nature and power of science that it moves forward through the systematic discovery and acknowledgment of its own errors.* The point under discussion is sufficiently important to warrant status as a design corollary to Principle 3.

> *Corollary 3.1.* Every research design for the study of human development should provide for the possibility of differences in process and outcome associated with the factors of gender, age, and race, to the extent that they differ within the research sample.

With this paradoxically specific universal injunction, we conclude our analysis of the properties of the person as viewed from an ecological perspective. As the analysis has revealed, that perspective incorporates a universal injunction of its own that is far more general. Stated in the form of a fourth and final principle, that universal tenet reads as follows:

> *Principle 4.* No characteristic of the person exists or exerts influence on development in isolation. Every human quality is inextricably embedded, and finds both its meaning and fullest expression, in particular environmental settings, of which the family is a prime example. As a result, there is always an interplay between the psychological characteristics of the person and of a specific environment; the one cannot be defined without reference to the other.

This phenomenon of interaction is of course fundamental to an understanding of how human beings develop. An adequate conceptualization of it must simultaneously take into account diverse properties of the person and of the environment in which the person is embedded. Having completed an analysis of the former, I turn next to an elaboration and, in some instances, reformulation of the environmental paradigms set forth in *The Ecology of Human Development* (Bronfenbrenner, 1979).

V. Parameters of Context From a Developmental Perspective

As previously noted, because of the one-sided emphasis given to the environment in the aforementioned work, there already exists a working taxonomy of contexts that can serve as a basis for further work. As originally formulated, the taxonomy consisted of a hierarchy of systems at four levels moving from the most proximal to the most remote. The systems were identified by the successive prefixes *micro-*, *meso-*, *exo-*, and *macro*. While these environmental constructs appear to have stood the test of trial and time, my subsequent efforts to right the imbalance on the organism side of the ecological equation have unexpectedly led to an expansion and reformulation on the context side as well. The most conspicuous of these changes involves the introduction of significant new elements in the definition of the micro- and the macrosystem. These changes, and their rationale, are presented below.

A. The Microsystem Revisited and Revised

In its original form, the definition of this system read as follows:

A *microsystem* is a pattern of activities, roles, and interpersonal relations experienced by the developing person in a given face-to-face setting with particular physical and material features.

Examples of settings included home, school, peer group, and workplace.

With the sobering wisdom of hindsight, I find myself struck by what now appears as a glaring omission in this formulation. To the extent that the definition recognizes other human beings as existing in the setting, it is solely in terms of their social roles and relationships: that is, they have no existence as persons possessing distinctive characteristics of temperament, personality, or systems of belief. Thus the short shrift that had been given to the person side of the equation in the initial formulation of the ecological paradigm is reflected as well in the initial specification of the environment.

Unfortunately, the same one-sidedness is also found in contemporary empirical work. Relatively few studies of development in context examine the influence on psychological growth of the personality characteristics of significant others in the developing person's life. A signal exception appears in the recent work of Elder and his colleagues (Elder et al., 1986). Exploiting cross-generational data from the Berkeley Guidance Study, the investigators showed that the disruptive developmental effects of the Great Depression were particularly severe for children with irritable, explosive parents. As adults, these children were themselves likely to be more ill tempered. This general characteristic, in turn, affected both their marital relationship and their behavior as parents. Finally, upon looking at these parents' children and grandchildren, the researchers found evidence that "the legacy of undercontrolled behavior persists into the fourth generation" (p. 329). Note that this legacy was not simply a manifestation of the constancy of temperament over time but a product and projection (using these terms almost in their mathematical sense) of the initial combination of a particular kind of person in a particular kind of situation—specifically, a somewhat irascible adult male under economic duress.

Findings of this sort point to the importance of including within the formal definition of the developing person's immediate environment the developmentally relevant characteristics of the *other persons* present and participating in that environment. Potentially, such characteristics cover the same range of attributes as that set forth in the preceding section. Thus, depending on the research question being posed, they might include demographic features such as age and sex, cognitive abilities and skills, or, as in the study cited above, aspects of temperament or personality. As the foregoing study illustrates, the aspects of the person most likely to produce powerful interactive effects are what we have called *developmentally instigative* characteristics.

To highlight the potential importance for development of the personal characteristics of significant others in the immediate environment, I have added to the original definition of *microsystem* the final phase italicized below:

A microsystem is a pattern of activities, roles, and interpersonal relations experienced by the developing person in a given face-to-face setting with particular physical and material features *and containing other persons with distinctive characteristics of temperament, personality, and systems of belief.*[24]

The definitions of the next two systems levels remain unchanged and are repeated here solely for the reader's convenience.

The *mesosystem* comprises the linkages and processes taking place between two or more settings containing the developing person (e.g., the relations between home and school, school and workplace). In other words, a mesosystem is a system of microsystems.

The *exosystem*, encompasses the linkage and processes taking place between two or more settings, at least one of which does not ordinarily contain the developing person, but in which events occur that influence processes within the immediate setting that does contain that person (e.g., for a child, the relation between the home and the parent's workplace; for a parent, the relation between the school and the neighborhood group).

Ironically, the beginning effort to spell out developmentally relevant properties of the person had its greatest impact on the environmental side in enriching the theoretical conception and importance of the most distal and expansive region of the environment—the *macrosystem*. The impact has its origin mainly in two context-oriented definitions of person characteristics. The first source is Vygotsky's theory of the "sociohistorical evolution of the mind" (Luria, 1976, p. 5): in particular, his thesis that from earliest childhood onward the development of one's characteristics as a person depends in significant degree on the options that are available in a given culture at a given point in its history. The second source is the concept of *developmentally instigative personal characteristics,* in particular, systems of belief. As highlighted in the revised definition of the microsystem, such dynamic attributes are critical features not only of the developing person but also of significant others in the person's environment. Furthermore, with respect to macrosystems, consistent with Vygotsky's formulation, the repertoire of available belief systems, as well as their intensity, is defined by the culture or subculture in which one lives and hence may vary appreciably over both space and time. It is from this repertoire that parents, teachers, and other agents of socialization draw when they consciously or unconsciously define the goals, risks, and ways of raising the next generation. *It follows that scientific recognition of the belief systems prevailing in the world of the developing person is essential for an understanding of the interaction of organismic and environmental forces in the process of development.* Such belief systems therefore constitute a developmentally critical feature of every macrosystem.[25]

In addition, the concept of a cultural repertoire of belief systems raises the possibility of other kinds of repertoires that can create or constrain developmental opportunity. Thus there may be other features of the macrosystem that are not merely structural but also developmentally instigative. The application of this already familiar construct at the level of the macrosystem signals yet another instance of how efforts to expand the person side of the ecological equation have led to key expansions on the environmental side.

Specifically, consideration of these issues has resulted in the addition of a key dynamic complement to the formal definition of the macrosystem. The revised definition, with the addition italicized, reads as follows:

The *macrosystem* consists of the overarching pattern of micro-, meso-, and exosystems characteristic of a given culture, subculture, or other broader social context, *with particular reference to the developmentally instigative belief systems, resources, hazards, lifestyles, opportunity structures, life course options, and patterns of social interchange that are embedded in each of these systems.* The macrosystem may be thought of as a societal blueprint for a particular culture, subculture, or other broader social context.

Several aspects of this expanded definition merit further consideration. Thus we must ask: What are the "other broader social contexts" that also constitute macrosystems, and how do they differ from, and what do they share with, cultures and subcultures as macrosystems? To address the easiest part of this question first, what all macrosystems share are the elements specified in the above definition. Over and above these commonalities, cultures and subcultures have two distinguishing features. First, they constitute the highest-order, overarching macrostructures that encompass all other, intracultural forms. Second, they differ from these other constituent forms in possessing an additional, critical quality: namely, the patterns of belief and behavior characterizing the macrosystem are passed on from one generation to the next through processes of socialization carried out by various institutions of the culture, such as family, school, church, workplace, and structures of government.

Finally, to return to the initial part of the question: What are the principal types of macrosystems existing within a culture or subculture? Like these latter, superordinate systems, they are typically identified by proxy variables in the form of social address labels, such as social class, ethnicity, or region (e.g., rural vs. urban). Other possibilities include different professions (e.g., doctors vs. lawyers), or cohorts experiencing different historical events, epochs, or lifestyles (e.g., "Children of the Great Depression," "Vietnam veterans," "the Sixties generation," the "women's movement," "yuppies"). But, as previously noted, these are all class-theoretical concepts, mere labels that have no explanatory power in themselves. *In the last analysis, what defines the macrosystem is sharing the kinds of characteristics specified in the above formal definition (i.e., similar belief systems, social and economic resources, hazards, lifestyles, etc.). From this perspective, social classes, ethnic or religious groups, or persons living in particular regions, communities, neighborhoods, or other types of broader social structures constitute a macrosystem whenever the above conditions are met.* This also means that, over the course of history, newly evolving social structures have the potential of turning into subcultures by developing a characteristic set of values, lifestyle, and other defining features of a macrosystem. A case in point is the evolution, within the American middle class, of a new—and now predominating—family pattern, that of the two-wage-earner family. Another, contrasting example is the low-income, single-parent household. The test of whether the label of macrosystem is legitimately applied to each of these phenomena is the demonstration that they do in fact exhibit characteristic lifestyles, values, expectations, resources, and opportunity structures that distinguish them both from each other and from the more traditional family form in which the male is the sole breadwinner and "family head." There is a growing body of research evidence indicating that, in both instances, the criteria for the existence of a distinctive macrosystem are indeed well met.[26]

The critical, or merely curious, reader may ask why it is necessary to introduce the neologism of *macrosystem* when the already existing terms *culture* and *subculture* would seem to capture much the same concept. There is indeed some overlap, but it is far from complete. All cultures and subcultures qualify as macrosystems, but the reverse proposition does not hold. For instance, the former terms do not typically connote such social structures or institutions as neighborhoods, cohorts, family types, or systems of day care or education; yet, as some the foregoing examples reveal, such systems can, under certain circumstances, acquire the properties specified in the above definition of a macrosystem.

And, once evidence for the existence of a macrosystem is found, it becomes possible to investigate the nature of various aspects of that system as they affect developmental processes at more proximal levels. It becomes possible, but it is rarely done. To put it more precisely, in developmental research the analysis of macrosystem elements seldom goes beyond an operational definition based solely on a proxy variable (i.e., a social address), its use for purposes of statistical control, and a report of the effect on developmental outcomes associated with the label in question (e.g., class or ethnic differences in IQ or self-esteem).[27]

What else can and should be done? Stating the issue more broadly, what are the implications of the more differentiated conceptualizations of both person and environment set forth in the preceding pages for further advance in the scientific study of human development?

VI. Form and Substance for Future Research

Possible answers to the preceding question emerge from an integration of the formal ecological paradigms and models presented in the first part of this chapter (Sections I–III) with the structural and substantive aspects of person and context elaborated in the second part (Sections IV–V). I refer to "possible" answers because all of them are implications derived mainly from theoretical considerations. Relevant empirical evidence is lacking, or fragmentary at best. The justification for exploiting this lopsided state of affairs lies in the research potential of the possible answers. From its very beginning, the ecology of human development was defined as a scientific undertaking "in the discovery mode" (Bronfenbrenner, 1979, pp. 37–38). The aim was not to test hypotheses but to generate them. Even more broadly, the goal was to develop a theoretical framework that could provide both structure and direction for the systematic study of organism-environment interaction in processes of human development.

Given this objective, the "possible answers" take the form of a series of *priority principles,* each defining a particular element of the broader framework that, when operationalized in empirical work, could serve to illuminate developmental processes and permit the formulation of more fruitful and precise concepts and hypotheses. Hence, each principle consists of a theoretical statement, along with a specification of an operational research model suitable for investigating the principle in question. Thus, in this concluding section, issues of theory and research design are no longer treated separately (as principles vs. corollaries) but are presented together in a way that reveals the necessary close relation between the two.

For reasons that will become apparent, the principles begin with the outermost region of the environment—the macrosystem.

Principle 5. To the extent that is practically possible, every study of development in context should include a contrast between at least two macrosystems. In terms of research design, this means that, whatever questions or hypotheses are under investigation, the analysis is conducted separately for each macro-domain, thus making it possible to determine the extent to which the hypothesized processes operate in the same way in different macrosystems.

The preceding recommendation is not quite as demanding as might appear, for rarely would an investigator choose a sample so narrowly defined that it would not include within it substantial representation from two or more macrosystem domains. Moreover, the domains that occur most frequently are also those especially likely to offer contrasts in belief systems, resources, lifestyles, patterns of social exchange, and life course options that are especially significant for developmental processes and outcomes. For example, the contrasting macrosystems most salient in modern societies are those associated with differences in social class, family structure, gender, ethnicity, parental employment patterns, and linkages between home, school, and community. These are precisely the domains in which processes are apt to function differentially. Nevertheless, even if such contrasting groups are present in sufficient size, stratification of the sample inevitably reduces the statistical power of the design, while at the same time substantially increasing the scope and the cost of analysis.

What, then, would be the scientific yield of such expansion that could justify the increased expense? Fortunately, in this instance there is a concrete example that demonstrates the added gain. The example comes from a four-year longitudinal study conducted by Helen Bee and her associates (Bee et al., 1982). Relevant data were collected at five successive age periods during early childhood, beginning at birth. As we shall see shortly, the overall research findings testify to the developmental importance of aspects of both person and context delineated in the preceding pages. But first, we must take note of a distinctive feature of the investigation especially relevant for the topic at hand: the authors carried out a separate analysis of their data for mothers at each of two levels of schooling (those with some education beyond high school, in comparison with those with high school or less). The justification for conducting such a dual analysis was based not on the kinds of theoretical issues being raised here but on the more conventional ground of the need to control for what are viewed as possible confounding factors in order to establish the generality of the findings. In the authors' words, "[I]f we are to move closer to statements of causal connections between environmental measures and measures of the child's intellectual development, we must be able to show that the significant environmental variables are predictive within as well as across social class groups" (p. 1136).

The results of the analysis, however, revealed a rather different picture. In general, the predictive relationships were considerably stronger in the low-education group. Specifically, in predicting final outcome measures both of intelligence and receptive language, almost all of the correlations (10 in each case) were significant, ranging in magnitude from .20 to .63, with a median above .40. By contrast, in the high-education group, only three environmental predictors were significant, none above an r of .31.

The authors offer two explanations for this striking result:

First, it is possible that we are dealing here largely with differences in variance between the two groups. For example, most of the fathers in the high-education group were present during the pregnancy and were strongly supportive of the mother. Among the low-education group, there were a number of single mothers and others whose partners were less supportive. The fact that social support is predictive of IQ and language for the low-education group may, thus, be a simple reflection of the fact that only in that subgroup did the score vary widely.

An alternative explanation, however, is that there may be a different interactional dynamic operating in the high- and low-education families. For example, perhaps mothers with less education respond differently for high levels of life change or low levels of social support. These mothers may be less able to "buffer" the child against the vicissitudes in their own personal relationships. (p. 1152)

The authors' second explanation represents a classic example of process-context interaction. It would clearly be instructive were it possible to differentiate between the two alternative hypotheses through further analysis of the available data.

Fortunately, thanks to the care the authors took in reporting basic descriptive statistics, such a possibility exists. To begin with, an examination of the published standard deviations of the independent variables reveals that, in every case, the sigma is significantly greater for the low-education group. Hence, the authors' first alternative hypothesis finds empirical support.

But that is not the whole story. Although no regression coefficients are reported, the availability of the standard deviations along with the *r*s made it possible to calculate the regression of IQ and language scores on each independent variable, again separately for the two education groups.[28] The results of this reanalysis were indeed instructive. Certain variables did have greater impact per unit input in the low-education group: specifically, social supports, maternal expectations, and life changes. Certain other variables, however, had greater impact per unit input in the high-education group. These were measures of mother-infant interaction and of cultural resources present in the home [as assessed by Bradley and Caldwell's HOME scale (1977)].

While such essentially serendipitous findings obviously require cross-validation, they do exhibit a consistent pattern in terms of the theoretical framework presented in the preceding pages. Thus one might hypothesize that the developmental impact of *microsystem* processes within the family is enhanced by the kinds of resources that are associated with parents' education beyond the high school years. By contrast, the parent's linkages and orientations to the world outside the family (in this instance, in the form of social support, and belief systems about one's own and one's child's capacity to cope) have greater developmental power in families deprived of the resources that higher socioeconomic status might otherwise provide.[29]

My purpose here is not to claim validity for any particular hypothesis derived from this reanalysis of Bee's data but rather to illustrate the scientific importance of providing for the analysis of macrosystem contrasts in research on development in context. Such provision is highly desirable for several reasons. First, there is the danger, in the absence of one or more macrosystem contrasts, of overgeneralizing findings and conclusions. The reality of this risk is illustrated by the results of a recent study by Dornbusch and his colleagues of the relation of parenting style to adolescent school performance (Dornbusch, Ritter, Leiderman, Roberts, & Fraleigh, 1987). One of the most widely cited findings in the socialization literature is Diana Baumrind's demonstration, in a series of studies (Baumrind, 1971, 1973; Baumrind & Black, 1967), of the superiority of what she has called the "authoritative" pattern of child rearing, distinguished by a combination of firmness and support, as contrasted to more one-sided authoritarian or permissive styles. Dornbusch and his coworkers, employing a much larger and more representative sample of almost 8,000 subjects, obtained general support for Baumrind's thesis. "We found that both authoritarian and permissive parenting styles were negatively associated with grades, and authoritative parenting was positively associated with grades" (Dornbusch et al., 1987, p. 1244). The size and diversity of the sample, however, also permitted carrying out separate analyses for four ethnic groups: black, Asian, Hispanic, and non-Hispanic white. The results revealed that the expected relationships clearly held for whites and blacks but not for Asians or Hispanics. Asians, in particular, showed a widely discrepant pattern: the correlations of grades with both the authoritative and the permissive styles were near zero. Moreover, "compared to whites, the Asian high school students of both sexes reported that their families were higher on the index of authoritarian parenting and lower on the index of permissive parenting. Yet, counter to the general negative relation of such parenting patterns to academic achievement, the Asians as a group received high grades in school" (p. 1256). The authors acknowledge that "the success of Asian children in our public schools cannot be adequately explained in terms of the parenting styles we have studied" and suggest that "careful studies of the meaning of specific behaviors as interpreted by members of various social groups, particularly ethnic groups, could produce a major advance in our knowledge" (p. 1256).

The foregoing statement nicely captures Lewin's distinction between a class-theoretical model, in which ethnicity is treated simply as a social address, and a field-theoretical macrosystem model, which permits the analysis of the particular contextual elements and personal attributes and belief systems characterizing a particular ethnic group. Herein lies the second and more compelling reason for urging the introduction of macro-domains as a *common* denominator in studies of development in context.

The reason lies in the generative power of macrosystem designs in illuminating the sources and operation of forces affecting the pace and content of psychological growth. This potential cannot be realized, however, if the macrosystem is indexed only by its social address; the research design must *also* include provision *for assessing at least some of the substantive elements set forth in the formal definition of a macrosystem.* Unfortunately, most research models currently employed in studies of development in context do not incorporate these substantive features. From this viewpoint, the 1982 Bee study is a rare exception. The special strength of the work derives precisely from its comprehensiveness in obtaining and analyzing data at no less than three systems levels: micro- (e.g., mother-child interaction), exo- (e.g., mother's support networks), and macro- (e.g., contrasting levels of mother's education).

But even this outstanding study does not take advantage of some rewarding prospects that would have been provided by a more differentiated ecological paradigm. The first of these opportunities arises from the fact that, in the present research, the investigators moved quickly to more complex analyses, thus bypassing productive possibilities existing in the available data. For example, they were in a position to discover and describe the distinctive patterns of risk, belief systems, modes of mother-child interaction, and life changes that characterize families in the two macrosystems operationally defined by the proxy variable of maternal education. This could have been accomplished by examining differences in means for the two education groups on each of the environmental measures included in the study.

There was an even theoretically richer opportunity as well. It was created by the availability of data not only in the realm of context but also in the person domain. Beginning with the assessment of perinatal complications at birth, the investigators obtained successive measures of the young child's developmental status based on mental tests, mother's reports, and observations of language behavior. These data were used for the purpose of analyzing the relative predictive power, at successive ages, of the characteristics of the child as against those of the environment. The main finding in this regard was that "assessments of child performance were *poor* predictors prior to 24 months, but were excellent predictors from 24 months on" (Bee et al., 1982, p. 1134).

This finding may underestimate the importance for future development of the infant's early characteristics because of the restricted research paradigm guiding the analysis. What the paradigm overlooks is the possibility, indeed the likelihood, of an interaction, observable from the youngest ages onward, between the organism and the environment. For example, was the effect of mother-infant reciprocal activity the same for infants who had experienced perinatal complications versus those who had not? Analogous questions can be raised with respect to children who differed in developmental status at successive ages as assessed by tests or, perhaps more relevantly, as perceived by their mothers. Finally, returning to the level of the macrosystem, did these diverse developmental trajectories differ for children of mothers in the two educational groups? In sum, there was an opportunity to apply a full process-person-context model in their chronosystem design.

The preceding examples illustrate both the scientific need and the scientific gain of analyzing macrosystem contrasts in developmental research. All of the preceding investigations, however, were field studies concerned primarily with *social* processes. Is the injunction to employ macrosystem models equally applicable to research on basic cognitive processes in the laboratory? The results of previously cited studies bearing on this question (Bronfenbrenner, 1986a, 1986c) suggest that the case for employing macrosystem contrasts in the latter domain is equally if not more compelling. In terms of research design, two types of models merit consideration. The first, though more demanding, promises a richer scientific yield. It involves replicating each laboratory study in a natural setting with tasks that require analogous processes but draw on the subjects' experience in everyday life. The second, more economical strategy extends to the laboratory the principle of exploiting macrosystem contrasts already present within the sample, perhaps strengthened through the selection of subjects in a stratified design. There is good reason to believe that the systematic application of one or both of these models in studies of such basic cognitive processes as memory, concept formation, logical operations, and reasoning will not only challenge existing conceptions and conclusions but—more importantly—lead to more sophisticated formulations that, when implemented in appropriate research designs, will significantly enhance our understanding and knowledge of cognitive development in context.

The next principle takes as its point of departure a feature previously incorporated as a new element in the revised definition of the microsystem: namely, the recognition of the developmental importance of the characteristics of significant others in one's life. This same element also has key relevance for the nature of the proxy variables employed to identify macrosystems. At the present time, these variables are typically limited to background characteristics of the research subjects themselves, such as their social class, ethnicity, and place of residence. An ecological perspective suggests, however, that equally pertinent would be the background characteristics of the *other persons* living in the same environment: for example, neighbors, friends, associates at work. I have been able to find few investigations that have taken such factors into account; but when this was done, the effects were substantial. An early example is a study by Kawi and Pasamanick (1959) on the role of prenatal factors in the development of childhood reading orders. The sample was drawn from the greater Baltimore area and consisted only of white males. Instead of using a conventional measure of social class based on parents' education and occupation, the investigators classified families on the basis of census tracts ranked by decile in terms of the median rental cost. In other words, the index took into account the socioeconomic status not only of the subjects' families but also of their neighbors. Within each decile, children with and without reading problems (retardation of two years or more) were matched on an impressive array of background variables. For example, the control group was selected on the basis of the next birth in the same hospital (i.e., a child of the same age), of the same sex, and at the same mother's age as the index child.

The effect of class background in this study was much greater than is usually obtained in developmental research. Moreover, the influence of what, from a macrosystem perspective, one might call different socioeconomic macrosystems was reflected not only in a marked contrast in levels of both prenatal complications and reading disorders but also in the relation between these two factors. For example, the ratio of birth complications among nonreaders versus matched controls was 12 to 1 in the two lowest census tract deciles, but 1 to 1 in the top two. In other words, in the latter case, there was no difference at all; as in Drillien's (1957, 1964) work cited earlier, families living in good ecologies are in a position to avoid any serious problems for their children's later development arising from complications of pregnancy.

A second instructive example appears in a comparative study by Blau (1981) of competence, socialization, and social structure in a sample of black and white children and their families. As one measure of socioeconomic status, Blau calculated "the proportion of close neighbors in white-collar occupations, of college educated neighbors, and of neighbors with a child who has gone to college" (p. 18). She appropriately called the measure "social milieu" and, perhaps more precisely, "middle-class exposure." In a multiple regression of the five "best" predictors for IQ and achievement test scores in the sample as a whole, this index had an independent effect second only to race and slightly ahead of both education and occupational status. The impact of middle-class exposure was especially strong in the black subsample.

The preceding theoretical and empirical considerations lead to the following principle:

> *Principle 6.* The concept of macrosystem includes not only the subculture in which the person has been raised but also the subculture in which the person lives. The latter is defined by the personal and background characteristics of those with whom the person associates in the settings of everyday life. Any research design that includes a macrosystem contrast should therefore, to the extent possible, provide for securing identifying criteria from both of these domains. This provision is especially important when the person has been raised, or lives in, two different subcultures (as in the case of minority or immigrant groups).

The recommendation to include a macrosystem contrast in every study of development in context accords special importance to the structure and substance of the particular macrosystems in question. The next principle addresses this issue by taking cognizance of the fact that the macrosystem, as the outermost region of the environment, encompasses all the other systems.

> *Principle 7.* The macrosystem is defined by the structure and content of constituent systems, with particular reference to the developmentally instigative belief systems, resources, hazards, lifestyles, patterns of social exchange opportunity structures, and life course options that are embedded in each of these systems. The power of a macrosystem model is therefore enhanced to the extent that provision is made for assessing the foregoing characteristics in the research design for constituent micro-, meso-, or exo-systems.

Accordingly, the next set of principles deals with these constituent systems, proceeding in descending order.

Exo- and mesosystems have a key feature in common: both deal with the *relations between two or more settings*. In my 1979 monograph, I pointed out that such interesting linkages could take a number of forms, among them the participation of the same persons in more than one setting, communications between settings, and the availability of information in one setting about the other. The preceding principles dealing with the macrosystem call attention to yet another key dimension of relations between settings. The domain constitutes the focus of the next principle.

> *Principle 8.* The nature and power of developmental processes at the level of the meso- or the exosystem are influenced to a substantial degree by the

belief systems and expectations existing in each setting about the other. Provision for assessing such bidirectional orientations should therefore be incorporated as a key element in research designs involving the relation between two settings.

Existing empirical evidence for the above principle is as yet only indirect, being based solely on research findings, such as those previously cited, indicating the developmental importance of belief systems, first at the personal and then at the cultural level. Despite the extensive research literature in such areas as the relation between family and day care, home and school, school and peer group, and family and workplace, I have been unable to find any study that systematically addressed the issue of intersecting beliefs and expectations.

I turn next to a set of three principles pertaining to the microsystem. As the reader will observe, all of them reflect, and indeed follow from, the four principles (and their associated design corollaries) that emerged from the effort above to construct a tentative topology of the developmentally relevant characteristics of the person.

Principle 9. In a microsystem paradigm, the developing person is viewed as an active agent who inevitably plays some part in any developmental process taking place in the microsystem. Any research design for a microsystem must therefore take this active role into account. In addition, the scientific power of a microsystem model is enhanced to the extent that it provides for each of the following:

- The assessment of cognitive competence, socioemotional attributes, and context-relevant belief systems of the developing person, with particular emphasis on those qualities that meet criteria for being characterized as developmentally instigative;
- The assessment and interpretation of personal characteristics from the differing viewpoints of the person him- or herself, familiar significant others in the setting, and a trained observer, as well as from the perspective of the culture(s) and subculture(s) in which the developing person has been raised and has lived.

Principle 10. The developmental processes taking place within a setting can vary substantially as a function of the personal attributes of significant others present in the setting. Of particular significance are qualities of others that are developmentally instigative for the subject. The scientific power of a microsystem model is therefore further increased to the extent that such characteristics are assessed.

Principle 11. Each member of a microsystem influences every other member. In terms of research design, it is therefore important to take into consideration the influence of each relationship on other relationships: for example, within the family the effect of the husband-wife relationship on the parent-child relationship, the effect of the mother-child relationship on the father-child relationship, and vice versa.[30] The appropriate design for this purpose is a process-person-context model in which each relationship is treated as a context for processes taking place in the others.

The eighth and final principle is all-pervasive, for it invokes a parameter that is critical to the functioning of every ecological system in all of its parts. I refer to *the stability and predictability of the system's operation.* In short, does the system operate consistently over time? The most extensive evidence bearing on this issue comes from a longitudinal study conducted by the Finnish psychologist Lea Pulkkinen. Beginning when the children were eight years of age, she investigated the effect of environmental stability and change on the development of children through adolescence and young adulthood. The "steadiness" versus "unsteadiness" of family living conditions was measured by the frequency of such events as the following: the number of family moves, changes in day care or school arrangements, extent of family absence, incidence of divorce and remarriage, and altered conditions of maternal employment. Greater instability in the family environment was associated with greater submissiveness, aggressiveness, anxiety, and social problems among children in later childhood and adolescence, leading to higher risks of violence and criminal behavior in early adulthood (Pulkkinen, 1983; Pulkkinen & Saastamoinen, 1986). Moreover, the factor of stability of family living conditions appeared to be a stronger determinant of subsequent development than was the family's socioeconomic status.

Other findings pointing to the disruptive effect of environmental instability on developmental processes come from a variety of sources. For example, in her classic study of the developmental sequelae of low birth weight, Drillien (1964) investigated the role of what she called "family stress" in increasing the risk that the child would experience subsequent problems in development. Her index of stress was quite similar to that developed by Pulkkinen a decade later in Finland, including such items as divorce or separation, employment of the mother, and placement of the child in a residential nursery. (Pulkkinen does not seem to have been familiar with Drillien's earlier investigation.) When related to behavioral outcomes, Drillien's measure of family stress proved to be an even stronger predictor of developmental problems than socioeconomic status.

In particular, the tendency of children of low birth weight to exhibit problem behavior in school was especially strong for those youngsters who had grown up in unstable family environments.

Analogous findings for the contemporary American scene were obtained by Moorehouse (1986) in a study of how stability versus change over time in the mother's work status during the child's preschool years affected patterns of mother-child communication and how these patterns in turn influenced the child's achievement and social behavior in the first year of school. A key analysis involved a comparison between mothers who had maintained the same employment status over the period of the study and those who had changed in either direction: that is, to working more hours, fewer hours, or none at all. The results revealed that significant effects of work status were pronounced only in the group that had changed their working status. Although the disruptive impact was greatest among those mothers who had moved into full-time employment, it was still present even for those who had reduced their working hours or had left the labor force. Moorehouse concluded that "instability, on the whole, is associated with less favorable school outcomes than stability" (p. 103).

Further support for this conclusion emerged from a reanalysis of data reported in the previously cited study by Dornbusch and his colleagues (1987). The results indicated that by far the lowest school grades were obtained by adolescents whose parents had exhibited mixed or inconsistent child-rearing styles. At the same time, there is evidence from this same investigation that too much rigidity in a given system may also lead to developmental dysfunction. The reader will recall that, in the reported results, the poorest performance was shown by adolescents whose parents consistently exhibited an authoritarian pattern of child rearing, a result in accord with the earlier findings of Baumrind (Baumrind 1971, 1973; Baumrind & Black, 1967). At a broader level, an investigation conducted in rural and urban areas of Switzerland (Meili & Steiner, 1965; Vatter, 1981) indicated that the superior cognitive functioning observed in city children was a function of the richer and more diversified environment typifying the urban scene. Not only were these results independent of social class, but the community factors exerted a stronger influence than intrafamilial variables.

Such findings point to some optimal middle ground between extreme fluidity of systems, on the one hand, and extreme rigidity, on the other. This point is incorporated in the following principle.

Principle 12. The degree of stability, consistency, and predictability over time in any element of any level of the systems constituting an ecology of human development is critical for the effective operation of the system in question. Extremes either of disorganization or rigidity in structure of function represent danger signs for potential psychological growth, with some intermediate degree of system flexibility constituting the optimal condition for human development. In terms of research design, this proposition points to the importance of assessing the degree of stability versus instability, with respect to characteristics both of the person and of context, at each level of the ecological system.

Some readers may regard the preceding principle as too indeterminate to warrant scientific status, particularly as the final statement in a series of precepts defining directions for future research. In response, I can do no better than quote the succinct and elegant answer given to this same question by the philosopher of language John Searle (1983): "It is a condition of the adequacy of a precise theory of an indeterminate phenomenon that it should precisely characterize that phenomenon as indeterminate" (p. 72).

Retrospect and Prospect

The preceding series of propositions marks the completion of the task undertaken in this chapter. How close has the effort come to achieving its aim? One way to answer this question is to look again at our disembodied Lewinian equation and ask to what extent it is now possible to substitute concrete substance for the empty symbols. Here, once again, is the reformulated formula:

$$D_t = f_{(t-p)} \, (PE)_{(t-p)}$$

At first glance, it would appear that all is well. In every domain, including the previously neglected sphere of properties of the person, there is now much material. Indeed, the supply may even exceed the demand; there may not be enough researchers to go round. All any one of them need do is to choose a research question that fits the magic paradigm and apply the mighty process-person-context model—perhaps even with a timely chronosystem component—and a rich research reward is sure to come.

But that is only on the first glance. Alas, a second look reveals a new lacuna. The all-essential key to scientific discovery is missing. In all the preceding pages, what is there to substitute for the fateful "f" in the formula? What is the *process* that person and context are to generate? The original monograph of a decade ago contained no less than 50 hypotheses—all neat and numbered. The hopeful reader who looks back through the preceding pages will find nary a one. The task, however, is not being neglected; it is the subject of a book manuscript to which this chapter is but a prologue. I offer the prologue now, in advance, in the hope that others too may be moved to get into the act. "The play's the thing."

Notes

1. Bronfenbrenner (1982, 1985a, 1985b, 1986b, 1986c, 1986d, 1987, 1988a, 1988b, 1988c); Bronfenbrenner and Crouter (1983); Bronfenbrenner, Kessel, Kessen, and White (1986); Bronfenbrenner, Moen, and Garbarino (1982); Silbereisen (1986).

2. What is being criticized here is the failure to give adequate consideration to the developmental impact of the person *in contemporary ecological research*. Personal characteristics have of course received an enormous amount of attention in traditional studies of personality development, but relatively few such investigations have been conducted from an ecological perspective. A number of researches that do examine the *joint* contribution of person and context to development are cited below.

3. The exposition that follows draws on and extends a formulation first introduced in Bronfenbrenner (1988b).

4. The issue here raised is one that Lewin himself never fully addressed, or—perhaps putting it more precisely—it is an issue that he finessed by defining psychology as an ahistorical science. Lewin's failure to include this factor in his formula was not accidental but deliberate. In his view, science was by its very nature ahistorical. In psychology as in physics, he argued, present events can be influenced only by forces existing in the present situation. In psychology, however, the latter consisted of what Lewin called the "psychological field": that is, the situation not as deemed objectively but as perceived by the person. Hence, historical events could become "field forces" only to the extent that they existed in the person's present awareness. It was perhaps Lewin's predilection for the paradigms of physics, and their ahistorical orientation, that led him, and many other psychologists as well, to be far more interested in the study of behavior than of development. For further discussion of these issues, see Bronfenbrenner (1951, esp. pp. 210–216); Lewin (1931, 1951).

5. Henceforth, the term *paradigm* will be used to refer to the *conceptual* definition of the general paradigm or any of its components, whereas the term *model* will be applied to denote *operational* definitions of these concepts.

6. Although the social address model has limited scientific utility, it is useful as a marker for identifying what I have called *macrosystems*, overarching environmental structures at the level of the culture and subculture that define the nature of more proximal systems (see Section V).

7. For more detailed discussion of the nature, uses, and limitation of social address and personal attribute models, see Bronfenbrenner and Crouter (1983) and Bronfenbrenner (2001).

8. See Bronfenbrenner and Crouter (1983, pp. 192–193).

9. It is an interesting question whether the effects are as severe today [1989], given the subsequent progress in scientific knowledge and treatment strategies. Unfortunately, the absence of comparable data does not permit an answer.

10. The analysis involved comparing the children's school performance to what would have been expected on the basis of their scores on an intelligence test.

11. Regrettably, the analyses did not include any breakdown by birth weight, age, or sex of child.

12. For additional discussion of these issues, see Rutter and Pickles (in press [1991]).

13. The term *chronosystem*, which characterizes a particular type of research design, is not to be confused, through "clang association," with a series of concepts employed in the 1979 monograph, as well as later in this chapter, to differentiate various types of environmental systems (micro-, meso-, exo-, and macro-) that serve as contexts of development (see Section V). The chronosystem is a methodological construct; the remaining four are theoretical but can also become substantive when put to empirical use.

14. For a summary of Elder's original studies, see Bronfenbrenner (1979, pp. 273–284).

15. For reviews, see Bullinger and Chatillon (1983); Case (1985); Gelman and Baillargeon (1983).

16. For a comprehensive review of this literature, see Rest (1983).

17. The same consideration also applies to more objective measures of ability and achievement to the extent that the individual's scores become known to teachers or superiors or are used as the basis for selection or recommendation. Such possibilities are often not taken into account by researchers, especially in the interpretation of measures of mental ability.

18. The theory was first introduced to American psychologists in the late 1920s in a series of two articles, both under the same title, in the *Journal of Genetic Psychology*. The first article was authored by Luria (1928), the second by Vygotsky himself (Vygotsky, 1929).

19. In a preface to the English edition of the full report of the research, Luria (1979, p. v) indicates that the original idea for the study was suggested by Vygotsky.

20. The publication of the study in the Soviet Union was held up for more than three decades. The reasons for the delay are described by Michael Cole in his preface to the American edition: the status of national minorities has long been a sensitive issue in the USSR (not unlike the issue of ethnic minorities in the United States). It was all well and good to show that uneducated, traditional peasants quickly learned the modes of thought characteristic of industrialized socialist peoples, but it was definitely not acceptable to say anything that could be

interpreted as negative about these people at a time when their participation in national life was still so tenuous (for source, see Luria, 1978, p. xiv).

21. A promising strategy for future work in both of these is the application of what I have called meso- and exosystem models that link the family to other principal contexts of development such as school, peer group, and the parents' workplace (see Bronfenbrenner 1986a, 1986c).

22. For a comprehensive review of this literature, see Rest (1983).

23. For documentation, see Plant (1937).

24. This revised definition, along with that for the macrosystem to follow, has important implications for research design. Because these implications involve research models that relate systems properties of the environment to characteristics of the person, specification of these designs is deferred to the final section of this chapter, which deals with paradigms and models for future research.

25. In a sense, a place for this feature was accorded in the original definition of macrosystem through reference to "belief systems or ideology." But the reference was little more than that, since no implications were spelled out.

26. For reviews of the research literature on both of these new family forms, see Bronfenbrenner and Crouter (1982) and Hetherington, Cox, and Cox (1982).

27. Often this last seemingly basic feature is left unspecified; the text will merely state that a given hypothesis was (or was not) supported after control for a set of background variables, without indicating whether the latter had any effects and what they were.

28. The raw (unstandardized) regression coefficient measures the change in the dependent variable for each unit change in the independent variable, irrespective of the degree of variation in the latter. In short, it may be thought of as measuring "the bang for the buck." Ordinarily, this statistic is not useful for purposes of comparison, since regression coefficients are specific to the particular pair of independent and dependent variables involved. In the present instance, however, the same variables appear at each education level. Hence, it becomes possible to compare the relative impact of each environmental factor in the two education groups.

29. Support for this tentative hypothesis also emerged in an analysis of the effects of mother-infant interaction on the child's subsequent adjustment upon entering school. The mother's joint activity with her baby at age three significantly facilitated early school performance and behavior, but only in families in which the mother had had some education beyond high school (see Bronfenbrenner, 1986d).

30. The proposition addresses what I referred to in my 1979 monograph as the *second-order* or *third-party* effect, defined as "the indirect effect of third parties on the interaction between members of a dyad" (see Bronfenbrenner, 1979, pp. 68, 77–81).

References

Allport, G. W. (1937). *Personality: A psychosocial interpretation.* New York: Holt.
Baldwin, A. L. (1947). Changes in parent behavior during pregnancy. *Child Development, 18,* 29–39.

Bandura, A. (1977). Self-efficacy: Toward a unifying theory of behavior change. *Psychological Review, 84*, 191–215.

Bandura, A. (1982). Self-efficacy mechanism in human agency. *American Psychologist, 37*, 122–147.

Baumrind, D. (1971). Current patterns of parental authority. *Developmental Psychology Monograph, 4*, 1–103.

Baumrind, D. (1973). The development of instrumental competence through socialization. In A. D. Pick (Ed.), *Minnesota symposia on child psychology* (Vol. 7, pp. 3–46). Minneapolis: University of Minnesota Press.

Baumrind, D., & Black, A. E. (1967). Socialization practice associated with dimensions of competence in preschool boys and girls. *Child Development, 38*, 291–327.

Bee, H. L., Barnard, K. E., Eyres, S. J., Gray, C. A., Hammond, M. A., Spietz, A. L., Snyder, C., & Clark, B. C. (1982). Prediction of IQ and language skill from perinatal status, child performance, family characteristics, and mother-infant interaction. *Child Development, 53*, 1134–1156.

Blau, Z. B. (1981). *Black children/white children: Competence, socialization, and social structure.* New York: Free Press.

Block, J. H., & Block, J. (1980). The role of ego-control and ego-resiliency in the organization of behavior. In W. A. Collins (Ed.), *Minnesota symposia on child psychology* (Vol. 13, pp. 39–101). Hillsdale, NJ: Lawrence Erlbaum.

Block, J., Block, J. H., & Keyes, S. (1988). Longitudinally foretelling drug usage in adolescence: Early childhood personality and environmental precursors. *Child Development, 59*, 336–355.

Bradley, R. H., & Caldwell, B. M. (1977). Home observation for measurement of the environment: A validation study of screening efficiency. *American Journal of Mental Deficiency, 81*, 417–420.

Bronfenbrenner, U. (1951). Toward an integrated theory of personality. In R. R. Blake & G. V. Ramsey (Eds.), *Perception: An approach to personality* (pp. 206–257). New York: Ronald.

Bronfenbrenner, U. (1979). *The ecology of human development: Experiments by nature and design.* Cambridge, MA: Harvard University Press.

Bronfenbrenner, U. (1982). Child development: The hidden revolution. *Issues and studies* [National Research Council], *1*, 41–45.

Bronfenbrenner, U. (1985a). Contextos de crianza del nino: Problemas y prospectiva. *Infancia y Aprendizaje, 29*, 41–55.

Bronfenbrenner, U. (1985b). Midtveis i den menneskelige utviklings okologi [The ecology of human development in mid-passage]. In I. Bo (Ed.), *Barn i miljo* [Children in the environment] (pp. 36–69). Oslo: J. W. Cappelens.

Bronfenbrenner, U. (1986a). Alienation and the four worlds of children. *Phi Delta Kappan, 67*, 430–436.

Bronfenbrenner, U. (1986b). Dix années de recherche sur l'ecologie du developpement humain. In M. Crahay & D. Lafontaine (Eds.), *L'art et la science de l' enseignement* (pp. 283–301). Brussels: Editions Labor.

Bronfenbrenner, U. (1986c). Ecology of the family as a context for human development. *Developmental Psychology, 22*, 723–742.

Bronfenbrenner, U. (1986d). Recent advances in research on human development. In R. K. Silbereisen, K. Eyferth, & G. Rudinger (Eds.), *Development as action in context: Problem behavior and normal youth development* (pp. 287–309). New York: Springer-Verlag.

Bronfenbrenner, U. (1987). La cambiante ecologia de la infancia: Implicaciones en el terreno del la ciencia y de la accion. In A. Alvarez (Ed.), *Psicologia y education: Realizaciones y tendencies actuales en la investigacion y en la practica* (pp. 44–56). Madrid: Mec y Visor Libros.

Bronfenbrenner, U. (l988a). Foreword. In A. R. Pence (Ed.), *Ecological research with children and families* (pp. ix–xix). New York: Columbia University Teachers' College Press.

Bronfenbrenner, U. (1988b). Interacting systems in human development: Research paradigms: Present and future. In N. Bolger, A. Caspi, G. Downey, & M. Moorehouse (Eds.), *Persons in context: Developmental processes* (pp. 25–49). New York: Cambridge University Press.

Bronfenbrenner, U. (1988c). Paradoxes of prenatal care: A case for vitality from our vital statistics. *Early Childhood Update, 4,* 2–7.

Brofenbrenner, U. (2001). Growing chaos in the lives of children and families. How can we turn it around? In J. C. Westman (Ed.), *Parenthood in America* (pp. 115–125). Madison: University of Wisconsin Press.

Bronfenbrenner, U., & Crouter, A. C. (1982). Work and family through time and space. In S. B. Kamerman & C. D. Hayes (Eds.), *Families that work: Children in a changing world* (pp. 39–83). Washington, DC: National Academy Press.

Bronfenbrenner, U., & Crouter, A. C. (1983). The evolution of environmental models in developmental research. In P. H. Mussen (Series Ed.) & W. Kessen (Vol. Ed.), *Handbook of child psychology: Vol. 1. History, theory, and methods* (4th ed., pp. 357–414). New York: John Wiley.

Bronfenbrenner, U., Kessel, F., Kessen, W., & White, S. (1986). Toward a critical history of developmental psychology. *American Psychologist, 41,* 1218–1230.

Bronfenbrenner, U., Moen, P., & Garbarino, J. (1982). Child, family, and community. In R. D. Parke (Ed.), *Review of child development research: Vol. 7. The family* (pp. 283–328). Chicago: University of Chicago Press.

Brown, A. L., Bransford, J. D., Ferrara, R. A., & Campione, J. C. (1983). Learning, remembering, and understanding. In P. H. Mussen (Series Ed.) & J. H. Flavell & E. M. Markman (Vol. Eds.), *Handbook of child psychology: Vol. 3. Cognitive development* (4th ed., pp. 77–166). New York: John Wiley.

Bullinger, A., & Chatillon, J. F. (1983). Recent theory and research of the Genevan school. In P. H. Mussen (Series Ed.) & J. H. Flavell & E. M. Markman (Vol. Eds.), *Handbook of child psychology: Vol. 3. Cognitive development* (4th ed., pp. 231–262). New York: John Wiley.

Campbell, D. T., & Fiske, D. W. (1959). Convergent and discriminant validation by the multitrait-multimethod matrix. *Psychological Bulletin, 56,* 81–105.

Campos, J. J., Caplovitz, C., Lamb, M. E., Goldsmith, H. H., & Stenberg, C. (1983). Socioemotional development. In P. H. Mussen (Series Ed.) & M. M. Haith &

J. J. Campos (Vol. Eds.), *Handbook of child psychology: Vol. 2: Infancy and developmental psychobiology* (4th ed., p. 832). New York: John Wiley.

Carraher, T. N., Carraher, D. W., & Schliemann, A. D. (1985). Mathematics in the streets and in schools. *British Journal of Developmental Psychology, 3,* 21–29.

Case, R. (1985). *Intellectual development birth to adulthood.* Orlando, FL: Academic Press.

Caspi, A., Elder, G. H., Jr., &. Bem, D. J. (1988). Moving away from the world: Life-course patterns of shy children. *Developmental Psychology, 24,* 824–831.

Catto-Smith, A. G., Yu, V. Y., Bajusk, B., Orgill, A. A., & Astbuty, J. (1985). Effect of neonatal periventricular haemorrhage on neurodevelopmental outcomes. *Archives of Disease in Childhood, 60,* 8–11.

Ceci, S. J. (1996). *On intelligence: A bioecological view of intellectual development.* Cambridge, MA: Harvard University Press.

Ceci, S. J., & Bronfenbrenner, U. (1985). "Don't forget to take the cupcakes out of the oven": Prospective memory, strategic time-monitoring, and context. *Child Development, 56,* 150–165.

Ceci, S. J., Bronfenbrenner, U., & Baker, J. G. (1988). Memory in context: The case of prospective memory. In F. Weinert & M. Perlmutter (Eds.), *Universals and changes in memory development* (pp. 243–256). Hillsdale, NJ: Lawrence Erlbaum.

Ceci, S. J., & Liker, J. (1986). A day at the races: IQ, expertise, and cognitive complexity. *Journal of Experimental Psychology: General, 115,* 255–266.

Clarke, A. M., & Alan, D. B. (1988). The adult outcome of early behavioral abnormalities. *International Journal of Behavioral Development, 11,* 3–19.

Clausen, I. A. (1986). *The life course: A sociological perspective.* Englewood Cliffs, NJ: Prentice Hall.

Cole, M. J., Gay, J., Glick, I., & Sharp, D. W. (1971). *The cultural context of learning and thinking.* New York: Basic Books.

Cole, M., & Scribner, S. (1974). *Culture and thought.* New York: John Wiley.

Cottrell, L. S. (1942). The analysis of situational fields in social psychology. *American Sociological Review, 7,* 370–382.

Crockenberg, S. B. (1981). Infant irritability, other responsiveness, and social support influences on the security of infant-mother attachment. *Child Development, 52,* 857–865.

Dornbusch, S. M., Ritter, P. L., Leiderman, P. H., Roberts, D. F., & Fraleigh, M. J. (1987). The relation of parenting style to adolescent school performance. *Child Development, 58,* 1244–1257.

Drillien, C. M. (1957). The social and economic factors affecting the incidence of premature birth. *Journal of Obstetrical Gynaecology, 64,* 161–184.

Drillien, C. M. (1964). *The growth and development of the prematurely born infant.* London: E. & S. Livingston.

Elder, G. H., Jr. (1974). *Children of the Great Depression.* Chicago: University of Chicago Press.

Elder, G. H., Jr. (1985). Perspectives on the life course. In G. H. Elder Jr. (Ed.), *Life course dynamics* (pp. 23–49). Ithaca, NY: Cornell University Press.

Elder, G. H., Jr., & Caspi, A. (1988). Stressful times in children's lives. In N. Bolger, A. Caspi, G. Downey, & M. Moorehouse (Eds.), *Persons in context: Developmental processes* (pp. 77–113). New York: Cambridge University Press.

Elder, G. H., Jr., Caspi, A., & Downey, G. (1986). Problem behavior and family relationships: Life course and intergenerational themes. In A. Sorensen, F. Weinert, & L. Sherrod (Eds.), *Human development and the life course: Multidisciplinary perspectives* (pp. 293–340). Hillsdale, NJ: Lawrence Erlbaum.

Elder, G. R., Jr., van Nguyen, T. V., & Caspi, A. (1985). Linking family hardship to children's lives. *Child Development, 56,* 361–375.

Gelman, R., & Baillargeon, R. (1983). A review of some Piagetian concepts. In P. H. Mussen (Series Ed.) & J. H. Flavell & E. M. Markman (Vol. Eds.), *Handbook of child psychology: Vol. 3. Cognitive development* (4th ed., pp. 167–230). New York: John Wiley.

Hetherington, E. M., Cox, M., & Cox, R. (1982). Effects of divorce on parents and children. In M. Lamb (Ed.), *Nontraditional families* (pp. 233–288). Hillsdale, NJ: Lawrence Erlbaum.

Hinde, R. A., & Tobin, C. (1988). Temperament at home and behavior at preschool. In G. A. Kohnstamm (Ed.), *Temperament discussed* (pp. 123–132). Lisse, the Netherlands: Swets & Zeitlinger.

Jones, W. H., & Briggs, S. R. (1984). The self-other discrepancy in social shyness. In R. Schwarzer (Ed.), *The self in anxiety, stress, and depression* (pp. 93–108). Amsterdam: North Holland.

Kagan, J., Moss, H. A., & Sigel, I. E. (1963). Psychological significance of styles of conceptualization. In J. C. Wright & I. Kagan (Eds.), *Basic cognitive processes in children* (Monographs of the Society for Research in Child Development, Vol. 28, No. 2, pp. 73–124). Lafayette, IN: Child Development Publications.

Kawi, A. A., & Pasamanick, B. (1959). *Prenatal and paranatal factors in the development of childhood reading disorders* (Monographs of the Society for Research in Child Development, Vol. 24, No. 4). Lafayette, IN: Child Development Publications.

Kogan, N. A. (1973). Creativity and cognitive style: A life span perspective. In P. B. Baltes & K. W. Schaie (Eds.), *Life span developmental psychology: Personality and socialization* (pp. 146–180). New York: Academic Press.

Kogan, N. A. (1983). Stylistic variation in childhood and adolescence. In P. H. Mussen (Series Ed.) & J. H. Flavell & E. M. Markman (Vol. Eds.), *Handbook of child psychology: Vol. 3. Cognitive development* (pp. 695–706). New York: John Wiley.

Laboratory of Comparative Human Cognition. (1983). Culture and cognitive development. In P. H. Mussen (Series Ed.) & W. Kessen (Vol. Ed.), *Handbook of child psychology: Vol. 1. History, theory, and methods* (pp. 295–356). New York: John Wiley.

Lancy, D. F., & Strathem, A. J. (1981). Making two's: Pairing as an alternative to the taxonomic mode of representation. *American Anthropologist, 83,* 773–795.

Lave, J. (1977). Tailor-made experiments and evaluating the intellectual consequences of apprenticeship training. *Quarterly Newsletter of the Institute for Comparative Human Development, 1*, 1–3.

Lave, J., Murtaugh, M., & de la Roche, D. (1984). The dialectic of arithmetic in grocery shopping. In B. Rogoff &. J. Lave (Eds.), *Everyday cognition: Its development in social context.* Cambridge, MA: Harvard University Press.

Leontiev, A. N. (1932). The development of voluntary attention in the child. *Journal of Genetic Psychology, 40*, 52–83.

Leontiev, A. N. (1959). *Problemy razvitiya psikhiki* [Problems of mental development]. Moscow: Izdatel'stvo Moskovskogo Gosudarstvennogo Universiteta. Published in English (1982) as *Problems in the development of mind.* Moscow: Progress Publishers.

Leontiev, A. N. (1975). *Deyte/'nost,' soznanie, lichnost'* [Activity, consciousness, personality]. Leningrad: Izdatel'stvo Polilticheskoi Literaturi. Published in English (1978) as *Activity, consciousness, personality.* Englewood Cliffs, NJ: Prentice Hall.

Lewin, K. (1931). The conflict between Aristotelian and Galilean modes of thought in contemporary psychology. *Journal of Genetic Psychology, 5*, 141–177.

Lewin, K. (1935). *A dynamic theory of personality.* New York: McGraw-Hill.

Lewin, K. (1951). *Field theory in social science.* New York: Harper & Brothers.

Luria, A. R. (1928). The problem of the cultural behavior of the child. *Journal of Genetic Psychology, 35*, 493–506.

Luria, A. R. (1931). Psychological expedition to Central Asia. *Science, 74*, 383–384.

Luria, A. R. (1976). *Cognitive development.* Cambridge, MA: Harvard University Press.

Luria, A. R. (1978). *Cognitive development: Its cultural and social foundations.* Cambridge, MA: Harvard University Press.

Luria, A. R. (1979). *The making of mind.* Cambridge, MA: Harvard University Press.

Luria, A. R. (1982). *Language and cognition.* New York: Wiley Intersciences.

Matheny, A. P., Jr., Wilson, R. S., Dolan, A. B., & Krantz, J. Z. (1981). Behavioral contrasts in twinships: Stability and patterns of differences in childhood. *Child Development, 52*, 579–588.

Mead, G. H. (1934). *Mind, self, and society.* Chicago: University of Chicago Press.

Meili, R., & Steiner, H. (1965). Eine Untersuchung zum Intelligenzniveau elf-jähriger der deutschen Schwei z. *Schweizerische Zeitschrift für Psychologie und ihre Anwendungen, 24*(1), 23–32.

Messick, S. (1983). Assessment of children. In P. H. Mussen (Series Ed.) & W. Kessen (Vol. Ed.), *Handbook of child psychology: Vol. 1. History, theory, and methods* (4th ed., pp. 477–526). New York: John Wiley.

Moorehouse, M. (1986). *The relationships among continuity in maternal employment, parent-child communicative activities, and the child's school competence.* Unpublished doctoral dissertation, Cornell University.

Murtaugh, M. (1985, Fall). The practice of arithmetic by American grocery shoppers. In "The social organization of knowledge and practice: A symposium." *Anthropology and Educational Quarterly, 16*, 171–213.

Newman, R. S. (1984). Children's achievement and self-evaluations in mathematics: A longitudinal study. *Journal of Educational Psychology, 76*, 857–873.

Plant, J. S. (1937). *Personality and the cultural pattern.* New York: Commonwealth Fund.

Plomin, R., & Nesselrode, J. R. (In press [published 1990]). Behavior genetics and personality change. *Journal of Personality, 58*(1), 191–220.

Plomin, R., & Rowe, D. C. (1979). Genetic and environmental etiology of social behavior in infancy. *Developmental Psychology, 15*, 62–72.

Pulkkinen, L. (1983). Finland: The search for alternatives to aggression. In A. P. Goldstein & M. Segall (Eds.), *Aggression in global perspective* (pp. 104–144). New York: Pergamon.

Pulkkinen, L., & Saastamoinen, M. (1986). Cross-cultural perspectives on youth violence. In S. J. Apter & A. P. Goldstein (Eds.), *Youth violence: Programs and prospects* (pp. 262–281). New York: Pergamon.

Rest, J. R. (1983). Morality. In P. H. Mussen (Series Ed.) & J. H. Flavell & E. M. Markman (Vol. Eds.), *Handbook of child psychology: Vol. 3. Cognitive development* (4th ed., Vol. 3, pp. 556–629). New York: John Wiley.

Rivers, W. H. R. (1926). *Psychology and ethnology.* New York: Harcourt Brace.

Rotter, J. (1966). Generalized expectancies for internal versus external locus of control of reinforcement. *Psychological Monographs: General and Applied, 80*, 1–28.

Rutter, M. J., & Pickles, A. (In press [1991]). Person-environment interaction: Concepts, mechanisms, and implications for data analysis. In T. Wachs & R. Plomin (Eds.), *Conceptualization and measurement in organism-environment interaction* (105–141). Washington, DC: American Psychological Association.

Scribner, S., & Cole, M. (1981). *The psychology of literacy.* Cambridge, MA.: Harvard University Press.

Searle, J. (1983, October 27). The world turned upside down. *New York Review of Books,* pp. 74–79.

Silbereisen, R. K. (1986). Entwicklung und ökologischer Kontext: Wissenschaftsgeschichte im Spiegel persönlicher Erfahrung—Ein Interview mit Urie Bronfenbrenner [Development in ecological context: History of psychological science through the mirror of personal experience—An interview with Urie Bronfenbrenner]. *Psychologische Erziehung und Unterricht, 33*, 241–249.

Stewart, A. (1983). Severe perinatal hazards. In M. L. Rutter (Ed.), *Developmental neuropsychiatry* (pp. 15–31). New York: Guilford.

Super, C. M. (1980). Cognitive development: Looking across at growing up. In C. Super & M. Harkness (Eds.), *Anthropological perspectives on child development* (New Directions for Child Development, No. 8, pp. 59–69). San Francisco: Jossey-Bass.

Thomas, W. I. (1927). *The unadjusted girl.* Boston: Little, Brown.

Thomas, W. I., & Thomas, D. S. (1928). *The child in America.* New York: Knopf.

Thomas, W. I., & Znaniecki, F. (1927). *The Polish peasant in Europe and America.* Chicago: University of Chicago Press.

Tulkin, S. R. (1973). Social class differences in infants' reactions to mother's and stranger's voices. *Developmental Psychology, 8*(1), 137.

Tulkin, S. R. (1977). Social class differences in maternal and infant behavior. In P. H. Leiderman, A. Rosenfeld, & S. R. Tulkin (Eds.), *Culture and infancy* (pp. 495–537). New York: Academic Press.

Tulkin, S. R., & Cohler, B. J. (1973). Child-rearing attitudes and mother-child interaction in the first year of life. *Merrill-Palmer Quarterly, 19,* 95–106.

Tulkin, S. R., & Covitz, F. E. (1975). *Mother-infant interaction and intellectual functioning at age six.* Paper presented at the meeting of the Society for Research in Child Development, Denver.

Tulkin, S. R., & Kagan, J. (1972). Mother-child interaction in the first year of life. *Child Development, 43,* 31–41.

Vatter, M. (1981). Intelligenz und regionale Herkunft: Eine Langsschnittstudie im Kanton Bern. In A. H. Walter (Ed.), *Region und sozialisation* (Vol. 1, pp. 56–91). Stuttgart: Frommann-Holzboog.

Vygotsky, L. S. (1929). II. The problem of the cultural development of the child. *Journal of Genetic Psychology, 6,* 415–434.

Vygotsky, L. S. (1978). *Mind in society.* Cambridge, MA: Harvard University Press.

Werner, E. E., & Smith, R. S. (1982). *Vulnerable but invincible.* New York: McGraw-Hill.

Whiting, B. B., & Whiting, J. W. M. (1975). *Children of six cultures: A psychocultural analysis.* Cambridge, MA: Harvard University Press.

Whiting, J. W. M., & Whiting, B. B. (1973). Altruistic and egoistic behavior in six cultures. In L. Nader & T. W. Maretzki (Eds.), *Cultural illness and health: Essays in human adaptation.* Washington, DC: American Anthropological Association.

Witkin, H., Dyk, R. B., Faterson, H. F., Goodenough, D. R., & Karp, S. A. (1962). *Psychological differentiation.* New York: John Wiley.

Article 11

Heredity, Environment, and the Question "How"

A First Approximation

Urie Bronfenbrenner and Stephen J. Ceci

In this article, Stephen J. Ceci and I proposed the forerunner of what was to be our formal bioecological model, published a year later in the *Psychological Review*. Departing from the routine question "How much do heredity and environment contribute to development?" here we asked, "How do they contribute? What are the proximal mechanisms through which genotypes are transformed into phenotypes?" As has been my frequent approach, I focus here on a single study, not well known, to throw light on the question's answer. The study is that of Cecil Mary Drillien, a little-known Scottish researcher who had the perspicacity to include in her model person, process, and context factors as well as time. In this preview of what was to become the full bioecological model, we present for the first time a number of concepts and hypotheses. For example, we assert that proximal processes' greatest impact for positive outcomes is to be found in the best environments,

Source: Bronfenbrenner, U., & Ceci, S. J. (1993). Heredity, environment and the question "how": A first approximation. In R. Plomin & G. E. McClearn (Eds.), *Nature, nurture, and psychology* (pp. 313–323). Washington, DC: APA Books. Copyright © 1995 by the American Psychological Association. Reprinted with permission.

whereas their greatest impact for negative outcomes (e.g., crime, teenage pregnancy) is to be found in the poorest environments, a claim that is theoretically coherent but perhaps not intuitive.

T hree and a half decades ago, Anne Anastasi (1958), the then-outgoing president of the American Psychological Association's Division of General Psychology, posed the question "How do heredity and environment contribute to development?" as a challenge to psychological science as a whole. Anastasi offered few answers. Instead, she urged her scientific colleagues to pursue this question, which she saw as a more rewarding and necessary scientific goal than attempting to determine *how much* of the variance was attributable to heredity and how much to environment. The question "How?" offers a more fruitful approach than the question "How much?" since there is still much to be learned about the specific modus operandi of hereditary and environmental factors in the development of behavioral differences before we can assign proportions to their contributions.

Today, 35 years later, Anastasi's challenge still stands, despite the fact that recent developments in both science and society give it renewed importance. Thus, over the past decade, research in the fields of both behavioral genetics and human development has placed increased reliance on the traditional percentage-of-variance model (Plomin & Bergeman, 1991; Plomin, DeFries, & McClearn, 1990; Scarr, 1992; "Special Section," 1992). The extensive body of research guided by this model—in particular, some of the general conclusions drawn from it—has evoked criticism, not only on scientific grounds but also on social and ethical grounds ("Special Section," 1991).

Social and ethical concerns notwithstanding, in our view, although the traditional model has made important contributions to the understanding of not only genetic but also environmental influences on human development (e.g., Plomin & Daniels, 1987), it nevertheless remains incomplete. In addition, some of its basic assumptions are subject to question. At the core of the problem lies precisely Anastasi's issue: the need to identify the mechanisms through which genotypes are transformed into phenotypes.

Overview

In this chapter, we take a first step in addressing that need by offering a possible conceptual framework for constructing a more systematic theoretical and operational model of genetic-environment interaction. Based on a bioecological perspective (Bronfenbrenner, 1989a, 1993; Ceci, 1990), the proposed framework replaces some of the key assumptions underlying the traditional paradigm of human behavioral genetics with formulations that we believe to be more consonant with contemporary theory and research in the field of human development. In addition to incorporating explicit measures of the environment conceptualized in systems terms and allowing for nonadditive synergistic effects in genetic-environment interaction, the model specifically posits empirically assessable mechanisms, called *proximal processes,* through which genotypes are transformed into phenotypes.

It is further argued, on both theoretical and empirical grounds, that heritability, defined by behavioral geneticists as "the proportion of the total phenotypic variance that is due to additive genetic variation" (Cavelli-Sforza & Bodmer, 1971), is in fact highly influenced by events and conditions in the environment. We propose that heritability (h^2) can specifically be shown to vary substantially as a direct function of the magnitude of proximal processes and the quality of the environments in which they occur, potentially yielding values of h^2 that, at their extremes, are appreciably both higher and lower than those heretofore reported in the research literature. Furthermore, what h^2 in fact measures is the proportion of variance attributable to observed individual differences in actualized genetic potential. It follows that the amount of unactualized potential remains unknown and cannot be inferred from the magnitude of h^2.

In formal expositions of the established behavioral genetics model, the point is usually made that the model is intended to apply only to individual differences in developmental outcome and not to differences between groups. Yet, to our knowledge, no systematic theoretical framework has been proposed by behavioral geneticists for conceptualizing and analyzing the role of heredity and environment in producing group differences in developmental outcomes. By contrast, a bioecological model explicitly conceptualizes both kinds of differences as interactive products of genetic-environment interaction and suggests research designs that permit the simultaneous investigation of both types of variation. In the case of group differences, it is as yet possible to demonstrate environmental effects only; the assessment of the genetic contribution to group differences must wait on advances in molecular genetics and related fields (see the discussion of Hypothesis 5 later in this chapter).

Finally, there is evidence that social changes taking place over the past two decades in developed societies as well as developing societies have undermined conditions necessary for the operation of proximal processes (Bronfenbrenner, 1989b, 1992). Hence, if it is valid, then the proposed model has importance for both science and society because it implies that humans have genetic potentials, in terms of both individual and group differences, that are appreciably greater than those that are currently realized and that progress toward such realization can be achieved through the provision of environments in which proximal processes can be enhanced, but which are always within the limits of human genetic potential.

Bioecological Model

As previously noted, at the core of a bioecological model of human development is the concept of proximal process. At the outset, it is important to clarify how such processes differ from the classic physiopsychological processes of perception, cognition, emotion, and motivation. These processes are usually thought of as occurring primarily within the brain, which is also viewed as the "place" where development occurs. But, in our view, this is not the whole story because perception, cognition, emotion, and motivation involve psychological content: They are about *something*. And from the beginning, much of that content is in the outside world. More specifically, in humans, the content turns out, early on, to be mainly about people, objects, and symbols. These entities exist initially only in the environment: that is, outside the organism. Hence from its beginnings, development involves interaction between organism and environment. Moreover, interaction implies a two-way activity. The external becomes internal and becomes transformed in the process. But because, from its beginnings, the organism begins to change its environment, the internal becomes external and becomes transformed in the process.

Thus far, we have been speaking in metaphors and deliberately so. We wish to convey to the reader a sense of the general schema in which our more systematic, substantive framework is cast. But the metaphor must also have some correspondence with reality, and for that purpose, it must take on more concrete forms. To make this transition from the abstract to the concrete, we return to the concept of interactive proximal processes and examine how they relate to the genetic endowment of the person on the one hand and to the environment on the other.

Genetic potentials for development that exist within humans are not merely passive possibilities but active dispositions expressed in selective patterns of attention, action, and response. However, these dynamic potentials do not spring forth full-blown like Athena out of Zeus's head from a single blow of Hephaestus's hammer. The process of transforming genotypes into phenotypes is neither so simple nor so quick. The realization of human genetic potentials and predispositions for competence, character, and psychopathology requires intervening mechanisms that connect the inner with the outer in a two-way process that occurs not instantly but over time. This process is the focus of the first defining property of a bioecological model, which is formulated as follows.

Proposition 1

Especially in its early phases, and to a great extent throughout the life course, human development takes place through processes of progressively more complex reciprocal interaction between an active evolving biopsychological human organism and the persons, objects, and symbols in its immediate environment. To be effective, the interaction must occur on a fairly regular basis over extended periods of time. Such enduring forms of interaction in the immediate environment are referred to henceforth as proximal processes. Examples of enduring patterns of proximal process are found in parent-child and child-child activities, group or solitary play, reading, learning new skills, studying, athletic activities, and performing complex tasks.

Thus, to the extent that they occur in a given environment over time, proximal processes are postulated as the mechanisms through which human genetic potentials for effective psychological functioning are actualized. In short, proximal processes are the primary engines of development. But, like all engines, they cannot produce their own fuel, nor are they capable of self-steering. A second defining property identifies the threefold source of these dynamic forces.

Proposition 2

The form, power, content, and direction of the proximal processes that affect development vary systematically as a joint function of the characteristics of the developing person and the environment (both immediate and more remote) in which the processes are taking place and the nature of the developmental outcomes that they produce.

Illustrative Research Designs and Hypotheses

Among the most consequential personal characteristics that affect the form, power, content, and direction of proximal processes is genetic inheritance.

As yet, however, there are no concrete examples in which the bioecological model has been applied to samples composed of groups of contrasting consanguinity (e.g., identical vs. fraternal twins, biological vs. adopted children). Given the absence of such studies, we proceed as follows to illustrate the kinds of research designs that might be used for analyzing genetic-environment interaction in a bioecological model. First, we present a concrete example of findings obtained with what we call a *process-context model*: one in which the characteristics of the person (in this instance, children who differ in degree of consanguinity) have not yet been included in the design. We then present some examples of hypotheses derived from a bioecological model that could be tested once family members representing contrasting degrees of consanguinity have been incorporated into the design.

The results of the first step are shown in Figure 11.1. The data are drawn from a classic longitudinal study by Drillien (1964) of factors affecting the development of children of low birth weight compared with those of normal birth weight.

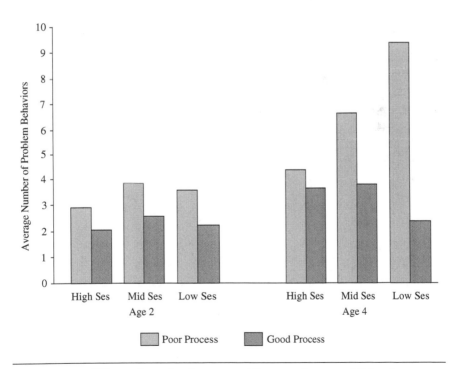

Figure 11.1   Effects of proximal process at 2 years of age on children's problem behaviors at 2 and 4 years of age by socioeconomic status (SES).

For present purposes only the data for the latter are shown. The figure depicts the impact of the quality of mother-infant interaction at two years of age on a number of observed problem behaviors at four years of age as a function of social class. As can be seen, in accord with Proposition 1, a proximal process (in this instance, mother-infant interaction across time) emerges as the most powerful predictor of developmental outcome. Furthermore, as stipulated in Proposition 2, the power of the process varies systematically as a function of the environmental context (in this instance, social class). Note also that proximal process has the general effect of reducing or buffering against environmental differences in developmental outcome.

Finally, the proximal process appears to have the greatest impact in the most unfavorable environment. From the perspective of a bioecological model, however, the greatest effectiveness of proximal processes in poorer environments is to be expected only for indices of developmental dysfunction.[1] For outcomes reflecting developmental competence, proximal processes are expected to have greater impact in more advantaged environments, primarily because the achievement of competence requires resources that exist in, and are drawn from, the broader external environment. For example, when the outcome is superior school achievement, mother-child interaction is most effective in families in which mothers have had some education beyond high school (Small & Luster, 1992).

In our second step, incorporating children of contrasting consanguinity into the research design would require the introduction of an additional dimension. Specifically, each of the six cells of the longitudinal design (two levels of care × three levels of social class) would now be further stratified by the degree of genetic relationship (e.g., monozygotic vs. dizygotic twins, biological vs. unrelated children living in the same family). One would then proceed to calculate the value of h^2 for each of the original six cells.

What would be the anticipated results viewed from the perspective of a bioecological model? The expectations are based on two of the model's key assumptions: first, that proximal processes actualize genetic potentials for developmental competence and thereby reduce developmental dysfunction and, second, that h^2 is correctly interpreted as the proportion of trait variance attributable to actualized genetic potential. Given these assumptions, the bioecological model generates a series of empirically testable hypotheses. We cite five of them as examples.

Hypothesis 1

With respect to outcomes that reflect developmental competence, h^2 will be greater when levels of proximal process are high and smaller when such processes are weak. This prediction follows from the principle that proximal processes actualize genetic potentials for developmental competence, which thereby reduces variation attributable to the environment.

Hypothesis 2

The values of h^2 that are associated with high and low levels of proximal process will be more extreme (greater and smaller, respectively) than those previously reported in the literature (when proximal process was not taken into account). This hypothesis follows from Proposition 1, which stipulates that proximal processes have more powerful effects on development than do the characteristics of either the environment or the person.

Hypothesis 3

The power of proximal processes to actualize potentials for developmental competence will be greater in advantaged and stable environments than in those that are impoverished and disorganized. For example, with respect to outcomes such as competence, we predict that the difference between values of h^2 that are associated with high versus low levels of proximal process will be even greater in middle-class environments than in lower-class environments.

Hypothesis 4

Conversely, the power of proximal process to buffer genetic potentials for developmental dysfunction (such as Drillien's 1964 index of children's problem behaviors) will be greater in disadvantaged and disorganized environments. Thus, for such outcomes, we predict that the difference between values of h^2 that are associated with high levels versus low levels of proximal process will be greater in lower-class environments than in middle-class environments.

A final hypothesis, and its empirical investigation, are made possible by the specification of proximal processes as the mechanisms through which genetic potentials are actualized. Such processes not only exist in nature but also can be produced experimentally. For example, two randomly assigned groups, each including the same contrast in consanguinity but comparable in other respects, could be exposed to intervention strategies systematically differing in the degree to which they encourage the involvement of children in proximal processes in the home or other child care settings. Although it would be difficult to assemble and sustain a sample of twins for this purpose, recent demographic changes in the United States are creating other research opportunities on a much larger scale. Thus, the growing number of families that contain both biological and stepchildren or adopted children can provide the contrasts in consanguinity necessary to assess the impact of proximal processes on the actualization of genetic potential (as assessed by the value of corresponding h^2).

The applicability of an experimental strategy makes possible two important scientific gains. First, it provides a more rigorous test of the types of hypotheses already cited. The desirability of such a test arises from the following considerations. Although research has shown that environmental factors exert a substantial influence on proximal processes (Bronfenbrenner, 1986a, 1986b, 1989a, 1992), in accord with the bioecological model such processes—like all forms of human behavior—must necessarily also have a significant genetic component. Hence, stratification by levels of proximal process also results in some unknown level of genetic selection. By varying such levels experimentally, one avoids this source of bias. If, under these circumstances, groups that are randomly assigned to high versus low levels of proximal process show corresponding differences in levels of h^2, then this would constitute strong experimental evidence in support of the proposed conceptual framework.

Applying an experimental strategy can also shed light on the role of genetic-environment interaction in producing group differences in developmental outcomes. Thus, to the extent that experimentally induced increases in level of proximal process can significantly reduce developmental differences that are associated with socioeconomic status, family structure, or other environmental contexts, this finding would indicate that such environmental differences are primarily a reflection of variation in proximal processes. These considerations lead to the final hypothesis.

Hypothesis 5

Similarly high experimentally induced levels of proximal process will substantially reduce differences between groups (e.g., social class effects) in the degree of actualized genetic potential. Such reduction will be manifested with respect to group differences in both developmental competence and developmental dysfunction. Conversely, similarly low levels of proximal process will substantially increase such group differences.

The last hypothesis has an unfortunate shortcoming. Unlike the others, it cannot be rigorously tested, at least as yet. It is surely possible to determine whether proximal processes reduce group differences in developmental outcome. Indeed, the results shown in Figure 11.1 illustrate precisely such an effect. Moreover, these results would be consistent with the last hypothesis. But research findings that are merely "consistent" with a particular hypothesis are of course not sufficient to establish its validity. Thus, in the present instance, true validation of the hypothesis requires an assessment of the extent of actualized genetic potential in groups that do not differ systematically in degree of consanguinity. In this case, no such assessment is possible at present (i.e., there is no way to calculate an estimate corresponding to an h^2). The issue cannot be resolved solely on the basis of phenotypic data and must wait on further scientific advances in methods for analyzing human genotypes.

It is appropriate that we end this chapter on a note of uncertainty, for it sounds the underlying theme of the chapter as a whole. We would of course be gratified if our theoretical constructs and hypotheses turned out to have some validity. But that is not the main purpose of the undertaking. Indeed, our aim, and that of developmental science as well, might be better served if the concepts and hypotheses were to be found wanting. For our principal intent is not to claim answers but to provide a theoretical framework that might enable our colleagues in the field and ourselves to make further progress in discovering the processes and conditions that define the scope and limits of human development, and to develop a corresponding operational model that permits our position to be falsified. We hope that our colleagues will be sufficiently intrigued, or perhaps provoked, to join in that effort.

Note

1. This formulation leaves unanswered the question of what mechanisms lead to the actualization of genetic potentials for functioning incompetence. This issue is addressed in a more extended exposition of the bioecological model in Bronfenbrenner and Ceci (1993).

References

Anastasi, A. (1958). Heredity and environment, and the question "How?" *Psychological Review, 65*, 197–208.

Bronfenbrenner, U. (1986a). Ecology of the family as a context for human development. *Developmental Psychology, 22*, 723–742.

Bronfenbrenner, U. (1986b). Recent advances in research on the ecology of human development. In R. K. Silbereisen, K. Eyforth, & G. Rudiger (Eds.), *Development as action in context* (pp. 287–309). Berlin: Springer Verlag.

Bronfenbrenner, U. (1989a). Ecological systems theory. In R. Vasta (Ed.), *Six theories of child development: Revised formulations and current issues* (pp. 185–246). Greenwich, CT: JAI.

Bronfenbrenner, U. (1989b). *Who cares for children?* Invited address to UNESCO. Bilingual Pub. No. 188. Paris: UNESCO.

Bronfenbrenner, U. (1992). Child care in the Anglo-Saxon mode. In M. Lamb, K. J. Sternberg, C. P. Hwang, & A. G. Broberg (Eds.), *Child care in context: Cross-cultural perspectives* (pp. 281–291). Hillsdale, NJ: Lawrence Erlbaum.

Bronfenbrenner, U. (1993). The ecology of cognitive development: Research models and fugitive findings. In R. H. Wozniak & K. Fischer (Eds.), *Thinking in context* (pp. 3–24). Hillsdale, NJ: Lawrence Erlbaum.

Bronfenbrenner, U., & Ceci, S. J. (1993). *Nature-nurture reconceptionalized: Toward a new theoretical and operational model.* Manuscript submitted for publication.

Cavelli-Sforza, L. L., & Bodmer, W. F. (1971). *The genetics of human populations.* San Francisco: W. H. Freeman.

Ceci, S. J. (1990). *On intelligence . . . more or less: A bioecological treatise on intellectual development.* Englewood Cliffs, NJ: Prentice Hall.

Drillien, C. M. (1964). *The growth and development of prematurely born infants.* Edinburgh: Livingston.

Plomin, R., & Bergeman, C. S. (1991). The nature of nurture: Genetic influence on environmental measures. *Behavioral and Brain Sciences, 14,* 373–427.

Plomin, R., & Daniels, D. (1987). Why are children in the same family so different from one another? *Behavioral and Brain Sciences, 10,* 1–16.

Plomin, R., DeFries, J. C., & McClearn, G. E. (1990). *Behavior genetics.* New York: W. H. Freeman.

Scarr, S. (1992). Developmental theories for the 1990s: Development and individual differences. *Child Development, 63,* 1–19.

Small, S., & Luster, T. (1992). *Effects of parental monitoring on adolescent development: The process-person-context model applied.* Unpublished manuscript, University of Michigan.

Special section: Ability testing. (1992). *Psychological Science, 3,* 266–278.

Special section: Commentary on Plomin & Bergeman. (1991). *Behavioral and Brain Sciences, 14,* 386–414.

Growing Chaos in the Lives of Children, Youth, and Families

How Can We Turn It Around?

Most of the contemporary challenges to the healthy development of humans across the life span are identical to the challenges facing the American family at the beginning of the new millennium. This excerpt frames much of what the ecology of human development perspective offers to scholars and practitioners by explaining how theoretically predicated research can advance understanding of the bases of the challenges, indeed the disarray, confronting contemporary families and, in turn, can offer ideas for policies and programs that can actualize humans' self-constructive potential for positive development.

This article consists of three parts that lay the foundation for understanding and improving the present state of parenthood in America. In addition to analyzing the developmental disarray of children, youth, and families, today's researchers need to pay more attention to the scientific bases and strategies for turning it around and thereby to draw upon as yet untapped constructive potentials.

Source: Bronfenbrenner, U. (2001). Growing chaos in the lives of children, youth, and families: How can we turn it around? In J. C. Westman (Ed.), *Parenthood in America* (pp. 197–210). Madison: University of Wisconsin Press.

The Growing Chaos

Before we can try to turn the chaos around, we need to know what it is. In 1996 my Cornell colleagues and I published a volume documenting the marked changes that have taken place over the past four decades in the lives of children and youth growing up in economically developed nations, particularly in the United States (Bronfenbrenner, McClelland, Wethington, Moen, & Ceci, 1996).

Two main trends reinforce each other over time. The first trend reveals growing chaos in the lives of children, youth, and families. The second trend is the progressive decline in the competence and character of successive generations as they move into the twenty-first century.

Among the most prominent developmental trends are the following:

- Over the past two decades, systematic studies based on nationally representative samples document increasing cynicism and disillusionment among American adolescents and youth manifested in a loss of faith in others, in the basic institutions of their society, and in themselves. For example, over a 12-year period beginning in the 1980s the percentage of U.S. high school seniors agreeing with the statement "Most people can be trusted" fell from 35 to 15 percent.
- A complementary theme is increasing self-centeredness and disregard for the needs of others. Consider the change over time in response to the following questionnaire item: "A man and a woman who decide to have and raise a child out of wedlock are 'doing their own thing and not affecting anyone else.'" One wonders what the picture is now.
- More and more youth are spending their formative years in prison.
- Although declining somewhat since 1994, rates of teenage births remain higher than 10 years ago.
- Standardized measures of school achievement have been falling, even for students in the top 10 percent of distribution.

These findings indicate that the rising developmental disarray in the lives of children, youth, and families is the product of marked and continuing changes, taking place over the same time period, in the social institutions and informal structures that have greatest impact on the development of competence and character in the next generation. One explanation for this can be found in observations made by Alexis de Tocqueville in the 1830s (1835/1961). He noted that the young United States of America had two distinctive national characteristics. First, it was the most individualistic society in human history; second, it also was the most "volunteeristic." As I wrote some years ago: "We Americans are all the descendants of those who couldn't stand authority, and of those whom authority couldn't stand" (Bronfenbrenner, 1992, p. 288).

There are of course many ways of knowing: philosophy, literature, art, history, and so on. However, *science* does differ from these fields because it is the only way of knowing in which you are obligated to try to prove yourself wrong. As Albert Einstein noted: "In science, more important than finding the right answers is asking the right questions." How does one find the right questions about how human beings develop?

Developmental Science in the Discovery Mode

How is this domain defined? Human development is the scientific study of the conditions and processes shaping the biopsychological characteristics of human beings through the life course and across successive generations.

Here the principal aim is not the customary one of verifying hypotheses already formulated. It is a more extended process involving a series of progressively more differentiated formulations, with the results at each successive step setting the stage for the next round. The corresponding research designs, therefore, must be primarily generative rather than confirming versus disconfirming. Thus, the procedure is not the usual one of testing for statistical significance. Rather, the research designs must provide a framework for carrying out an equally essential prior stage of the scientific process: that of developing hypotheses of sufficient explanatory power and precision to warrant being subjected to empirical test. In short, we are dealing with science in the *discovery* mode rather than in the *verification* mode.

At the same time, as in any scientific endeavor, it is essential that the successive formulations and the corresponding research designs be made explicit. It is necessary to have a systematic conceptual framework within which evolving formulations and designs can be classified and ordered in terms of their stage of scientific development in the discovery process (Bronfenbrenner & Morris, 1998).

The Bioecological
Model of Human Development

The characteristics of the person appear twice in the bioecological model: first as one of the four principal elements—process, person, concept, and time (PPCT)—influencing the form, power, content, and direction of the proximal processes; and then again as the "developmental outcome"—that is, a quality of the developing person that emerges at a later point in time as the result of the mutually influencing effects of the four principal elements of the bioecological model. In sum, the characteristics of the person function both as an indirect producer and as a product of development.

How does the bioecological model fare when analyzed in a PPCT framework? Which elements are present, and how are they presumed to relate to each other? Two studies conducted some years ago, when analyzed in PPCT terms, come close to meeting the requirements of this theoretical model and its corresponding research design.

Drillien's Study

The first example dates from the late 1950s and early 1960s. At that time, Cecil Mary Drillien, a physician and professor of child life and health at the University of Edinburgh in Scotland, carried out a seven-year longitudinal investigation of psychological development in two groups: 360 children of low birth weight and a control group selected by taking the next mature birth from the hospital admission list (Drillien, 1957, 1964).

Drillien's interest was twofold: (a) to analyze the impact of the quality of mother-infant interaction at age two on the frequency of problem behaviors observed in the infant at age two and again at age four; and (b) to examine how this relationship varied as a joint function of the family's social class and three levels of infant birth: underweight by a pound or more, underweight by up to one pound, and normal weight. Assessments of maternal interactions were based on observations in the home and interviews with the mother.

Drillien's measure of social class took into account not only parental income and education but also the socioeconomic level of the neighborhood in which the family lived. The quality of interactions was assessed in terms of the extent to which the mother was responsive to changes in the state and behavior of the infant. Finally, the measure of the developmental outcome was based on the frequency of reported behavior disturbances, such as hyperactivity, overdependence, timidity, and negativism.

This research design includes all four elements of the bioecological model. Drillien's measure of maternal responsiveness closely approximates the definition of proximal process as the mechanism driving human development on a fairly regular basis over extended periods of time. To complete the picture, the remaining two elements of the characteristics of the person and of the environmental context appear respectively in the form of the infant's birth weight and of social class. Finally, as previously noted, a characteristic of the person appears again, but now in the role of a developmental outcome: in this instance, any lasting change in behaviors exhibited at age two and then again at age four.

With theory and design in place, we turn to the results. In all three social class levels, the infants who had experienced low levels of maternal responsiveness at age two showed higher levels of problem behavior two years later, especially those youngsters growing up in the poorest environments. The proximal process (maternal responsiveness) markedly reduced the frequency of later problem behaviors, but the moderating factor was in a different quarter. Whereas maternal responsiveness made its greatest impact on those children growing up in the most disadvantaged environment, within that environment youngsters with normal birth weights benefited most from the developmental process.

Maternal responsiveness across time still emerged as an exceptionally powerful predictor of developmental outcome. In all instances, responsive maternal interactions reduced significantly the degree of behavioral disturbance exhibited by the child.

Herein lies the main justification for distinguishing between proximal processes, on the one hand, and the environments in which the processes occur, on the other. The former turn out to be an especially potent force influencing the developmental outcome (in this case, the frequency of problem behaviors two years later, when the children were four years old). Furthermore, the power of the process varies systematically as a function both of the environmental context (i.e., social class) and of the characteristics of the person (i.e., weight at birth).

However, one other key element of the bioecological model still remains to be considered. Proposition 2 stipulates that the "form, power, content, and direction of proximal processes effecting development" also "vary systematically both as a function of . . . the nature of the developmental outcomes under consideration." Our next research example speaks to this issue. It also illustrates a "next stage" of developmental science in the discovery mode.

Small and Luster's Study

Specifically, we anticipate on theoretical grounds that the greater developmental impact of proximal processes on children growing up in poorer environments is to be expected only for outcomes reflecting developmental dysfunction (Small & Luster, 1990).

In this context, the term *developmental dysfunction* refers to the manifestation of difficulties in maintaining control and integration of behavior across a variety of situations. In contrast, *competence* refers to knowledge and skills—whether intellectual, physical, emotional, or a combination of them (for example, learning how to care for an infant involves all three).

The theoretical expectation that proximal processes will differ in their developmental effects depending on the quality of the environment rests on the following basis. In deprived and disorganized environments, manifestations of dysfunction in children are likely to be both more frequent and more severe, with the result that they attract more attention and involvement from parents; whereas in advantaged and more stable environments, such manifestations are less intense, and parents are more likely to be attracted by and to respond to gratifying signs, such as clear evidence of their children's developmental progress.

Although most parents have the capacity and the motivation to respond to the immediate physical and psychological needs of their children, the situation is rather different with respect to enabling their children to acquire new knowledge and skills. In these domains, the parents must themselves possess the desired knowledge and skills, or they must have access to resources outside the family that can provide their children with the experiences needed to develop competence, or both.

Taken together, the foregoing considerations lead to a working hypothesis regarding the differential impact of proximal processes as a joint function of the quality of the environment in terms of available resources, on the one hand, and, on the other, the nature of the outcome in terms of dysfunction versus competence.

The results of such strategies are documented by Stephen Small and Thomas Luster (1990) of the University of Wisconsin Department of Child and Family Studies. Their work reports the differential effects of parental monitoring on the school achievement of high school students living in the three most common family structures found in a total sample of more than 4,000 cases. The sample is further stratified by two levels of mother's education, with completion of high school as the dividing point. *Parental monitoring refers to the effort by parents to keep informed about and set limits on their children's activities outside the home.*

Once again, the results reveal that the effects of proximal processes are more powerful than those of the environmental contexts in which they occur. In this instance, however, the impact of the proximal process is greatest in what emerges as the most advantaged ecological niche: families with two biological parents in which the mother has had some education beyond high school. In single-parent and stepfamilies, the same degree of active effort yields a somewhat smaller result. In this case, for pupils who are not doing so well in school, parental monitoring can apparently accomplish a great deal by ensuring stability of time and place so that some learning can occur. In addition, however, superior school achievement would clearly require high levels of motivation, focused attention, knowledge, and, especially, *actually working with the material to be learned*—all qualities that stability of time and place by themselves cannot provide.

In the same Small and Luster study, within each family structure, parental monitoring exerted a more powerful effect on the school achievement of girls than of boys—a result that is paralleled by corresponding differences in average GPA for the two sexes. In each of the three family structures, girls received higher grades than boys, with the difference being most pronounced in two-parent households and lowest in single-mother families.

A distinctive feature of the pattern for girls is a marked flattening of the curve of scholastic achievement, especially for daughters of single-parent mothers. This result suggests that, in each of the three family structures, better-educated mothers may push their already successful daughters too hard, to the point where conformity to maternal control no longer brings educational returns, particularly when the mother is the only parent.

An analysis of data on students whose mothers had no more than a high school education showed a similar general pattern, but the effects were less pronounced. The influence of monitoring was appreciably weaker, and its greater benefit to girls also was reduced. Nevertheless, girls with less educated mothers both in single-parent families and in stepfamilies still had higher GPA scores than boys.

Nature-Nurture From the Bioecological Perspective

A growing body of research claims strong evidence for the view that individual and group differences in a wide range of developmental outcomes are mainly driven by genetic endowment. In response, my colleagues have proposed an empirically testable theoretical model that (a) goes beyond the established behavioral genetics paradigm by allowing for nonadditive synergistic effects, direct measures of the environment, and mechanisms of organism-environment interaction (namely, proximal processes); (b) hypothesizes that estimates of heritability increase markedly with the magnitude of proximal processes; (c) demonstrates that heritability represents the proportion of variation in individual differences attributable only to actualized potential, with the degree of nonactualized potential remaining unknown; and (d) proposes that, by enhancing proximal processes, it is possible to increase the extent of actualized potentials for reducing developmental dysfunction and for increasing developmental competence.

The examples considered thus far are essentially "experiments of nature." That is, they show how development is influenced by variation in the elements of the bioecological model occurring in already existing social conditions. But they tell us nothing about whether, to what extent, or how these elements and their combinations can be changed. This limitation applies particularly to the most consequential component of the bioecological model, proximal processes. The most effective way to answer this question would be to conduct an experiment, with subjects randomly assigned to different experimental conditions, including a control group. Such an experiment has been carried out.

Riksen-Walraven's Experiment

In 1978, Marianne Riksen-Walraven, a developmental psychologist in the Dutch city of Nijmegen, reported an experiment she had conducted with a sample of 100 nine-month-old infants and their mothers. All subjects came from working-class families because this was seen as the group in greatest need. In the research design, mother-infant pairs were randomly assigned to one of three groups. Those who ended up in what Riksen-Walraven called the "stimulation group" were given a "Workbook for Parents," with drawings to match, emphasizing the importance of mothers providing their infants with a variety of experiences that captured the baby's attention, such as pointing to and naming objects and persons and speaking a lot to their infants.

By contrast, the workbook for mothers in the "responsiveness" group stressed the idea that "the infant learns most from the effects of its own behavior." Accordingly, caregivers were advised not to direct the children's activities too much but to give the children opportunities to find out things for themselves and then to respond to the child's initiatives.

Finally, mothers in the third experimental group were given pages from both workbooks, in effect recommending that the mothers use both strategies. How did the three groups come out in the follow-up three months later? Which group did the best, and which did the worst?

All three experimental groups were influenced by the workbooks they were given. However, it was the children in the responsiveness group who showed the strongest and most pervasive effects on laboratory measures of young children's cognitive development that were administered at the end of the experiment. Specifically, they exhibited the highest gains on measures of exploratory behavior, were more likely to prefer a novel object to one that was already familiar, and obtained higher scores on a learning task. The stimulation group placed second; and the one relying on both stimulation and responsiveness did least well. These results suggest the possibility of designing home-based intervention programs that could operate effectively at much lower cost and reach many more families in need than those requiring on-site professional staff on a regular basis.

A key question, however, is how long the effects can last. Fortunately, the original investigator, together with a colleague, provided an answer in a longitudinal follow-up study of the same families when the children were 7, 10, and 12 years of age, using measures based on teachers' ratings (Van Aken & Riksen-Walraven, 1992). At these later ages only the girls from the original responsiveness group showed any effects of the original experimental intervention. Specifically, at all three later ages they were rated by teachers as more "competent and skillful," "curious and exploring," "resourceful in initiating activities," "better able to handle stressful situations," "less dependent on adults for help," and "less anxious." In addition, by age 12, these girls were described by their teachers as more "attractive, interesting and energetic children."

The authors offer the following speculations about why the responsiveness program was particularly effective for girls and not for boys:

We suggest that different parental attitudes towards competence striving in boys and girls may have contributed to this finding. Striving for competence, independence, and self-reliance are part of the traditional masculine stereotype, which was still current in the early seventies when our intervention started. . . . This means that initially competent boys will have more opportunities to experience themselves as effective agents than initially competent girls. . . . It thus seems possible that competence motivation can maintain itself in young girls only when it is at an "extra" high level and only when the parents are "extra" willing to accept their daughters' autonomy and independent exploration. (Van Aken & Riksen-Walraven, 1992, p. 111)

In sum, from the perspective of the bioecological model, we have evidence for the power of an experimentally induced proximal process in furthering young girls' psychological development. This result was accomplished by changing the belief systems of mothers, thereby leading them to provide a different kind of experience for their young daughters over an extended period of time. Thus, taken as a whole, the findings encompass all four defining properties of the bioecological model and its corresponding PPCT design, with developmental context deliberately limited to working-class families as the group most in need of assistance. The fact that the long-range effects of the intervention were limited to girls poses an unanswered question regarding the nature of proximal processes that might achieve similar developmental gains for boys.

Vygotsky's Experiment

Is there a known strategy that can reverse disruptive changes that are powerful and widespread in a society? Yes, there is, and it has a long history. But I know of only one instance in which such a strategy was conceived and carried out by developmental scientists. The strategy was based on theory, refined in an "experiment of nature," and applied in an "experiment by design." The central figure in this remarkable achievement was the developmental psychologist Lev Semyonovitch Vygotsky (Vygotsky & Luria, 1930 [Russian back-translation, Vygotsky & Luria, 1994]; Vygotsky, 1978). The central idea underlying the entire enterprise was Vygotsky's concept of the "transforming experiment." By this he meant an experiment that restructures the environment to produce a new configuration that activates the previously unrealized developmental potential of the persons living in that environment.

Alexander Romanovich Luria, one of Vygotsky's best-known students, tells the story of Vygotsky's experiment in his autobiography. The time was the early 1930s in the Soviet Union.

> We conceived the idea of carrying out the first far-reaching study of intellectual functions. . . . By taking advantage of the rapid cultural changes that were then in progress in remote parts of our country, we hoped to trace the changes in thought processes that are brought about by technological change. . . . At that time, many of our rural areas were undergoing rapid change with the advent of collectivization and the mechanization of agriculture. (Luria, 1979, p. 60)

The basic research design took advantage of the fact that the process of modernization had not been introduced in all areas of the Soviet Union at the same time. As a result, it became possible to carry out a comparison of cognitive functioning in communities differing in their degree of exposure to social change. Vygotsky died of tuberculosis before this extraordinary investigation was completed. The following is Luria's summary of the findings:

> Our data indicate that decisive changes can occur in going from graphic and functional—concrete and practical—methods of thinking to much more

theoretical modes of thought brought about by changes in social conditions, in this instance by the socialist transformation of an entire culture. (Luria, 1976, p. vi)

The publication of the study in the Soviet Union was held up for more than three decades. The reasons for the delay are perceptively described by Michael Cole in his preface to the American edition of Luria's book:

The status of national minorities has long been a sensitive issue in the USSR (not unlike the issue of ethnic minorities in the United States). It was all well and good to show that uneducated, traditional peasants quickly learned the modes of thought characteristics of industrialized socialist peoples, but it was definitely not acceptable to say anything that could be interpreted as negative about these people at a time when their participation in national life was still so tenuous. (Luria, 1976, p. xiv)

Conclusion

America has yet to confront the reality that the growing chaos in the lives of our children, youth, and families pervades too many of the principal settings in which we live our daily lives: our homes, health care systems, child care arrangements, peer groups, schools, neighborhoods, workplaces, and means of transportation and communication among all of them.

These are the settings in which our society has concentrated fragmented resources and efforts to reverse the mounting developmental disarray. Even though the United States experienced an economic upswing in the late 1990s, the sparse bits of recent demographic data give little indication of a true and lasting turnaround. The rising trend of chaos and its consequences also extend to other spheres of our society.

Not long ago, one of our nation's leading corporate executives gave a major lecture at Cornell's Graduate School of Management. His title was "Growing Chaos in America's Corporate Enterprises." He said that no sooner is a new production policy implemented after weeks of planning and testing than an order comes down from above "to scrap the whole thing" because the policy has been changed.

Transforming experiments have been carried out in the United States, but their developmental effects have never been investigated systematically. Perhaps one of the most successful was the G.I. Bill, which gave educational and housing benefits and hope to a whole generation of World War II veterans and their families. The same deserved legacy was not bestowed on their comrades-in-arms in the wars that followed.

A second example is Head Start. But from what I know both from looking at its budgets and its mounting bureaucratic controls and from personal experience as an external member of a Head Start Parents' Policy Committee, the prospects for the future are hardly rosy. Head Start parents are today drawing on their own meager resources to continue some of the programs that are needed most, and they take time off from jobs (when they have them) to help fellow families in emergencies because of illness or the desperate need for childcare.

Such heroic acts are signals to the rest of American society. They sound a call for a transforming experiment in strengthening parenthood, one that can draw on the deepest sources of our national strength. As yet, this call is not being heard, either by our scientists or by our citizens. We do not heed the immortal words of John Donne: "Do not ask for whom the bell tolls; it tolls for thee."

References

Bronfenbrenner, U. (1992). Child care in the Anglo-Saxon mode. In M. E. Lamb, K. J. Sternberg, C.-P. Hwang, & A. G. Broberg (Eds.), *Child care in context: Cross-cultural perspectives* (281–291). Hillsdale, NJ: Lawrence Erlbaum.

Bronfenbrenner, U., McClelland, P., Wethington, E., Moen, P., & Ceci, S. J. (1996). *The state of Americans: This generation and the next.* New York: Free Press.

Bronfenbrenner, U., & Morris, P. (1998). The ecology of developmental processes. In W. Damon (Series Ed.) & R. M. Lerner (Vol. Ed.), *Handbook of child psychology: Vol. 1. Theoretical models of human development* (5th ed., pp. 993–1028). New York: John Wiley.

Drillien, C. M. (1957). The social and economic factors affecting the incidence of premature birth. *Journal of Obstetrical Gynaecology, British Empire, 64,* 161–184.

Drillien, C. M. (1964). *Growth and development of the prematurely born infant.* Edinburgh: E. & S. Livingston.

Luria, A. R. (1976). *Cognitive development: Its cultural and social foundations.* Cambridge, MA: Harvard University Press.

Luria, A. R. (1979). *The making of mind: A personal account of Soviet psychology.* Cambridge, MA: Harvard University Press.

Riksen-Walraven, J. M. (1978). Effects of caregiver behavior on habituation rate and self-efficacy in infants. *International Journal of Behavioral Development, 1,* 105–130.

Small, S., & Luster, T. (1990, November 27). *Youth at risk for parenthood.* Paper presented at the Creating Caring Communities Conference, Michigan State University, East Lansing.

Tocqueville, A. de (1961). *Democracy in America.* New York: Schocken. (Original work published 1835)

Van Aken, M. A., & Riksen-Walraven, J. M. (1992). Parental support and the development of competence in children. *International Journal of Behavioral Development, 15*(1), 101–123.

Vygotsky, L. S. (1978). *Mind in society: The development of higher psychological processes.* Cambridge, MA: Harvard University Press.

Vygotsky, L. S., & Luria, A. R. (1930). *Tools and symbols in child development.* Unpublished manuscript in English.

Vygotsky, L. S., & Luria, A. R. (1994). *Tool and symbol in child development.* In L. S. Vygotsky, R. van der Veer, & J. Valsiner (Eds.) & T. Prout (Trans.), *The Vygotsky reader* (pp. 99–174). Cambridge, MA: Basil Blackwell.

SECTION II

Using the Ecology of Human Development to Enhance the Human Condition

*T*he Ecology of Human Development (1979) not only set out a series of propositions and hypotheses about interactive influences on human development but also proposed that scholars wishing to understand human development should engage directly with programs and policies, especially those aimed at promoting development. Articles in this section use the ecological perspective to call attention to large-scale societal changes affecting children and families in the United States. The consistent theme is that parents need more support to do what they want and need to do.

As a society that values independence and self-reliance, we are reluctant to assume responsibility for supporting parents, but the price of that reluctance can be seen in crime, school failure, neglected children, fractured marriages and relationships, and other trends that weaken the values we hold dear. Scholars can attempt to correct or at least ameliorate these problems by sharing their knowledge with policy makers and citizens and by conducting research that guides and assesses new policies and practices.

Article 13

The Split-Level
American Family

When one understands the family's influence on children's development
as itself embedded in larger circles of influence, including influences
such as television, parents' jobs and job prospects, and community
cohesion, then indicators of troubled development can no longer be
attributed simply to uncaring parents. Likewise, "peer pressure" must be
accepted as a source of both positive and negative influence, depending in part on the structures for peer interaction that adults create. The
concluding prescription of "engaging children and adults in common
activities," subsequently formalized in terms of "proximal processes,"
remains valid despite the changes that have occurred since it was
propounded.

C hildren used to be brought up by their parents. It may seem pre-
sumptuous to put that statement in the past tense. Yet it belongs to
the past. Why? Because de facto responsibility for upbringing has shifted
away from the family to other settings in the society. While the family still
has the primary moral and legal responsibility for developing character in
children, the power or opportunity to do the job is often lacking in the

Source: Bronfenbrenner, U. (1967, October 7). The split-level American family.
Saturday Review, 60–66. Reprinted 1974 in S. Coopersmith & R. Feldman (Eds.), *The
formative years: Principles of early childhood education* (pp. 73–85). San Francisco:
Albion.

home, primarily because parents and children no longer spend enough time together in those situations in which such training is possible. This is not because parents don't wish to spend time with their children. It is simply that conditions of life have changed.

As the stable world of the small town has become absorbed into an ever-shifting suburbia, children are growing up in a different kind of environment. Urbanization has often reduced the extended family to a nuclear one with only two adults, and the friendly neighborhood—where it has not decayed into an urban or rural slum—has withered to a small circle of friends.

Neighborhood experiences available to children are often limited nowadays but this really doesn't matter, for children aren't home much, anyway. A child leaves the house early in the day on a school-bound bus, and it's almost suppertime when he gets back. There may not be anybody home when he gets there. If his mother isn't working at least part time (more than a third of all mothers are), she's out a lot because of community obligations.

If a child is not with his parents, with whom does he spend his time? With other children—in school, after school, over weekends, on holidays. Today's schools, however, have brought homogeneous grouping by age and, more recently, segregation of children by levels of ability. It doesn't take the children very long to learn: *Latch on to your peers.* In short, whereas American children used to spend much of their time with parents and other grownups, more and more waking hours are now lived in the world of age mates.

What do we know about the influence of the peer group, especially when parents are away from home? Some relevant studies have been carried out in our own society. For example, along with others, I have done research on a sample of American adolescents from middle-class families. We found that children who reported their parents away from home for long periods of time rated significantly lower on such characteristics as responsibility and leadership. Perhaps because it was more pronounced, absence of the father was more influential than that of the mother, particularly in its effect on boys. Similar results have been reported in studies of the effects of father absence among soldiers' families during World War II, in homes of Norwegian sailors and whalers, and in African American households with absent fathers from the United States. In general, father absence contributes to low motivation for achievement, inability to defer immediate for later gratification, low self-esteem, susceptibility to peer group influence, and juvenile delinquency. All of these effects are much more marked for boys than for girls.

These findings lead us directly to the question of the impact of the peer group on the child's attitudes and behavior. The first systematic research on this question was carried out by two University of North Carolina sociologists, Charles Bowerman and John Kinch, in 1959. Working with a sample of several hundred students from the fourth to the tenth grades in the Seattle school system, these investigations reveal a turning point at about the seventh grade. Before that, the majority looked mainly to their parents as models, companions, and guides to behavior; thereafter, the children's peers had equal or greater influence.

The most comprehensive study relevant to the subject of our concern here was conducted by James Coleman (1966). The data were obtained from more than 600,000 children in Grades 1 to 12 in 4,000 schools carefully selected as representative of public education in the United States. An attempt was made to assess the relative contribution to the child's intellectual development (as measured by standardized intelligence and achievement tests) of the following factors: (a) family background (e.g., parents' education, family size, presence in the home of reading materials, records); (b) school characteristics (e.g., per-pupil expenditure, classroom size, laboratory and library facilities); (c) teacher characteristics (e.g., background, training, years of experience, verbal skills); and (d) characteristics of other children in the same school (e.g., their background, academic achievement, career plans).

Of the many findings of the study, two were particularly impressive; the first was entirely expected, the second somewhat surprising. The expected finding was that home background was the most important element in determining how well the child did at school, more important than any aspect of the school that the child attended. This generalization, while especially true for northern whites, applied to a lesser degree to southern whites and northern African Americans, for whom the characteristics of the school were more important than those of the home. The child apparently drew sustenance from wherever it was most available.

The second major conclusion concerned the aspects of the school environment that contributed most to the child's intellectual achievement. Somewhat surprisingly, such items as per-pupil expenditure, number of children per class, laboratory space, number of volumes in the school library, and the presence or absence of ability grouping were of negligible significance. Teacher qualifications accounted for some of the child's achievement. But by far the most important factor was the pattern of characteristics of the other children attending the same school. Specifically, if a lower-class child had schoolmates who came from advantaged homes, he did reasonably well; but if all the other children also came from deprived backgrounds, he did poorly.

What about the other side of the story? What happens to a middle-class child in a predominantly lower-class school? Do his classmates pull him down? According to Coleman's data, the answer is no; the performance of the advantaged children remains unaffected. It is as though good home background had immunized them.

How early in life are children susceptible to the influence of their classmates? Albert Bandura and his colleagues at Stanford University have conducted some experiments that suggest that the process is well developed at the preschool level (Bandura, Ross, & Ross, 1961, 1963). The basic experimental design involves the following elements. The child finds himself in a familiar playroom. As if by chance, in another corner of the room a person is playing with toys. Sometimes this person is an adult (teacher), sometimes another child. This other person behaves very aggressively. He strikes a large Bobo doll (a bouncing inflated figure), throws objects, and mutilates dolls and animal toys, with appropriate language to match. Later on, the experimental subject (i.e., the child who "accidentally" observed the aggressive behavior) is tested by being allowed to play in a room containing a variety of toys, including some similar to those employed by the aggressive model. With no provocation, perfectly normal, well-adjusted preschoolers engage in aggressive acts, not only repeating what they have observed but also elaborating on it. Moreover, the words and gestures accompanying the actions leave no doubt that the child is living through an emotional experience of aggressive expression.

Bandura used both a live model and a film of a cartoon cat that said and did everything the live model had said and done. The films were presented on a TV set left on in a corner of the room, as if by accident. When the children were tested, the TV film turned out to be just as effective as the real people. The cat aroused as much aggression as the human model.

As soon as Bandura's work was published, the television industry issued a statement calling his conclusions into question on the interesting ground that the children had been studied "in a highly artificial situation," since no parents were present either when the TV was on or when the aggressive behavior was observed. "What a child will do under normal conditions cannot be projected from his behavior when he is carefully isolated from normal conditions and the influences of society," the statement declared. Since then, Bandura has shown that only a 10-minute exposure to an aggressive model still differentiates children in the experimental group from their controls (children not subjected to the experiment) six months later.

At what age do we become immune from contagion to violence on the screen? Richard Walters of Waterloo University in Canada, and his associate, Llewllyn Thomas (Walters & Thomas, 1963), showed two movie films to a group of 34-year-old hospital attendants. Half of these adults were shown a knife fight between two teenagers from the picture, *Rebel Without a Cause;* the other half saw a film depicting adolescents engaged in artwork. Subsequently, all the attendants were asked to assist in carrying out an experiment on the effects of punishment in learning.

In the experiment, the attendants gave an unseen subject an electric shock every time the subject made an error. The lever for giving shocks had settings from 0 to 10. To be sure the assistant understood what the shocks were like, he was given several, not exceeding the level of 4, before the experiment. Since nothing was said about the level of shocks to be administered, each assistant was left to make his own choice. The hospital attendants who had seen the knife-fight film gave significantly more severe shocks than those who had seen the artwork film. The same experiment was repeated with a group of 20-year-old females. This time the sound track was turned off so that only visual cues were present. But neither the silence nor the difference in sex weakened the effect. The young women who had seen the aggressive film also administered more painful shocks.

These experiments point to the same conclusion. At all age levels, pressure from peers to engage in aggressive behavior is difficult to resist. Now if the peer group can propel its members into antisocial acts, what about the opposite possibility? Can peers also be a force for inducing constructive behavior?

Evidence on this point is not so plentiful, but some relevant data exist. To begin with, experiments on conformity to group pressure have shown that the presence of a single dissenter—for example, an "assistant" who refuses to give a severe shock—can be enough so that the subject no longer follows the majority. The only research explicitly directed at producing moral conduct as a function of group experience is a study conducted by Muzafer Sherif and his colleagues at the University of Oklahoma and known as the "Robber's Cave Experiment" (Sherif, Harvey, Hoyt, Hood, & Sherif, 1961). In the words of Elton B. McNeil (1962),

War was declared at Robber's Cave, Oklahoma, in the summer of 1954. Of course, if you have seen one war you have seen them all, but this was an interesting war, as wars go, because only the observers knew what the fighting was about. How, then, did this war differ from any other war? This one was caused, conducted, and concluded by behavioral scientists. After years of religious, political, and economic wars, this was, perhaps, the first scientific war. It wasn't the kind of war that an adventurer could join just for the thrill of it. To be eligible, ideally, you had to be an eleven-year-old, middle-class, American, Protestant, well-adjusted boy who was willing to go to an experimental camp. (p. 77)

Sherif and his associates wanted to demonstrate that within the space of a few weeks they could produce two contrasting patterns of behavior in this group of normal children. They could first bring the group to a state of intense hostility and then completely reverse the process by inducing a spirit of warm friendship and active cooperation. The success of their efforts can be gauged by the following two excerpts describing the behavior of the boys after each stage had been reached. After the first experimental treatment of the situation was introduced,

> Good feeling soon evaporated. The members of each group began to call their rival "stinkers," "sneaks," and "cheaters." They refused to have anything more to do with individuals in the opposing group. The boys . . . turned against buddies whom they had chosen as "best friends" when they first arrived at the camp. (Sherif, 1956, p. 57)

But after the second treatment,

> The members of the two groups began to feel more friendly to each other. For example, a Rattler whom the Eagles disliked for his sharp tongue and skill in defeating them became a "good egg." The boys stopped shoving in the meal line. They no longer called each other names, and sat together at the table. New friendships developed between the individuals in the two groups.
>
> In the end the groups were actively seeking opportunities to mingle, to entertain and "treat" each other. They decided to hold a joint campfire. They took turns presenting skits and songs. Members of both groups requested that they go home together on the same bus rather than on the separate buses in which they had come. (Sherif, 1956, p. 58)

How were each of these effects achieved? Treatment One has a familiar ring:

> To produce friction between the groups of boys we arranged a tournament of games: baseball, touch football, a tug-of-war, a treasure hunt, and so on. The tournament started in a spirit of good sportsmanship. But as the play progressed good feeling soon evaporated. (Sherif, 1956, p. 57)

How does one turn hatred into harmony? Before undertaking this task, Sherif wanted to demonstrate that, contrary to the views of some students of human conflict, mere interaction— pleasant social contact between antagonists—would not reduce hostility.

> [W]e brought the hostile Rattlers and Eagles together for social events: going to the movies, eating in the same dining room, and so on. But far from reducing conflict, these situations only served as opportunities for the rival groups to berate and attack each other. (Sherif, 1956, p. 57)

How was conflict finally dispelled? By a series of stratagems, of which the following is an example:

> Water came to our camp in pipes from a tank about a mile away. We arranged to interrupt it and then called the boys together to inform them of the crisis. Both groups promptly volunteered to search the water line for the trouble. They worked together harmoniously, and before the end of the afternoon they had located and corrected the difficulty. (Sherif, 1956, p. 58)

To move from practice to principle, the critical element for achieving harmony in human relations, according to Sherif (1956), is joint activity in behalf of a superordinate goal. "Hostility gives way when groups pull together to achieve overriding goals which are real and compelling for all concerned" (p. 58).

Here, then, is a solution for the problems posed by autonomous peer groups and rising rates of juvenile delinquency: Confront the youngsters with some superordinate goals, and everything will turn out fine.

This writer disagrees. Challenging activities for children can be found, but their discovery requires breaking down the prevailing patterns of segregation identified earlier in this essay—segregation not merely by race (although this is part of the story) but to an almost equal degree by age, class, and ability. I am arguing for greater involvement of adults in the lives of children and, conversely, for greater involvement of children in the problems and tasks of society.

We must begin by engaging children and adults in common activities. Here, integration across class and culture is not enough. In line with Sherif's findings, contact between children and adults, or between economically advantaged and disadvantaged, will not of itself reduce hostility and evoke mutual affection and respect. What is needed in addition is a context in which adults and children can pursue together a superordinate goal, for there is nothing so "real and compelling to all concerned" as the need of a young child for the care and attention of his elders. The difficulty is that we have not yet provided the opportunities—the institutional setting—that would make possible the recognition and pursuit of such cross-generational experiences on a regular basis.

The beginnings of such an opportunity structure, however, already exist in our society. They are to be found in the poverty program, particularly those aspects of it dealing with children: Head Start, which involves parents, older children, and the whole community in the care of the young. The program has two stages: (a) Follow Through, which extends Head Start into the elementary grades; and (b) Parent and Child Centers, which provide a neighborhood center where all generations can meet to engage in community activities.

The need for such programs is not restricted to the nation's poor. So far as alienation of children is concerned, the world of the disadvantaged reflects in more severe form social problems that have affected the entire society. Such programs are needed by the middle class as much as by the economically less favored. Again, the principal purpose of these programs is not remedial education but giving children and their families, from all levels of society, a sense of dignity, purpose, and meaningful activities.

Service to the very young is not the only superordinate goal potentially available to children in our society. The very old also need developmental support. In segregating them in their own housing projects and, indeed, in communities, we have deprived both them and the younger generation of an essential cross-generational human experience. We need to find ways in which children once again can assist and comfort old people and, in return, gain insight to character development that occurs through such shared experiences. Participation in constructive activities on behalf of others may also reduce the growing tendencies to aggressive and antisocial behavior.

Such proposals for the future may appear to some as a pipe dream, but they need not be a dream. For just as autonomy and aggression have their roots in the American tradition, so have neighborliness, civic concern, and devotion to the young and old. By re-exploring these domains, we can rediscover our moral identity as a society and as a nation.

References

Bandura, A., Ross, D., & Ross, S. A. (1961). Transmission of aggression through imitation of aggressive models. *Journal of Abnormal and Social Psychology,* *63*(3), 575–582.

Bandura, A., Ross, D., & Ross, S. A. (1963). Imitation of film-mediated aggressive models. *Journal of Abnormal and Social Psychology, 66*(1), 3–11.

Bowerman, C. E., & Kinch, J. W. (1959). Changes in family and peer orientation of children between the fourth and tenth grades. *Social Forces, 37,* 206–211.

Coleman, J. S. (1966). *Equality of educational opportunity.* Washington, DC: Government Printing Office.

McNeil, E. B. (1962). Waging experimental war: A review. *Journal of Conflict Resolution, 6,* 77–81.

Sherif, M. (1956). Experiments in group conflicts. *Scientific American, 195,* 54–58.

Sherif, M., Harvey, O. J., Hoyt, B. J., Hood, W. R., & Sherif, C. W. (1961). *Intergroup conflict and cooperation: The Robbers' Cave experiment.* Norman: University of Oklahoma Book Exchange.

Walters, R. H., & Thomas, E. L. (1963). Enhancement of punitiveness by visual and audiovisual displays. *Canadian Journal of Psychology, 17*(2), 244–255.

Article 14

Minority Report of Forum 15

1970 White House Conference on Children

Urie Bronfenbrenner

Forum 15 Chairman

In 1970 I participated in Forum 15, "Children and Parents," of the White House Conference on Children. The following minority report sets forth my differences with the majority report that the forum produced. I argue that although the challenges facing American families are greatest for those facing the largest disadvantages, including both poverty and discrimination, the assumption that only those families are threatened ignores both the impact of their difficulties on everyone else and the extension of many of the same kinds of threats into the general population. Children suffer when their parents neglect them, whether because of the distresses of unemployment or from long hours of rewarding work.

I take issue with the working draft of the original *Majority Report of Forum 15* on two major counts.

Source: Bronfenbrenner, U. (1970). "Minority report of Forum 15." In White House Conference on Children, *Report to the President: Child Development Recommendations*. Washington, DC: Government Printing Office.

First, the report, in my judgment, fails to convey the urgency and severity of the problem confronting the nation's families and their children. Second, the document underestimates and consequently fails to alert the reader to the critical role played by business and industry—both private and public—in determining the lifestyle of the American family and the manner in which parents and children are treated in American society. I shall speak to each of these points in turn.

The National Neglect of Children

The draft of the working draft of the original Forum 15 Task Force report began with the following statement:

> America's families, and their children, are in trouble, trouble so deep and pervasive as to threaten the future of our nation. The source of the trouble is nothing less than national neglect of children and those primarily engaged in their care—America's parents.

The Editorial Committee objected to this statement on the grounds that it applied only to a minority of the nation's children and that, therefore, no note of urgency was justified. I strongly disagree.

To assess danger, and to avert it, one must be aware of not only where we are but in what direction we are moving. From this perspective, the picture is hardly reassuring. The evidence indicates that American society, whether viewed in comparison to other nations or to itself over time, is according progressively less attention to its children. The trend is already apparent when the child is born. America, the richest and most powerful country in the world, stands thirteenth among the nations in combating infant mortality. Even East Germany does better. Moreover, our ranking has dropped steadily in recent decades.[1] The situation is similar with respect to maternal and child health, day care, children's allowances, and other basic services to children and families.

But the figures for the nation as a whole, dismaying as they are, mask even greater inequities. For example, infant mortality for non-whites in the United States is almost twice that for whites, and in several states the ratios are considerably higher. Ironically, of even greater monetary cost to the society than the infants who die are the many more who sustain injury but survive with some disability. Many of these suffer impaired intellectual function and behavioral disturbance including hyperactivity, distractibility, and low attention span, all factors contributing to school retardation and problem behavior. Again, the destructive impact is greatest on the poorest segments of the population, especially nonwhites. It is all the more tragic that this massive damage and its subsequent cost in reduced productivity, lower income, unemployability, welfare payments, and institutionalization are avoidable if adequate family and child services are provided, as they are in a number of countries less prosperous than ours.

But it is not only children from disadvantaged families who show signs of progressive neglect. For example, a survey by this writer of changes in child-rearing practices in the United States over a 25-year period reveals a decrease, especially in recent years, in all spheres of interaction between parent and child. A similar conclusion is indicated by data from cross-cultural studies comparing American parents with those from Western Europe. Moreover, as parents and other adults move out of the lives of children, the vacuum is filled by the peer group. Recently, my colleagues and I completed a study showing that, at every age and grade level, children today show a greater dependence on their peers than they did a decade ago. Our evidence indicates that susceptibility to group influence is higher among children from homes in which one or both parents are frequently absent. In addition, "peer-oriented" youngsters describe their parents as less affectionate and less firm in discipline. Attachment to age mates appears to be influenced more by a lack of attention and concern at home than by any positive attraction of the peer group itself. In fact, these children have a rather negative view of their friends and of themselves as well. They are pessimistic about the future, rate lower on such traits as responsibility and leadership, and are more likely to engage in such antisocial behavior as lying, teasing other children, "playing hooky," or "doing something illegal." In short, we see here the roots of alienation. The more serious manifestations are reflected in the rising rates of youthful drug abuse, delinquency, and violence documented in charts and tables specially prepared for the White House Conference. According to these data, the proportion of youngsters between ages 10 and 18 arrested for drug abuse doubled between 1964 and 1968; since 1963, juvenile delinquency has been increasing at a faster rate than the juvenile population; over half the crimes involve vandalism, theft, or breaking and entry; and, if present trends continue, one out of every nine youngsters will appear in juvenile court before age 18. These figures index only detected and prosecuted offenses. How high must they run before we acknowledge that they reflect deep and pervasive problems in the treatment of children and youth in our society?

The Effect of Business on Family Life

In the original Task Force report, the first and longest series of recommendations was addressed to business, industry, and government as employers. In the present document, this section has been drastically reduced and relegated to an inconspicuous position in the total report. Yet it is American business and industry that has the power to reverse the present trend and to place families and children at the center rather than the periphery of our national life. They can do so by recognizing the full measure of their responsibility for the stressful conditions in which many families are forced to live and changing the organization and demands of work in such a way as to make it possible for children and parents to spend more time together.

Specifically, the Planning Committee for Forum 15 originally recommended the following measures in addition to those covered in the majority report.

Minimizing Out-of-Town, Weekend, and Evening Obligations

A parent who cannot be at home for extended periods with his children, no matter how excellent he may be in other respects, cannot fulfill his role as a parent. The introduction of a family-oriented personnel policy that minimizes such obligations not only would counteract these effects but—if offered as a fringe benefit—would help attract and hold more able personnel, for the most capable and responsible staff are also likely to be those who care about their families.

Reducing Frequent Geographic Moves

The policy followed by some large organizations of often transferring personnel from one city or region to another is disruptive to family life. The impact is hardest on children, since healthy psychological development requires some degree of stability and continuity in the social environment from childhood through adolescence. A pattern of life that repeatedly tears the child away from familiar friends, schools, and neighborhoods increases the likelihood of the child's alienation both inside and outside the family.

Leave and Rest Privileges for Maternal and Child Care

Business and industrial organizations share with other institutions in society responsibility for the birth of a healthy child. In view of the cost to society of welfare and institutionalization of children born with prenatal damage, these organizations have the obligation to develop policies of leave and rest for mothers during pregnancy and early months of infant care without jeopardy to their employment or income status.

Day Care Facilities

To increase opportunities for parents and to spend time with their children, day care facilities should be established within or near the place of work, but with independent administrative arrangements that allow parents a voice in the planning and execution of the program. Parents and other employees should be encouraged to visit the day care facility during the lunch hour or coffee breaks and to participate in activities with the children.

Note

1. The comparative data cited in this commentary are documented in Bronfenbrenner (1970, esp. pp. 95–124).

Reference

Bronfenbrenner, U. (1970). *Two worlds of childhood: U.S. and U.S.S.R.* New York: Russell Sage Foundation.

Two Worlds of Childhood

U.S. and U.S.S.R.

with the assistance of John Condry, Jr.

The two worlds in the title, the United States and the Soviet Union, were in conflict at the time this book was written. The following excerpt conveys how an examination of child-rearing methods carefully and consistently aimed at producing a particular kind of society can reveal gaps and inconsistencies between what we believe we want for our children and what actually happens to them. The comparison is not political or ideological; it instantiates the ecological perspective on human development through a systematic contrast between two ecosystems. The article closes with a postscript describing research on adolescents since the breakup of the Soviet Union.

This book is the outgrowth of three sets of scientific adventures. The first is a research project, entitled "Cross-Cultural Studies in Child Rearing," conducted for the past five years under a grant from the National Science Foundation. Fundamentally, this volume is the product and by-product of that endeavor. It has provided the basic comparative data. More importantly, it was the exposure to patterns of upbringing in other cultures, especially in the U.S.S.R., that alerted me to the impressive power—and

Source: Bronfenbrenner, U. (1970). *Two worlds of childhood: U.S. and U.S.S.R.* New York: Russell Sage Foundation.

even greater potential—of models, peers, and group forces in influencing the behavior and development of children (Bronfenbrenner, 1966). Finally, it was this comparative research that sensitized me to the disruptive trends in the process of socialization in American society and spurred involvement in the design of counteractive programs. Thus, in the last analysis, not only many of the facts but many more of the ideas presented in this volume were derived from cross-cultural research.

The second scientific adventure was the offspring of the first: namely, a series of seven visits to the U.S.S.R., which have enabled the author to acquire the background for, develop, and finally carry out the field observations, interviews, and experiments on which the analysis of Soviet methods of upbringing and their effects is based. The writer made his first trip to the Soviet Union in 1960 as one of several scientists asked by the American Psychological Association to assess Soviet work in this field. The second journey was made in 1961 as a member of an official United States exchange mission in the field of public health. These visits provided an opportunity to arrange for a scientific exchange between Cornell University and the Institute of Psychology in Moscow. This exchange has made possible a series of five visits, ranging in length from a few weeks to several months, in the course of which the more systematic aspects of the research were carried out. These field trips were supported by grants from the National Science Foundation, the Russell Sage Foundation, and the Committee on Soviet Studies of Cornell University.

A Criterion for Two Cultures

How can we judge the worth of a society? Many indices could be used for this purpose, among them the Gross National Product, the birth rate, crime statistics, and mental health data. In this book we propose yet another criterion: *the concern of one generation for the next*. If the children and youth of a nation are afforded opportunity to develop their capacities to the fullest, if they are given the knowledge to understand the world and the wisdom to change it, then the prospects for the future are bright. In contrast, a society that neglects its children, however well it may function in other respects, risks eventual disorganization and demise.

We shall explore the "concern of one generation for the next" in the Soviet Union and the United States. We shall examine what each country does for and with its children both intentionally and, perhaps, unintentionally. Then, drawing upon existing research and theory in the behavioral sciences, we shall ask what are, or might be, the consequences of the modes of treatment we observed: that is, what values and patterns of behavior are being developed in the new generation in each society.

In the language of developmental science, this volume is concerned with the process of socialization, the way in which a child born into a given society becomes a social being—a member of that society. It should be clear that being socialized is not necessarily the same as being civilized. Nazi youth were also products of a socialization process. The example is instructive, for it reminds us that the family is not the only possible agent of upbringing. The process typically begins in the home but does not end there. The outside world also has a major impact, as the child becomes exposed to a succession of persons, groups, and institutions, each of which imposes its expectations, rewards, and penalties on the child and thus contributes to shaping the development of skills, values, and patterns of behavior.

Our selection of the Soviet Union as the object of paired comparison was dictated not by considerations of power politics but by those of science. We wished to profit from the contrasting perspective provided by a society that differs substantially from our own in the process and context of socialization but at the same time faces similar problems as an industrialized nation with developed systems of technology, education, and mass communication. In terms of socialization, the major difference between the two cultures lies in the localization of primary responsibility for the upbringing of children. In the United States, we ordinarily think of this responsibility as centered in the family, with the parents playing the decisive part as the agents of child rearing and other persons or groups outside the family serving supplementary roles. Not so in the Union of Soviet Socialist Republics. The difference is nowhere better expressed than in the following passage from one of the most influential Soviet publications in this sphere: *A Book for Parents* by Anton Semyonovich Makarenko (1954; American ed., 1967), an eminent educator whose methods for rehabilitating juvenile delinquents in the 1920s and 1930s became the primary basis for the techniques of collective upbringing employed in all Soviet nurseries, schools, camps, children's institutions, and youth programs. In this volume, which came to be regarded as a guide to ideal Soviet family life, Makarenko defined the role of the family as follows:

> Our family is not a closed-in collective body, like the bourgeois family. It is an organic part of Soviet society, and any attempt it makes to build up its own experience independently of the moral demands of society is bound to result in disproportion, discordant as an alarm bell.

Our parents are not without authority either, but this authority is only the reflection of social authority. In our country the duty of a father toward his children is a particular form of his duty toward society. It is as if our society says to parents:

You have joined together in goodwill and love, rejoice in your children, and expect to go on rejoicing in them. That is your own personal affair and concerns your own personal happiness. But in this happy process you have given birth to new people. A time will come when these people will cease to be only a joy to you and become independent members of society. It is not at all a matter of indifference to society what kind of people they will be. In handing over to you a certain measure of social authority, the Soviet state demands from you correct upbringing of future citizens. Particularly it relies on a certain circumstance arising naturally out of your union—on your parental love.

If you wish to give birth to a citizen and do without parental love, then be so kind as to warn society that you wish to play such an underhanded trick. People brought up without parental love are often deformed people. (Marakenko, 1954, p. xi–xii)

Upbringing in the Soviet Family

Patterns in Maternal Care

We begin with a discussion of parental treatment in infancy and early childhood.

Physical contact. Russian babies receive substantially more physical handling than their American counterparts. To begin with, breast feeding is highly recommended and virtually universal. And even when not being fed, Russian babies are still held much more of the time. The nature of this contact is both highly affectionate and restricting. On the one hand, in comparison with American babies, the Russia child receives considerably more hugging, kissing, and cuddling. On the other hand, the infant is held more tightly and given little opportunity for freedom of movement or initiative. Manuals on child care, prepared by the Academy of Pedagogical Sciences, frequently inveigh against this practice. Witness the following excerpt:

There are still mothers who, when the child is not asleep, never allow him to remain in his bed but continually hold him in their arms. They even cook holding the child with the left arm. Such a position is very harmful to the child, since it leads to curvature of the spine. (Volkova, 1961, p. 15)

Solicitousness. The mobility and initiative of the Soviet child are further limited by a concerted effort to protect him from discomfort, illness, and injury. There is much concern about keeping him warm. Drafts are regarded as especially dangerous. Once the child begins to crawl or walk, there is worry lest he hurt himself or wander into dangerous territory. For example, children in the park are expected to keep in the immediate vicinity of the accompanying adult, and when our youngsters—aged nine and four—would run about the paths, even within our view, kindly citizens of all ages would bring them back by the hand, often with a reproachful word about our lack of proper concern for our children's welfare.

Values and Techniques of Discipline

It would be a mistake to conclude that the affection and solicitousness that Russians, in particular Russian mothers, lavish on children imply permissiveness or indulgence with respect to conduct. On the contrary, much emphasis is placed, no less by parents than by professional educators, on the development of such traits as obedience and self-discipline.

What is meant concretely by these terms? For an answer we turn to the authoritative volume, *Parents and Children* (1961), prepared by a group of specialists from the Academy of Pedagogical Sciences with the aim of "helping parents to bring up their children properly so that they can grow up to be worthy citizens of our 'socialist nation.'" In a chapter on discipline, we read the following:

> What is necessary and possible to demand of young children? First of all, a child must be *obedient* toward his parents and other adults, and treat them with respect. . . . The child must fulfill requests that adults make of him—this is the first thing the child must be taught. The child must fulfill the demands of his elders. In following the orders, instructions, and advice of grownups, the child manifests obedience. By becoming accustomed to obey from early childhood, to react to the demands of adults as something compulsory, the child will begin successfully to fulfill later demands made of him in family and school. (Volkova, 1961, p. 120)

But to obey is not enough; the child must also develop *self-discipline.* On this score, the manual speaks as follows:

> It is necessary as early as possible to develop in the young child an active, positive relation to the demands of adults, the desire to act in accordance with these demands, to do that which is necessary. Herein lies the great

significance of our efforts in developing conscious self-discipline, indeed its very elements. Every person, including the young school-age child, will better, more quickly, and more joyously fulfill demands and rules once he has a desire to do so. (p. 126)

In other words, in the parlance of Western psychology, self-discipline is internalized obedience—fulfilling the wishes of adults not as commands from without but as internally motivated desires.

A recent work by one of the Soviet Union's most popular writers on child rearing, I. A. Pechernikova (1965) (the first edition of 150,000 copies sold out in a few months), reiterates much the same idea and then poses a critical question.

Obedience in young children provides the basis for developing that most precious of qualities: self-discipline. Obedience in adolescents and older school children—this is the effective expression of their love, trust, and respect toward parents and other adult family members, a conscious desire to acknowledge their experience and wisdom. This is an important aspect of preparing young people for life in a Communist society. We shall be asked: what about developing independence in children? We shall answer: if a child does not obey and does not consider others, then his independence invariably takes ugly forms. Ordinarily this gives rise to anarchistic behavior, which can in no way be reconciled with laws of living in Soviet society. Where there is no obedience, there is no self-discipline; nor can there be normal development of independence. Training in obedience is an essential condition for developing the ability of self-discipline. (p. 7)

We cannot risk our children's future by allowing their upbringing to be determined by spontaneous drift. The school and the parents [note the order] must hold the reins of upbringing in their own hands and take all measures necessary to insure that children obey their elders. (p. 123)

What measures are these? On first glance, we recognize familiar phrases "reprimand," "dressing down," "deprivation of privileges": that is, the usual armamentarium of frustrated parents everywhere. But a more careful reading reveals a special emotional tone somewhat alien to present-day parental practices in our own country.

Upbringing in Collective Settings

Training in the first year of life involves two major features. The first is early experience in collective living. The infants are placed in group playpens with six to eight children in each. To permit face-to-face interaction between staff members and children, the pens are raised on legs, the one for the three- to six- month-olds being higher than that for the near-toddlers. At these age levels, there is one "upbringer" for every four charges.

The second core principle of upbringing is the so-called *regime*. Each child is on what a Western psychologist would view as a series of reinforcement schedules: that is, the upbringer spends a specified amount of time in stimulating and training sensory-motor functions.

Probably the most important difference between Soviet and American schools is the emphasis placed in the former not only on subject matter but equally on *vospitanie*, a term for which there is no exact equivalent in English; it might best be translated as "upbringing" or "character education." *Vospitanie* has as its stated aim the development of "communist morality." The nature of communist morality, its component traits, and the specific techniques for developing these traits in children are elaborated in great detail in an extensive literature including official manuals, books by leading authorities like Sukhomlinsky (1965), and innumerable articles in the popular press and in magazines totally devoted to the subject.

It is to be understood that all of the school and civic activities, including those carried out at home, are conducted in the context of the child's collective. Specifically, each classroom is a unit of the communist youth organization appropriate to that age level: the Octobrists for the first three grades (ages seven to nine), the Pioneers in grades four through eight (ages 10 to 15), and the Komsomol [Young Communist League] in the higher grades and beyond to the age of 28. Membership in the Octobrists and Pioneers is virtually universal. The Komsomol, which is selective, enrolls over half of those eligible by age, with the proportion being considerably higher among young people still in school.

The aims and values of these organizations, particularly at the school-age level, are of a piece with those promulgated for the school program itself. This is readily apparent from the codes of the Octobrists and the Pioneers, which every child must learn.

Laws of the Pioneers

1. A pioneer honors the memory of those who have given their life in the struggle for freedom and the flowering of the Soviet Motherland.

2. A pioneer is a friend to children of all the nations of the world.

3. A Pioneer studies diligently, is disciplined, and courteous.

4. A Pioneer likes to work and to take care of public property.

5. A Pioneer is a good friend, cares for younger children, and helps grownups.

6. A Pioneer develops courage and does not fear difficulties.

7. A Pioneer tells the truth and treasures the honor of his unit.

8. A Pioneer develops his physique, does physical exercises every day.

9. A Pioneer loves nature; he is a protector of green plants, useful birds and animals.

10. A Pioneer is an example to all children.

Some readers may be impressed by the similarity between the communist precepts for the young and those promulgated by Western youth organizations like the Boy Scouts. For example, the slogan on the emblem *Vsegda gotov* means "Always prepared." There are some possible differences, however, in interpretation. One of these is reflected in a poster illustrating the seventh law: "A Pioneer tells the truth and treasures the honor of his unit" (Figure 15.1).

As the drawing indicates, being truthful includes, as one Soviet educator preferred to put it, "expressing one's opinion publicly about a comrade's misconduct." (Note that the shamed seatmate had carved his name on the desk.) But there is a poster within the poster. It depicts a serious-faced Pioneer named Pavlik Morozov. Although the name is unfamiliar to most Westerners, it was a household word in the U.S.S.R. A young Pioneer during the period of collectivization, Pavlik denounced his own father as a collaborator with the Kulaks and testified against him in court. Pavlik was killed by people of the village for revenge and is now regarded as a martyr in the cause of communism. A statue of him in Moscow is constantly visited by children, who keep it bedecked with fresh flowers, and many collective farms, Pioneer palaces, and libraries bear his name.

Methods of Collective Upbringing

As already indicated, the organization of the youth groups parallels that of the school. The classes, designated as detachments, together compose the overall school organization known as *drushina*. In addition, each classroom is subdivided into *zvenya* [links], which typically correspond to the rows of double-seated school desks. It is this series of "nested" social units that constitutes the successive collectives of which each child is a member and that carries primary responsibility for guiding his behavior and character development.

Пионер ПАВЛИК МОРОЗОВ

ПИОНЕР
ГОВОРИТ
ПРАВДУ,
ОН ДОРОЖИТ
ЧЕСТЬЮ
СВОЕГО ОТРЯДА.

Figure 15.1   "A Pioneer tells the truth and treasures the honor of his unit."

The principles and methods employed are those developed by A. S. Makarenko early in his career. In the 1920s, as a young school teacher and devout communist, Makarenko was handed the assignment of setting up a rehabilitation program for some of the hundreds of homeless children who were roaming the Soviet Union after the civil wars. The first group of such children assigned to Makarenko's school, a ramshackle building far out of town, turned out to be a group of boys about 18 years of age with extensive court records of housebreaking, armed robbery, and manslaughter. For the first few months, Makarenko's school served simply as the headquarters for the band of highwaymen who were his legal wards. But gradually, through the development of his group-oriented discipline techniques, and through what can only be called the compelling power of his own moral convictions, Makarenko was able to develop a sense of group responsibility and commitment to the work program and code of conduct that he had laid out for the collective. In the end, his Gorky Colony became known throughout the Soviet Union for its high morale, for its discipline, and for the productivity of its fields, farms, and shops. Indeed, Makarenko's methods proved so successful that he was selected to head a new commune set up by the Ministry of Internal Affairs (then the Cheka, later to become the GPU and NKVD). Makarenko described his experiences, theories, and methods in an extensive series of semiautobiographical novels and essays, which take up seven volumes in the edition of 1957. His works are widely read not only in the Soviet Union but throughout the communist world. In the West, his principal writings have been published in all major countries, with the noted exception of the United States, where a first translation did not appear until 1967 (Makarenko, 1954, 1967).

By the time of my successive visits in the U.S.S.R., the systems of collective upbringing first introduced by Makarenko had become widespread. Here is an example of one of several that I had the opportunity of observing firsthand.

Swimming Without Supervision

I was attending the weekly assembly of the Pioneer organization in a school-of-the-prolonged-day. After the presentation of the colors, the commander of each class reported to the entire student body his collective's achievements for the week. One group had planted flowers in a new housing project, another had built bookcases for a nearby nursery, and so on. After the recital, the director of the school complimented the units on their accomplishments and then, turning to the assembled fifth graders, addressed their bright-eyed, twelve-year-old commander:

> Ivanov, on reporting on the achievements of your group, you omitted something. You failed to mention that only last evening you, the commander, and seven of your men went swimming without supervision. Such action reflects inadequacy not only in the class collective but in the entire Pioneer leadership and organization. I expect the Pioneers to deal appropriately with this matter.

After the meeting, I returned with the director to his office. There awaiting us was a group of half a dozen adults. These were the parents of the offending boys. They had been summoned from their place of work at the director's request. He received them in his office, one by one, as I sat by. His statement to each parent was almost the same. He spoke in a quiet, semiformal tone: "You are called here because yesterday your son participated in unsupervised swimming. I expect that you will give him appropriate punishment."

With only one exception, the responses of the parents were equally uniform. "Thank you, Comrade Director; the punishment will be administered," each one said and promptly left the director's office. One mother ventured an excuse, "I didn't know where he was." "Precisely," interrupted the director. "That is exactly the problem. Nothing could be more serious. I would rather be told that your son is getting failing grades, or that he spoke rudely to a teacher. But when it is a matter of endangering his life, that must not be permitted."

But punishment by the parents was only an ancillary penalty. The main disciplinary action, I learned, would take place at four that afternoon when the Soviet Druzhina, or executive council, of the school Pioneer organization would deliberate over Ivanov's case. Let us attend the meeting.

Ironically, Ivanov, as commander in the fifth-grade class, is a member of the group. Ivanov is asked to stand and tell the group what he has done. The answer is barely audible: "I went swimming."

As his answers are written down by the secretary, a girl asks: "You and who else?"

He names seven others.

Second girl: "Fine thing, you the commander leading your men."

A boy: "Do you realize that last year a child drowned in that very pond?"

The questions and accusations continue, mostly from the girls. The major effort is two-sided: first, to impress Ivanov with the fact that, in violating the rule, he has jeopardized the lives of his classmates as well as his own; second, that his act constituted a betrayal of the faith invested in him as a Pioneer commander. Ivanov is now speechless. He trembles slightly and is struggling to hold back the tears. The direction of questions shifts: "Who suggested the idea of going swimming in the first place?" Silence. "Was it you?" Ivanov shakes his head. "Then who was it?" No answer.

One of the older girls speaks up. She is a ninth grader and already a Komsomolka, or member of the Young Communist League. "All right, Ivanov, if you won't tell us, how would you like it if your whole class doesn't get to go on our five-day camporee next week?"

Another girl: "You will all just stay here and work."

Still another: "Think how the rest of your classmates will feel about you then."

Third girl: "Why punish the rest of the class? They didn't have anything to do with it."

Someone suggests punishing just the boys. Now the male council members, who have said very little, raise an objection. The full collective is responsible for the conduct of its members, they say. Besides, they argue, punishing only the boys would set up a division between the sexes, and that is against communist principles! During this discussion, the adult leader of the Pioneers, who came in some time after the session had started and has been listening attentively on the sidelines, asks for the floor. He suggests that it makes no sense to impose a punishment for the rest of the summer, since the offense itself will be forgotten and only the punishment remembered. As for finding the instigator, the rest of the offenders should be required to speak for themselves. "Let's call in the rest of them."

Seven boys file in. The previous procedure is repeated. Each one is asked if he participated in the swimming and each admits it. Then each is asked if he initiated the enterprise. All either deny it or refuse to answer. Again the council members explain the seriousness of the offense and discuss possible punishments. Again there is talk of forbidding the boys to attend the five-day camporee, the school's major spring outing. Mention is also made of special work assignments. And one new idea is introduced. A girl member proposes that until further notice the boys be deprived of the privilege of wearing their Pioneer kerchiefs. The boys are having a hard time facing their accusers. Some bow their heads; others give in at the knees.

Again it is the adult leader who eases the pressure. Although his voice is stern, the effect of his remarks is to set aside one of the severe suggestions: "This is certainly a serious matter. I would recommend that all eight of the offenders be placed on strict probation for the coming week, and if any one of them deviates so much as a jot or a tittle from the code of proper conduct, he will be deprived of the privilege of attending the camporee."

The council accepts the suggestion but in its final decision adds two further penalties. All the boys look up as sentence is passed in solemn instruction by Nadya, the council president: "Ivanov, first of all, it is your responsibility to see to it that beginning on Monday, neither you nor any of your men are to wear your Pioneer kerchiefs." The president continues, "Second, during the coming week while you are on probation, each of you is to carry out an extra work assignment by watering all the newly planted trees on the school grounds every day. Finally, before you go home this evening, all of you can scrub down and wax the floor in the school assembly."

Incidents of the type recorded above do not occur very often. For example, I looked through the minutes of the Pioneer Council that had tried Ivanov and his comrades. The last trial had occurred more than a year before; the culprits were two teenagers caught drinking a bottle of wine. In general the prevailing atmosphere in Soviet classrooms and other children's collectives is one of acceptance and approval for the work being done. The carrot is much more in evidence than the stick. What is distinctive, however, is the saliency of the collective as the focus of reward. For example, the great charts emblazoned "Who Is Best?" that bedeck the halls and walls of schools and classrooms have as entries the names not of individual pupils but of rows and links. It is the winning unit that is rewarded with a pennant or a special privilege or by having a picture taken.

Psychological Implications of Soviet Methods

What impressed this observer about Soviet youngsters, especially those attending schools of the new type, was their "good behavior." In their external actions, they are well-mannered, attentive, and industrious. In informal conversations, they reveal a strong motivation to learn, a readiness to serve their society, and—in general—ironically enough for a culture committed to a materialistic philosophy, what can only be described as an idealistic attitude toward life. In keeping with this general orientation, relationships with parents, teachers, and upbringers are those of respectful but affectionate friendship. The discipline of the collective is accepted and regarded as justified, even when severe as judged by Western standards. On the basis not only of personal observations and reports from Soviet educators but also of entries in the minutes of the Pioneer and Komsomol meetings which I had an opportunity to examine, it is apparent that instances of aggressiveness, violation of rules, or other antisocial behavior are genuinely rare.

The results of our systematic investigations point to similar conclusions. The most relevant data come from a series of experiments, some of them still in progress, carried out with children in a number of different countries, including the U.S.S.R.

Taken together, the results of these studies strongly indicate that collective upbringing does achieve some of its intended effects—at least at the school-age level. Not only does the peer group in the U.S.S.R. act to support behavior consistent with the values of the adult society, but it also succeeds in introducing its members to take personal initiative and responsibility for developing and retaining such behavior in others.

In the light of our earlier analysis, one other feature of the research results deserves comment. Of the various groups of boys and girls in the several countries in which we have worked (now numbering half a dozen), the Soviet girls show both the highest level of commitment to adult standards and the least individual variation within the classroom. In other words, our empirical findings confirm the impression that it is Soviet girls in particular who support the society's values and—both as individuals and in their collectives—exert pressure on others to conform to standards of good behavior. Though Soviet boys are not so committed as the girls, their responses, under all experimental conditions, were considerably more "adult oriented" than those of their Western counterparts.

In summary, considering both the observational and experimental data, it would seem that Soviet methods of upbringing, both within and outside the family, are accomplishing their desired objectives. The children appear to be obedient; they are also self-disciplined, at least at the level of the collective. But what about the individual? Is he capable of self-discipline when self-determination is required, particularly when the situation demands going it alone, perhaps in opposition to the group?

Some light is shed on this issue by a study conducted by Rodgers, Bronfenbrenner, and Devereux (1968) on standards of social behavior among schoolchildren in four cultures: England, Switzerland, the Soviet Union, and the United States. Again the subjects were sixth graders, with those from Switzerland and the U.S.S.R. coming from boarding schools and children's homes. The results showed that Soviet youngsters placed stronger emphasis than any other group on overt propriety, such as being clean, orderly, and well-mannered, but gave less weight than the subjects from the other countries to telling the truth and seeking intellectual understanding.

This result is, of course, not incompatible with the other data we have reported highlighting the obedience of Russian children. Indeed, another way of describing our findings as a whole is to say that, from a cross-cultural perspective, Soviet children in the process of growing up are confronted with fewer divergent views both within and outside the family and, in consequence, conform more completely to a more homogeneous set of standards.

The American Child

Particularly since World War II, many changes have occurred in patterns of child rearing in the United States, but their essence may be conveyed in a single sentence: *Children used to be brought up by their parents.* Over the years, de facto responsibility for upbringing has shifted away from the family to other settings in the society, some of which do not recognize or accept the task. While the family still has the primary moral and legal responsibility for the character development of children, it often lacks the power or opportunity to do the job, primarily because parents and children no longer spend enough time together in those situations in which such training is possible. This is not because parents do not want to spend time with their children. It is simply that conditions have changed.

Systematic evidence consistent with this conclusion comes from a survey of the changes in child-rearing practices in the United States over a 25-year period (Bronfenbrenner, 1958). As basis for the analysis, data were used from some 30 studies carried out during this interval by a variety of investigators. In the original publication, the data were interpreted as indicating a trend toward universal permissiveness in parent-child relations, especially in the period after World War II. "The generalization applies in such diverse areas as oral behavior, toilet accidents, dependency, sex, aggressiveness, and freedom of movement outside the house" (p. 424).

With the benefit of hindsight these same data admit of another interpretation, consistent with the trend toward permissiveness but going beyond it: namely, the same facts could be viewed as reflecting a progressive decrease, especially in recent decades, in the amount of contact between American parents and their children.

The same conclusion is indicated by data from another perspective— that of cross-cultural research. In a comparative study of parental behavior in the United States and West Germany, Devereux, Bronfenbrenner, and Suci (1962) found, somewhat to their surprise, that German parents not only disciplined their children more but also were more affectionate, offered more help, and engaged in more joint activities. The differences were especially marked in the case of father, with "Dad" perceived as appreciably less of a "pal" to his kids than *Vati* to his *Kinder*.

But even if Americans have to yield place to Germans in the matter of parental involvement, how do they stand in comparison to Russians? Specifically, given the prevalence of institutional upbringing in the U.S.S.R., one might conclude that American parents are closer to their children than their Russian counterparts. Paradoxically, although as yet we have no systematic data on this point, our field observations fail to support such a conclusion. Collective upbringing notwithstanding, emotional ties between Russian parents and children are, as we have seen, exceptionally strong. Maternal overprotection, overt display of physical affection, and simple companionship between parents and children appear more pronounced in Soviet society than in our own. Although, because of longer working hours and time lost in shopping and commuting, Soviet parents may spend less time at home, more of that time appears to be spent in conversation, play, and companionship with children than in American families.

In summary, whether in comparison to other contemporary cultures or to itself over time, American society emerges as one that gives decreasing prominence to the family as a socializing agent. This development does not imply any decrease in the affection or concern of parents for their children. Nor is it a change that we have planned or wanted. Rather it is itself the by-product of a variety of social changes, all operating to decrease the prominence and power of the family in the lives of children. Urbanization, the abolishment of the apprentice system, commuting, centralized schools, zoning ordinances, the working mother, the experts' advice to be permissive, the seductive power of television for keeping children occupied, the delegation and professionalization of child care—all of these manifestations of progress have operated to decrease opportunity for contact between children and parents, or, for that matter, adults in general.

Adults Versus Peers

In a recently completed study by Condry, Siman, and Bronfenbrenner (1968), 766 sixth-grade children reported spending, during the weekend, an average of two to three hours a day with their parents. Over the same period, they spent slightly more time than this with groups of friends and an additional two to three hours per day with a single friend. In short, they spent about twice as much time with peers, either singly or in groups, as with their parents. Moreover, their behavior apparently reflects preference as well as practice. When asked with whom they would rather spend a free weekend afternoon, many more chose friends than parents. An analysis of sex differences revealed that, although both boys and girls spent more time with peers, girls associated more with parents (especially mothers) during weekends than did the boys. Also, the boys associated more with a group, the girls with a single friend.

In this same study, the characteristics of predominantly "peer-oriented" and "adult-oriented" children were compared, and an attempt was made to answer the question of how the peer-oriented children "got that way." An analysis of data on the child's perception of his parents, his peers, and himself led us to conclude that the "peer-oriented" youngster was more influenced by a *lack* of attention and concern at home than by the attractiveness of the larger group. In general, the peer-oriented children held rather negative views of themselves and the peer group. They also expressed a dim view of their own future. Their parents were rated as lower than those of the adult-oriented children both in the expression of affection and support and in the exercise of discipline and control. Finally, in contrast to the adult-oriented group, the peer-oriented children reported engaging in more antisocial behavior such as "doing something illegal," "playing hooky," lying, and teasing other children. In summary, it would seem that the peer-oriented child is a product more of parental disregard than of the attractiveness of the peer group—that he turns to his age mates less by choice than by default. The vacuum left by the withdrawal of parents and adults from the lives of children is filled with an undesired—and possibly *undesirable*—substitute of an age-segregated peer group.

Postscript

A recent study[1] sheds a light on the changes in the lives and attitudes of adolescents in Russia since the breakup of the U.S.S.R. in December of 1991. Entitled *School Students in a Changing Society (1982–1997)* (2000), the investigation was carried out by Vadi Borisovich Ol'shanskii, Svetlana Gavrilovna Klimova, and Natalia Iuevna Volzhskaia with sixth through twelfth graders in Moscow schools in 1982 and again, six years after the regime change, in 1997. In the words of the authors: "The principal problem addressed by the survey was that of using comparison to determine how the values and attitudes of Moscow school students had changed over fifteen years under the influence of the changes in Russian society" (p. 45). The survey was carried out with uncompleted statements for the students to end with their own reactions to the issue. The statements vary from the personal: "The principal problem in my own personal life is . . ." to the more general: " These days relations among people . . ." (p. 48). The results of the survey indicate considerable change in the attitude of the students during this period of historic change. The replies given in the 1997 survey range from the practical, such as less time needed to shop for necessities, to the importance of money, status, and connections in the new Russia. In comparison, results from the 1982 survey included responses such as "to find a job where I can be useful" and "to be as creative as possible." In the 1997 survey, "the only moral qualities that were mentioned by the school students, . . . 'industriousness, persistence,' garnered no more than 1.3 percent. The moral factor stands opposed by material concerns" (p. 48).

Much of this change is blamed on the changes in the schools, where ability and performance have become less important in obtaining placement in institutions of higher learning or in good jobs than power and money. The authors blame this situation, in part, on changes that have taken place in the schools: "A substantial percentage of capable educators went into commercial companies in order to escape poverty. In many schools upbringing responsibilities were abandoned" (p. 52). The changes the authors suggest involve regulating corruption, such as "buying faculty" or using family wealth or connections for admission to institutes of higher education. The suggested countermeasures include better compensation for teachers, as well as encouraging ability and achievement as the educational goals for students.

Attitudes towards interpersonal relationships also changed dramatically between 1982 and 1997. In the first survey to be "competent and moral" had the highest rating; in the later survey, this was true for "having resources and advantages," methods of attraction, and secretiveness.

One must take into consideration that all the teachers, parents, as well as the researchers were brought up under the Soviet system, and the students were all born under that regime and many also attended preschool and the primary grades during that time.

How would American students or those from other Western countries have answered these queries in the year 2002 or earlier in the 1980s?

Note

1. English translation copyright © 2000 by M. E. Sharpe, Inc. From V. B. Ol'shanskii, S. G. Klimova, and N. I. Volzhskaia, "School Students in a Changing Society (1982–1997)," *Russian Education and Society*, vol. 42, no. 4 (April 2000), pp. 44–60. Used with permission.

References

Bronfenbrenner, U. (1958). Socialization and social class through time and space. In E. E. Maccoby, T. M. Newcomb, & E. L. Hartley (Eds.), *Readings in social psychology* (440–425). New York: Holt, Rinehart & Winston.

Bronfenbrenner, U. (1966, August). Response to pressure from peers versus adults among Soviet and American school children. In U. Bronfenbrenner, *Social factors in the development of personality,* Symposium 35, presented at the 18th International Congress of Psychology, Moscow. Reprinted 1967, *International Journal of Psychology, 2,* 199–207.

Condry, J. C., Jr., Siman, M. L., & Bronfenbrenner, U. (1968). *Characteristics of peer- and adult-oriented children.* Unpublished manuscript. Ithaca, NY: Department of Child Development, Cornell University.

Devereux, E. C., Jr., Bronfenbrenner, U., & Suci, G. (1962). Patterns of parent behavior in America and West Germany: A cross-national comparison. *International Social Science Journal, 14*(3), 488–506.

Makarenko, A. S. (1954). *A book for parents* [*Kniga dlya roditeleig*]. Moscow: Foreign Languages Publishing House.

Makarenko, A. S. (1967). *The collective family* (R. Daglish, Trans.). New York: Doubleday.

Ol'shanskii, V. B., Klimova, S. G., & Volzhskaia, N. I. (2000). School students in a changing society (1982–1997). *Russian Education and Society, 42*(4), 44–60.

Perchernikova, I. A. (1965). *Vospitanie poslushaniya i trudolyubiya u detei v semye* [The development of obedience and diligence among children in the family]. Moscow: Proveshchrnie.

Rodgers, R. R., Bronfenbrenner, U., & Devereux, E. C., Jr. (1968). Standards of social behavior among children in four cultures. *International Journal of Psychology, 3*(1), 31–42.

Sukhomlinsky, V. A. (1965). *Vospitanie lichnosti v sovetskoi shkole* [The upbringing of the personality in the Soviet school]. Kiev: Izdatelstvo Radyanska Shkola.

Volkova, E. I. (Ed.). (1961). *Roditeli i deti* [Parents and children]. Moscow: Academy of Pedagogical Sciences.

Is 80% of Intelligence
Genetically Determined?

All human behavior, including intelligence, develops through an integration of influences from all levels within the ecology of human development. Genes and environment are inseparable, then, in producing development. This excerpt critiques the lines of research that have been used to try to establish a split between genes and environment in the development of intelligence, evaluates the quality of the interpretations of the data derived from such research, and offers an alternative, bioecological view of the conjoined role of genes and environment in influencing intelligence.

Although Jensen's (1969a, 1969b) argument claiming genetically based race differences in intelligence has been repeatedly and forcefully attacked (e.g., Scarr-Salapatek, 1971b; Gage, 1972; Lewontin, 1970), his thesis that 80% of the variation in intelligence is determined by heredity has been cited as an unassailable fact by his supporters (e.g., Eysenck, 1971; Herrnstein, 1971; Shockley, 1972) and, by and large, has been left unchallenged by his critics (e.g., Lewontin, 1970; Scarr-Salapatek, 1971a). To quote but one representative statement from each quarter, Herrnstein (1971), a leading protagonist of Jensen's views, asserts, "Jensen concluded

Source: Bronfenbrenner, U. (1975). Is 80% of intelligence genetically determined? In U. Bronfenbrenner & M. A. Mahoney (Eds.), *Influences on human development* (pp. 91–100). Hillsdale, IL: Dryden.

(as have most other experts in the field) that the genetic factor is worth about 80 percent and that only 20 percent is left to everything else" (p. 56). Lewontin (1970), in his forceful critique and rejection of Jensen's argument for genetically based race differences, takes no issue with the latter's 80% figure for the contribution of heredity: "I shall accept Jensen's rather high estimate without serious argument" (p. 6).

Since Jensen takes his thesis of 80% genetic effect as the foundation both for his argument for innate differences in ability between the races and for his contention that intervention programs with disadvantaged groups have little hope of success, it becomes important, from the point of view both of science and of social policy, to examine the evidence and line of reasoning that underlie his initial thesis. Jensen's argument rests on inferences drawn primarily from three sets of data:

1. Studies of resemblance between identical twins reared apart

2. Studies of resemblance within families having own children versus adopted children

3. Studies of resemblance between identical versus fraternal twins reared in the same home

1. Identical Twins Reared Apart

Jensen's conclusion from these studies (Burt, 1966; Juel-Nielsen, 1965; Newman, Freeman, & Holzinger, 1937; Shields, 1962) that at least 75% of variance in intelligence is due to heredity is based on two critical assumptions. First, the environments of separated twins must be uncorrelated; in other words, there must be no tendency to place the twins in similar foster homes. Second, the range of environments into which twins are separated must be as great as that for unrelated children. There is evidence to indicate that neither of these assumptions is met. For example, in Newman et al.'s (1937) study, rated differences between the social or educational environments of each pair were usually small, and there was a correlation of .55 between separated twins in the number of years of schooling that each received. In addition, although separated, the twins were often brought up by related persons, such as a mother and an aunt. This was true in all four of the published studies. An examination of the 128 pairs of separated twins described in these investigations revealed that 42, or a third of all the cases, were brought up by relatives. In the three studies in which such information was made available, almost half

(44%) were found to have been brought up in the same town, and 31% attended the same school, usually in the same classroom.

Such findings illustrate the more general phenomenon of *selective placement,* which has been shown to operate whenever children are separated from their true parents and placed in foster homes or other settings (e.g., Skodak & Skeels, 1949). The effects of this process are manifested in correlations between the characteristics of the home into which the child was born and those of the foster home. The selection operates with respect to a variety of variables relevant to psychological development, including social status, religion, ethnicity, family structure, and, in particular, values and practices of child rearing. The operation of selective placement with respect to one or more such variables cannot be ruled out in any of the studies, and the resulting correlation between the environments means that estimates of 75% for genetic influence are confounded by environmental variance. Further evidence for the presence and effect of correlated environments is presented below.

The evidence also calls into question the assumption that the range of environments into which twins are separated is unrestricted. Findings from adoption studies indicate "a surprising uniformity among adoptive parents" (Pringle, 1966) in both their social and psychological characteristics.

The importance of degree of environmental variation in influencing the correlation between identical twins reared apart, and hence the estimate of heritability based on this statistic, is revealed by the following examples:

1. Among 35 pairs of separated twins for whom information was available about the community in which they lived, the correlation in Binet IQ for those raised in the same town was .83; for those brought up in different towns, the figure was .67.

2. In another sample of 38 separated twins, tested with a combination of verbal and nonverbal intelligence scales, the correlation for those attending the same school in the same town was .87; for those attending schools in different towns, the coefficient was .66. In the same sample, separated twins raised by relatives showed a correlation of .82; for those brought up by unrelated persons, the coefficient was .63.

3. When the communities in the preceding sample were classified as similar versus dissimilar on the basis of size and economic base (e.g., mining vs. agricultural), the correlation for separated twins living in similar communities was .86; for those residing in dissimilar localities the coefficient was .26.

4. In the Newman et al. (1937) study, ratings are reported of the degree of similarity between the environments into which the twins were separated. When these ratings were divided at the median, the twins reared in the

more similar environments showed a correlation of .91 between their IQs; for those brought up in less similar environments, the coefficient was .42.

The foregoing examples by no means exhaust the environmental variables in terms of which selection can occur in the placement of separated twins. As a result, the possible contribution of environment to differences between separated twins is considerably less than it would be in a population of unrelated children.

In view of these facts, the correlation of .75 or higher between IQs of identical twins reared apart cannot be interpreted as reflecting the proportion of variance attributable solely to heredity. There is no question that genetic factors play a significant role in the determination of intelligence. Witness the fact that the correlation in IQ between identical twins reared apart is greater than that for fraternal twins raised in the same home. But, for the reasons given, the conclusion that 70% to 80% of the variance in mental ability is due to heredity represents an inflated estimate.[1]

2. Children From Adoptive Families

Jensen (1969a) concludes that since the correlation between unrelated children brought up in the same home is only .24, the remaining fraction of .76 is due to heredity (pp. 50–51). This argument requires the rather extraordinary assumption that all differences between children raised in the same home are due only and entirely to genetic differences between them. The possible role of environment (in terms of such factors as differential treatment by parents, or varying experiences in school, peer group, or other settings) is ruled out of consideration. Clearly such an assumption is untenable.[2]

Jensen also relies heavily on studies reporting higher similarity among own versus adopted children, in particular the finding cited by Honzik (1957) that the correlation between IQ of adopted children was .40 with the IQ of their true mothers but unrelated to the educational level of the foster mothers. In point of fact, in the original study from which these data were taken, Skodak and Skeels (1949) had shown that the correlations for the mothers were significantly confounded by the selective placement of children of more intelligent and better-educated mothers in better foster homes. Moreover, the mean IQ of the foster children at age 12 was 106, whereas that of their true mothers was only 86. In an attempt to account for this marked difference, Skodak and Skeels analyzed the characteristics of the home environments among both true and foster families and concluded that the critical factor was the "maternal stimulation . . . and optimum security" provided in the foster homes as a group and especially in those in which the children had shown a marked gain in IQ over a 10-year period. None of these facts bearing on the substantial impact of the environment are reflected in Honzik's conclusions or Jensen's interpretation.

In sum, as in the case of identical twins reared apart, the data from studies of own versus adopted children likewise fail to support Jensen's claim that 80% of the variance in intelligence is genetically determined.

3. Identical Versus Fraternal Twins Reared Together

The most widely employed method for estimating the proportion of variance attributable to genetic factors is based on the comparison of within-pair differences for identical versus same-sex fraternal twins, both groups reared in their own homes. Without getting into technicalities, the basic argument runs as follows. Differences between identical twins can be attributable only to environment since their genetic endowments are the same. Differences between fraternal twins, however, reflect both environmental and genetic effects and are larger for that reason. Accordingly, if one subtracts the former variance from the latter, the resulting difference is the amount of variance attributable to heredity. By expressing this variance as a fraction of total variance among individuals, one obtains an estimate of the proportion of total variation attributable to genetic factors in fraternal twins. Since such twins have half their genes in common, the contribution of heredity to variation among unrelated children would be about twice as large. The resulting ratio is referred to as the *heritability coefficient* and is usually designated as h^2, after Holzinger (1929), who first developed such an index.

Drawing on the results from 25 studies of identical and fraternal twins reared together, as well as other kinship correlations, Jensen (1967) obtained a heritability coefficient of .80, which constitutes the primary basis of his claim.

The interpretation of the heritability coefficient as measuring the proportion of variance due to heredity rests on two critical assumptions. First, the environments of identical twins must be no more alike than those for fraternal twins. In the past, investigators have acknowledged that identical twins do grow up in more similar environments but have regarded the difference as a negligible one. An analysis of data published in the last decade reveals that the difference is in fact substantial and contributes significantly to the observed resemblance between identical twins. The analysis draws on three types of evidence. First, systematic studies of the environments of identical versus fraternal twins indicate that the former are more often placed in similar situations (Husen, 1959; Jones, 1946; Koch, 1966; Shields, 1954) and are consistently treated more similarly by their parents (Scarr, 1968).

Second, if their more similar environments have significant impact, then identical twins should resemble each other most in those characteristics that are the product of common experience in the family. For example, they should be more similar in verbal than in nonverbal tests of intelligence and in personality traits that relate to interpersonal relations (e.g., extraversion-introversion, dominance-submissiveness) than in intrapsychic qualities (e.g., anxiety, flexibility). Moreover, since parents do not treat boys and girls in the same way, male and female twins should differ in the abilities and traits in which they are most alike, with boys showing greater similarity, and therefore showing higher heritability coefficients, in mathematical ability or dominance, and girls in languages or sociability. The results of a series of independent studies (Gottesman, 1966; Husen, 1959; Nichols, 1965a, 1965b; Scarr, 1969; Scarr-Salapatek, 1971a) are in accord with these expectations.

Third, if their more similar environments affect their development, identical twins should be most alike in those social contexts in which parent-child interaction is most intensive, sustained, and focused on the development of the child. For example, the similarity of identical twins should vary directly with social class and, given present inequities in American society, should be greater among white than black families. In line with these expectations Scarr-Salapatek (1971a) reports greater similarity, and hence higher heritability coefficients, for twins from advantaged than from disadvantaged socioeconomic groups and in white as against black families. These findings indicate that the realization of genetic potential requires an appropriately complex, sustained, and stimulating environment. In accord with this principle, twins from lower-class black groups, who in our society live in suppressive environments, exhibit lower levels of ability and reduced genetic variability as reflected in lower heritability coefficients.

Independent confirmation for this conclusion comes from recent studies of intellectual development in children of mixed black-white marriages (Willerman, Naylor, & Myrianthopoulos, 1970). From the point of view of genetic theory, which parent is of which race should make no difference for the child's mental capacity. Yet the data showed a differential effect. Specifically, if the mother was black, then the child's IQ was closer to the average IQ for blacks than if the father was black. Since it is the mother who is the primary agent of child rearing, this result is consistent with the conclusion that the suppressive environments in which blacks grow up in our society disrupt the process of socialization, with the result that the child of the impoverished environment fails to realize his genetic potential.

The foregoing findings indicate that, contrary to Jensen's assumptions, the greater similarity of environments for identical twins contributes substantially to their greater psychological resemblance. As a result, the heritability coefficient again reflects substantial environmental as well as genetic variance.

Finally, Jensen's argument suffers from an even more serious restrictive condition. To the extent that it is a valid measure, the heritability coefficient reflects the relative contribution of genetic and environmental variance *within* but not *between* families. Yet it is precisely *between families* that most of the differences in ability occur. It may be true that individual differences among children *within the same family* are more influenced by genetic than by environmental factors, but such a finding implies nothing about variation among children from *different* families. Evidence for the effect of such environmental restriction on the magnitude of heritability coefficients based only on samples of twins can be obtained from data cited by Jensen himself. For example, twins are necessarily of the same age, a circumstance that obviously reduces differences in their environmental experience. Utilizing data provided by Jensen (1969a), one can compute a heritability coefficient from a comparison of siblings with unrelated children raised in the same family. Siblings, of course, are no more alike than fraternal twins. Just as identical twins have about twice as many genes in common as fraternal twins, so do the latter have about twice as many genes in common as children who are completely unrelated. Accordingly, from this point of view, the genetic contribution to differences in intelligence, as measured by the heritability coefficient, should be approximately the same in both cases. Of course, the critical element is the fact that we are now dealing with children who, though raised in the same family, are of different ages. Although just as similar genetically as fraternal twins, they do not look as alike *at the same point in time*. Hence they are more likely to be treated differently than fraternal twins are, so that the environmental variation is greater. This fact is reflected in the heritability coefficient computed by Jensen's formula from the data cited in his article on siblings versus unrelated children raised together. The obtained estimate of genetic effect was 68%, clearly lower than the 80% derived by Jensen from the data on twins. Which value is correct? Obviously, the answer depends on the range of variation present in the environment.

But the contribution of the environment to differences among children raised in the same family is of course less than would obtain for children raised in different households. As Newman et al. (1937) pointed out in their pioneering study, an unbiased estimate of the relative contribution of heredity and environment to differences between children raised in *different* families could be obtained from a heritability coefficient based on separated identical and separated fraternal twins (p. 347). They further speculated that, under these circumstances, the percentage of genetic effect, "instead of being about .75 as for twins reared together, might be of the order of .50 or even smaller. . . . The relative role of heredity and environment is thus a function of the type of environment" (p. 347).

It is surprising that no one has followed up on this suggestion. Nor do any published data exist on the degree of similarity between fraternal twins reared apart. Fehr (1969), however, has carried out an alternate analysis comparing separated identical twins with siblings reared apart. As Fehr acknowledges, such a comparison is biased toward heredity, since identical twins are probably more likely to come from and be placed in correlated environments and, unlike siblings, are always of the same age and sex (p. 576). As a result, a heritability coefficient based on a comparison of identical twins reared apart with separated siblings would be higher than one in which the contrast group was separated, same-sex fraternal twins. Even so, the estimate of heritability obtained by Fehr was .53, a value substantially below Jensen's figure of .80. Fehr's result also lends support to Newman et al.'s (1937) prediction of a coefficient of ".50 or even smaller" for separated twins of both types. But even this estimate cannot be generalized to the population at large, in view of the restricted range of environments into which foster children are placed.

We have now concluded our reexamination of evidence and assumptions underlying the thesis of Jensen and others that 80% of the variation in human intelligence is genetically determined. The results of our analysis lead to rejection of this thesis on both theoretical and empirical grounds. But what of the fundamental question to which Jensen was so ready to supply an answer? What can be said about the relative contributions of heredity and environment to psychological development? On the basis of the analysis we have undertaken, several conclusions appear to be in order:

1. There can be no question that genetic factors play a substantial role in producing individual differences in mental ability. Many research findings testify to the validity of this statement. Perhaps the most impressive is the fact that the similarity of identical twins reared apart is clearly greater than that of fraternal twins reared together.

2. It is impossible to establish a single fixed figure representing the proportion of variation in intelligence, or any other human trait, independently attributable to heredity versus environment. Even if one assumes the absolute degree of genetic variation to be a constant, the fact that the relative contribution of each factor depends on the degree of variability present in a given environment and its capacity to evoke innate potential means that the influence of genetic factors will vary from one environmental context to another. *Specifically, whereas the impact of hereditary endowment is considerable in accounting for individual differences among children raised in the same family, the relative importance of the environment becomes much greater in accounting for differences among children raised in different families. This fact is of special importance, since the greatest variation in human abilities occurs across families rather than within them.*

3. Any attempt to identify the independent contribution of heredity and environment to human development confronts the fact of a substantial correlation between these two factors. Moreover, the relation is not unidirectional. It is true, as Jensen (1969a) points out, that parents of better genetic endowment are likely to create better environments for their children and that the child, as a function of his genetic characteristics, in fact partially determines the environment that he experiences (p. 38). The genetically instigated greater environmental similarity of identical versus fraternal twins is a case in point. But Scarr-Salapatek's (1971a) research on this same phenomenon provides dramatic evidence that the environment can also determine the extent to which genetic potential is realized. This reverse relationship calls into question the legitimacy of including covariance between heredity and environment in the proportion of variance due solely to genetic factors, as Jensen (1969a) does (p. 39). The impossibility of assigning this covariance unequivocally to one or the other source is further ground for the conclusion that a fixed, single figure representing the proportion of variance attributable to genetic factors cannot be established.

4. For genetic potential to find expression in terms of level and diversity requires an appropriately complex and stimulating environment. This fact leads to a new and somewhat ironic interpretation of measures of heritability. Since heritability coefficients are lowest in environments that are most impoverished and suppressive, and highest in those that are most stimulating and enriched, *the heritability coefficient should be viewed not solely as a measure of the genetic loading underlying a particular ability or trait but also as an index of the capacity of a given environment to evoke and nurture the development of that ability or trait.*

5. Even when the heritability coefficient for a trait in a particular environment is very high, this in no way restricts what might occur in some new environment that might come about or be deliberately constructed. Specifically, contrary to Jensen's contention, *a high heritability coefficient for a particular ability or trait cannot be taken as evidence that the ability or trait in question cannot be substantially enhanced through environmental intervention.* An instructive example is cited by Gage (1972) in a reply to Shockley and Jensen. Gage calls attention to the striking gain in stature exhibited by adults in Western countries over the past 200 years as a function of improved conditions of health and nutrition. He notes further that the heritability of height as determined from twin studies is about .90 higher than that for IQ. "If this high heritability index had been derived in the year 1800, would it then have been safe to conclude that height cannot be increased through environmental influences? If that conclusion had been drawn, it would have been wrong" (p. 422).

6. If the heritability coefficient for a given ability or trait in a particular environment is low in comparison with other social contexts, this means that the environment is inadequate for the development of that capacity. Specifically, the low heritability coefficients and depressed levels of measured intelligence, observed in disadvantaged populations, especially blacks, indicate that the environments in which these persons live do not permit the realization of their genetic potential.

7. In terms of implications for social policy, the foregoing conclusions argue against reliance on methods of selective mating and population control and in favor of measures aimed at improving existing environments and even creating new ones better suited to evoke and nurture the expression of constructive. genetic potential.

Thus, our analysis has brought us to a paradoxical conclusion. An inquiry into the heritability of inborn capacities has shed new light on the power and potential of the environment to bring about the fuller realization of genetic possibilities.

Notes

1. A more detailed and technical analysis of evidence and argument bearing on the issues raised in this article is contained in Bronfenbrenner (1975).

2. Similar considerations apply to the interpretation of data on adopted versus own children. The fact that intrafamilial correlations in IQ tend to be higher for families with own than with adopted children is in part a function of the greater homogeneity of adoptive parents as a group in terms of both social background characteristics and values. Hence the greater similarity among blood-related versus adoptive family members cannot be attributed solely or even primarily to genetic factors.

References

Bronfenbrenner, U. (1975). Nature with nurture: A reinterpretation of the evidence. In A. Montagu (Ed.), *Race and IQ* (pp. 114–144). New York: Oxford University Press.

Burt, C. (1966). The genetic determination of differences in intelligence: A study of monozygotic twins reared together and apart. *British Journal of Psychology, 57,* 137–153.

Eysenck, H. J. (1971). *The IQ argument.* New York: Library Press.

Fehr, F. S. (1969). Critique of hereditarian accounts. *Harvard Educational Review, 39,* 571–580.

Gage, N. L. (1972, January). I.Q. heritability, race differences, and educational research. *Phi Delta Kappan,* pp. 297–307.

Gottesman, I. I. (1966). Genetic variance and adaptive personality traits. *Journal of Child Psychology and Psychiatry, 7,* 199–208.

Herrnstein, R. (1971, September). IQ. *Atlantic Monthly,* 43–64.

Holzinger, J. (1929). The relative effect of nature and nurture influences on twin differences. *Journal of Educational Psychology, 20,* 241–248.

Honzik, M. P. (1957). Developmental studies of parent-child resemblance in intelligence. *Child Development, 28,* 215–228.

Husen, T. (1959). *Psychological twin research.* Stockholm: Almqvist & Wiksell.

Jensen, A. R. (1967). Estimation of the limits of heritability of traits by comparison of monozygotic and dizygotic twins. *Proceedings of the National Academy of Sciences, 58,* 149–157.

Jensen, A. R. (1969a). How much can we boost I.Q. and scholastic achievement? *Harvard Educational Review, 39,* 1–123.

Jensen, A. R. (1969b). Reducing the heredity-environment uncertainty: A reply. *Harvard Educational Review, 39,* 449–483.

Jones, A. G. (1946). Environmental influences on mental development. In E. Carmichael (Ed.), *Manual of child psychology* (pp. 582–632). New York: Wiley & Sons.

Juel-Nielsen, N. (1965). *Individual and environment.* Copenhagen: Munksgaard.

Koch, H. T. (1966). *Twins and twin relations.* Chicago: University of Chicago Press.

Lewontin, R. C. (1970, March). Race and intelligence. *Bulletin of the Atomic Scientists, 26,* 2–8.

Newman, H. H., Freeman, F. N., & Holzinger, K. J. (1937). *Twins: A study of heredity and environment.* Chicago: University of Chicago Press.

Nichols, R. C. (1965a). The inheritance of general and specific abilities. *National Merit Scholarship Corporation Research Reports, 1,* 1–13.

Nichols, R. C. (1965b). The National Merit twin study. In G. Vandenberg (Ed.), *Methods and goals in human behavior genetics* (pp. 231–245). New York: Academic Press.

Pringle, M. L. K. (1966). *Adoption: Facts and fallacies.* London: Longmans, Green.

Scarr, S. (1968). Environmental bias in twin studies. *Eugenics Quarterly, 15,* 34–40.

Scarr, S. (1969). Social introversion-extroversion. *Child Development, 40,* 823–833.

Scarr-Salapatek, S. (1971a). Race, social class and IQ. *Science, 174,* 1285–1295.

Scarr-Salapatek, S. (1971b). Unknowns in the IQ equation. *Science, 174,* 1223–1228.

Shields, J. (1954). Personality differences and neurotic traits in normal twin school children. *Eugenics Review, 45,* 213–247.

Shields, J. (1962). *Monozygotic twins brought up apart and brought up together.* New York: Oxford University Press.

Shockley, W. A. (1972, March). Debate challenge: Geneticity is 80% for white identical twins I.Q.'s. *Phi Delta Kappan,* pp. 415–419.

Skodak, M., & Skeels, H. M. (1949). A final follow-up study of one hundred adopted children. *Journal of Genetic Psychology, 75,* 85–125.

Willerman, L., Naylor, A. F., & Myrianthopoulos, N. C. (1970). *Science, 170,* 1329–1331.

Article 17

The Future of Childhood

This article updates many of the points made in previous articles about the threats to families' capacity to nurture children but attends as well to the development of parents. Increases in rates and levels of mothers' employment and in the number of families headed by single parents reveal the importance of third persons in the parent-child system and of other supports to enable parents to perform their caring role and to gain the satisfactions that accrue from it. Four "preposterous proposals" point to needed changes.

I ask what, in the United States, would prove a provocative question. As you may know, all over the world 1979 was the Year of the Child. For us was it also the Year of the Family? As we sought to identify and to meet the needs of children, were we also seeking to identify and meet the needs of fathers, of mothers, child care workers, nurses, teachers, principals, and, for the United States, one would have to add bus drivers, probation officers, and policemen? In short, were we meeting the needs of all those to whom a society delegates, by decision or default, the responsibility for that crucial task that every culture must perform if it is to survive and flourish— *the process of making human beings?* For if the Year of the Child was not the Year of the Parent, the Year of the Preschool, the Year of the School, and again, at least in the United States, the Year of the Neighborhood and the Year of Flexible Schedules in the world of work—if it was the Year of the

Source: Bronfenbrenner, U. (1985). The future of childhood. In V. Greaney (Ed.), *Children: Needs and rights* (pp. 167–186). New York: Irvington Publishers, Inc.

246

Child alone—then it was another year of loneliness for children, and an ill omen for their future and ours. For then children were more talked about than talked to, and more influenced by a television set than by a human being.

Children in American Families

Some view the changes that have been taking place in the American family with dismay; others do not care one way or the other. As part of my work on a committee of our National Academy of Sciences, I carried out an analysis of the changes that have taken place in the American family and in the nation's children—changes over the last three and a half decades since World War II (Assembly of Behavioral and Social Sciences, 1976).

The primary reason mothers work is financial, especially for those who are single parents, for whom it may be a necessity. For many others, the rising cost of living makes a second wage earner essential if the family is to acquire and maintain what have come to be regarded as necessities—a car, gasoline, a vacation, a color TV. But there are other significant trends in the changing family that are not readily explainable by economic needs. As many more mothers go to work, the number of adults left in the home who might care for the child has been decreasing in two ways. First, there are fewer extended families: those that contain other relatives besides the parents have been gradually shrinking and disappearing.

Second, the shrinkage and disappearance have been even more pronounced in the so-called "nuclear family" consisting of mother, father, and children. In the United States today [1985] one in every five children is living in a single-parent family, with that one parent also being the head of the family, holding down a job (usually full time), and being the only adult in the household. Contrary to popular impression, single parenthood is usually not a temporary state, for on a national scale, the remarriage rate for women with children is substantially lower than that for men who have children. As a result the differential is increasing with only partial replacement. Our census statisticians are now estimating that over 50% of all children in the United States will be living in a single-parent household sometime during their childhood.

The fastest-growing component in this complex of single-parent families is the rocket rise in the number of unwed mothers. More and more young women are postponing the age of marriage but having children nonetheless. The trend began just after World War II but has accelerated rapidly since 1970. From 1970 to 1980, children under 18 in separated families increased by 29%, children of divorced families increased by 102%, and children of unwed mothers have increased by 239%, from 527,000 to 1,721,000. Most of these unwed mothers are teen-agers. By a standard now being considered by some as outmoded, they are children themselves.

As for the American family, it is getting smaller in terms of not only the number of children in the household but also the number of adults. The most significant manifestation of this trend is the one that has not received much publicity, despite the fact that it represents one of the most rapid changes taking place in American family demography. I refer to the dramatic rise in the number of persons living alone, especially those from 18 to 35 years of age, the prime childbearing years. Here the increase has been 233%, from 1,449,000 in 1970 to 4,820,000 in 1980, more than tripling the number over that period (U.S. Bureau of the Census, 1981).

Consequences of Changes in Families

What are the social consequences of the kinds of changes in the structure and role of the family that are now taking place in the United States and other modern industrialized societies? The answer to that question depends on what you view to be the function of the family in society. Some regard these changes as for the best. For example, they point out that the age of marriage is rising and marriage rates are increasing, primarily because of remarriage. Marriages are also lasting longer because people are living longer. And, if you do not stick to legalities and count it as a marriage when a man and woman live together, the number of "marriages" increases still further. What we are seeing are new family forms. In the words of a colleague, Mary Jo Bane of Harvard University, the family is "here to stay" (Bane, 1976). She argues that the family is simply changing its form. But what about its function? To be sure, if the main function of the family is seen as the satisfaction of heterosexual sexual drives, the family is not doing so badly. In the words of George Bernard Shaw, "The family is so popular because it combines the maximum of temptation with the maximum of opportunity." But for a student of human development like myself, the family has another function, more creative than sex, and even more critical for the well-being of a society and its individual members. In my view the family is the most effective and economical structure for nurturing and sustaining the capacity of human beings to function effectively in all domains of human activity—intellectual, social, emotional, and physiological.

In speaking of the enhanced effectiveness and development of human beings, I have in mind not only infancy, childhood, or youth—not just the formative years—but the entire life span to this very hour and beyond, from the moment life begins until the day we die. I suggest the family is crucial not only to the capacity of a child to learn to walk, talk, and learn in school *but also to the ability of an adult to perform on the job, to think clearly, to serve the community or society as a whole*. That capacity, I submit, is to a substantial degree motivated, mediated, and maintained by the family to which a person belongs—parents, spouse, children, relatives, partners— even though the members may not be physically present, or legally bound, or even still living.

Such a formulation implies a definition of the family that is somewhat unorthodox, since it views the family in functional rather than legalistic or structural terms. Specifically, from my perspective, as a researcher of human development, I define the family as *a group of persons who possess and implement an irrational commitment to each other's well-being*. Now it does make it easier to implement that commitment if members of the group are living together, and probably some structural, legal, and religious forms may be effective in maintaining and enhancing this irrational arrangement. But I shall argue that the main forces that keep the irrational arrangement irrational, implementable, and enduring are not to be found only within the structure itself; they also exist outside. Before we can understand these external circumstances we have to answer a prior question pertinent to the family's internal functioning. What is the price of irrational commitment? Who needs it?

To answer that question we have to return to the changes that have been taking place in the American family at an accelerating pace since World War II. First, we need to understand where those changes have been occurring, for, while found in all segments of a society, they have been occurring faster in some settings than in others.

Let me bring this concept down to earth by citing some concrete research findings. Hetherington, Cox, and Cox (1978, 1979a, 1979b) have just completed a brilliant investigation of the "aftermath of divorce" among families well above the poverty line.

Hetherington and her colleagues compared the experience of mothers, fathers, and their four- to six-year-old children in matched samples of divorced and intact families. Initially, it was the fathers who were hardest hit by the experience of separation. Feeling anxious, insecure, and inadequate, they engaged in a desperate search for a new identity in a variety of activities. But within a year the crisis had abated, primarily because they had established new heterosexual relationships. The problems experienced by the mothers and children, however, ran a longer course and were not so readily resolved. Placed in the unaccustomed position of family head, the mother usually also found it necessary, because of her reduced financial situation, to look for work or for a more remunerative job. At the same time, she had to care for the house and children, not to mention making a new personal life for herself. The result was a vicious circle. The children, in the absence of the father, demanded more attention, but the mother had other things that had to be done. In response, the children became more demanding. The research data reveal that in comparison with youngsters from intact families, the children of divorce were less likely to respond to the mother's requests. Nor did it make it any easier that similar requests were complied with when made by the divorced father. And even when the child was responsive to her, the divorced mother was less likely to acknowledge or reward the action. The researchers sum up the net effect by a quotation from one of the mothers: "It's like being bitten to death by ducks."

Hetherington et al. have followed the development of these children from home to preschool and to school. They found that children from these middle-class single-parent families did not function as effectively as those in the control group. They were less able to sustain attention and to establish relationships with teachers and peers and, therefore, did not progress as quickly in developing learning skills.

But fortunately Hetherington et al. did not stop at this discouraging point in their analyses. They noted that not all children from divorced families showed this maladaptive pattern. Some appeared to be developing as happy, competent youngsters. They found two sets of conditions that appeared to counteract the disruptive effects of divorce. The first, and by far the most powerful, was active assistance by the divorced father not so much to the child but to the mother herself, by backing her up in matters of discipline, doing errands, spelling her off, and providing needed advice and encouragement. In short, in accordance with our fourth proposition, whereas the parent-child dyad is the core context for human development, it takes a third party to enable the two-person system to function effectively. Like a three-legged stool, if one leg is broken or shorter than the others, the support is not very stable, and the structure tends to collapse.

But the third party need not be another parent. Yet another condition in which children of divorce seemed to function quite well was when the mother reported strong support from relatives, friends, and neighbors, as well as the local community and organizations. Professor Hetherington and her colleagues point out that the problem is not with divorced families as such; it is how we treat them in our society. Existing support systems are removed at divorce, and no substitute structures are provided.

Parent-child pairs require a third person if they are to operate effectively. Do three-person systems also demand certain conditions so that they can survive and function adequately? Unfortunately this is a question that has seldom been asked by students of human development. Some data bearing on the answer do exist, however, largely from studies designed for other purposes. My review of the research evidence (Bronfenbrenner, 1979) points to two major types of external systems that enable families to function. The first type is the more familiar, but not as powerful as the second. It is the formal institutions and programs designed to benefit families and children. In modern, industrialized societies, a number of such programs have been developed over the past decade in response to the kinds of social changes I have reported for my own country.

The most systematic account of this kind of assistance is found in an ongoing project led by Drs. Sheila Kamerman and Alfred J. Kahn of Columbia University (Kamerman, 1980; Kamerman & Kahn, 1978, 1981). The following is a quote from their preliminary findings:

> Mothers of very young children are working outside the home in growing numbers in all industrialized countries. Two-parent two-wage-earner families (and single-parent, sole-wage-earner families) are increasingly the norm. . . . In response to this development, some countries are expanding child care services as well as cash benefits to protect child and family life. . . .
>
> However, the U.S.A. lags far behind such major European countries as France, Sweden, and F.R. Germany in the west, and the German Democratic Republic and Hungary in the east, in providing either. (Kamerman & Kahn, personal communication, 1978)

But there is a second set of conditions even more important than the first. They have to do not with formal systems but with informal ones. Some evidence comes from a five-nation study my colleagues and I are [in 1985] conducting dealing with children and families in five modern industrialized societies. We asked parents in medium-sized cities what circumstances in their lives made it easier or harder for them to bring up their child in the way they would like to. The most intense source of stress, although not the most pervasive, was financial problems, in particular unemployment, lack of money to buy necessities for the child, and money to pay for food and housing. Next in line were two areas of strain that were less acute but more pervasive: circumstances at work, particularly working hours, and neighborhood conditions, with special emphasis on physical danger such as street violence and unfriendly neighbors.

The data on perceived supports were equally instructive. Contrary to the impression one might get from the mass media, parents identified as the most important source of encouragement the child himself. Next, in keeping with the principle affirmed earlier, parents in two-parent families saw strongest support coming from the spouse. For single-parent families it was the support of relatives, friends, and neighbors. For both groups, third place was accorded to availability of satisfactory child care arrangements. Also ranking high with both groups of families were community organizations concerned with family life.

Specifically, most of the changes I have described have been occurring more rapidly among younger families with small children. As so often happens, youth is the trend setter. But even more striking is the rapid increase in all these changes as a function of the degree of economic deprivation and urbanization. This means that all of these trends reach their maximum among low-income families living in the central core of larger cities. But these general trends are not limited to the urban poor; they apply to all strata of society. Indeed, in terms of such characteristics as the proportion of working mothers, the number of adults in the home, single-parent families, or children born out of wedlock, the middle-class family of today resembles the low-income family of the early 1960s.

What does it mean for children, what does it mean for parents, what does it mean for society that more and more mothers, especially mothers of preschoolers and infants, are going to work? What does it mean that as these mothers go to work, there is no compensatory trend for husbands to go back into the home in order to take over? And what does it mean when both parents work full time there are also fewer other adults in the home who might look after the child and that in ever more families there is only one parent, who is usually also the breadwinner, working full time, living in an independent household in which she is the only adult?

At the present time [1985] in the United States, the supply of substitute care for children, care of whatever form—nursery schools, group day care, family day care, or just a body to babysit—still falls far short of the need. That kind of objective need can now be measured in millions of children under the age of six, not to mention millions more of school-age youngsters, so-called "latchkey" children, who come home to empty houses and who contribute disproportionately to the ranks of pupils with academic and behavior problems, and who have difficulties in learning to read, who are dropouts, drug users, and juvenile delinquents.

This statement introduces our ultimate concern—the well-being of children. How are they affected by the changes that have been taking place in the structure and position of the American family? Unfortunately, the only evidence social scientists have provided for answering the question is sparse and its interpretation highly speculative, for the reason that the only data we have produced are correlational. The most salient facts bearing on the issue are the following: paralleling the changes in family structure in recent years are time-series data reflecting the impaired well-being and development of children as manifested in declining levels of academic performance and rising rates of child homicide, suicide, teenage pregnancy, drug use, and juvenile delinquency (Assembly of Behavioral and Social Sciences, 1976; Bronfenbrenner, 1975).

Many of these trends find their strongest expression in the social institutions of society bearing primary responsibility for the preparation of children and youth for participation in adult life—the nation's schools. The school situation was summarized by the title of a report of the U.S. Senate Committee on the Judiciary (1975): *Our Nation's Schools—A Report Card: "A" in School Violence and Vandalism*. The report documents that the unsatisfactory state of affairs in the schools is not restricted to large cities, slum areas, or particular ethnic groups. We are now dealing with a national phenomenon. The American school has become a major breeding ground of alienation, vandalism, and violence in American society (Wynne, 1980).

The negative trends are not limited to children living in deprived socioeconomic environments. The fact is perhaps most readily apparent from data on academic achievement among the college bound. The achievement measure is the Scholastic Aptitude Test (SAT), which the majority of high school students have to take if they wish to go to college. This is, of course, a select group. Since 1963 there has been a drop of over 30 points in mathematics scores (Bronfenbrenner, 1975; Bronfenbrenner & Crouter, 1981). That is substantial. Less well known is a comprehensive study sponsored by the Ford Foundation (Harnischfeger & Wiley, 1976), revealing that the decline in academic achievement is manifested among pupils from all segments of the society. No matter how the sophisticated statisticians tried to get rid of this downward trend, they could not do it. In the words of the report:

Beyond doubt beyond differences among assessment instruments, alterations in tests, or in pupil composition, *achievement test scores have been declining for about a decade in all grades from five upwards*. Score declines are more pronounced in higher grades and in recent years. They are more severe for tests probing verbal than mathematics achievements. . . . [T]hese are the facts and they describe a national phenomenon. . . . [W]e reported lowered test scores in diverse areas: English, writing, literature, vocabulary, reading, social studies, mathematics, and natural sciences. (pp. 115–116, 118)

The destructive consequences of poverty, educational impairment, and the hectic pace of daily life on the competence and character of future generations are so great that their elimination must be given priority at the national and international level. Such an undertaking is a long-term endeavor, and children can't wait.

Proposals for Reform

What supports can society give? I have four answers to that question. Each of them requires a change in our present way of life that is not likely to come to pass quickly, if at all. For this reason, I call them "preposterous proposals."

Preposterous Proposal I. It is now possible for a young person 18 years of age to graduate from an American high school without ever having had to do a piece of work on which someone else depended. Equally disastrous from this same perspective, it is possible for a young person, female as well as male, to graduate from high school, college, or university without ever having held a baby in his or her arms for longer than a few seconds, without ever having had to comfort or assist another human being who really needed help. Yet all of us, sooner or later, will desperately require such comfort and care, and no society can sustain itself unless its members have learned the motivations, sensitivities, and skills that such caring demands.

For some years I have been advocating the introduction in our schools, from the earliest grades onward, of what I have called a *curriculum for caring.* The purpose of this curriculum would be not to learn about caring but to engage in it: that is, children, boys as well as girls, would be asked to take responsibility for spending time with and caring for others—old people, younger children, the sick, and the lonely. The curriculum for caring has special significance for the increasing numbers of older children (and many of them not so old) who are in fact looking after their younger brothers and sisters in the absence of adequate and affordable day care services in our country. Obviously, such caring activities could not be restricted to the school; they would have to be carried out in the outside community. It would be desirable to locate caring institutions, such as day care centers, adjacent to or even within the school, but it would be even more important for the young caregivers to come to know the environments and the people in the lives of their charges. For example, older children taking responsibility for younger ones should come to know the latter's parents and become acquainted with the places where their charges live by escorting them home from school. In this way the children would come to know firsthand the living conditions of the families in their community. This is surely an essential aspect of public education in a free society; yet it is one that we have neglected almost completely.

The consequences of this neglect are now before us—a generation of Americans, and of American leaders, many of whom do not understand the hard realities of what it means to be the parent of a young child; to be poor; to be sick; to be unable to get a job; or to ensure food, shelter, and health for one's family. That neglect has a terrible economic cost that, like inflation, escalates with each succeeding year. If we wish to preserve our vitality as a nation, we cannot afford to pay the price.

Preposterous Proposal II. This proposal addresses the great American dilemma of the 1980s: the conflict between the demands of work and family. One effective, but unlikely, solution to the problem requires a radical change in the American way of life such that the prevailing pattern of employment for both men and women is to work three-quarters time. The remaining quarter would be free for family activities, visiting friends and relatives, participating in the life of one's neighborhood and community, and looking at the sunset—in short, a quarter of one's life for living. The introduction of such a pattern would have the additional fringe benefit of reduced unemployment, since new cadres would be needed to maintain national levels of production.

Under what circumstances could such a revolutionary proposal be adopted in American society? This query brings us to the next and even more outlandish proposal.

Preposterous Proposal III. In order to meet the needs of families created by the rapid and profound social changes that have been taking place in recent years, it will be necessary to introduce significant changes in public policy and practice in domains outside the family itself. Such innovations will require broad vision and hard-headed decisions by those persons who occupy positions of power and responsibility in both the public and the private sectors. Despite the impressive achievements of the women's movement, the fact remains that the overwhelming majority of persons in such influential positions today are men.

Given the prevailing pattern in the upbringing of children and youth in American society, males are particularly likely, from earliest childhood, to have been isolated from experiences of caring or from close association with those needing care (Gilligan, 1977). As a result, men are less able to understand the needs of such persons, the circumstances in which they live, their human potential, the necessity and nature of the support systems required to realize this potential, and the very practical social and economic gains that would be achieved as a result. In contrast, those in our society who possess such experience and knowledge are predominantly women, not due to innate sex differences in caring aptitude but because women confront these situations more often than men in the course of their lives. Women, however, typically do not occupy the positions of power that would permit their experience and knowledge to be translated into public policy and practice. This state of affairs calls for a substantial increase in the number of women in positions of decision making and power both in the public and private sector.

Preposterous Proposal IV. The basis for this final and most pressing recommendation is found in a research trajectory reaching back almost half a century. My Cornell colleague Glen Elder (Elder, 1974, 1979; Elder & Rockwell, 1979) has been exploiting archival data from two longitudinal studies in order to trace the impact of the Great Depression on the subsequent development of children whose families had been subjected to severe economic stress. Elder took advantage of this natural experiment to divide each of the two samples into two otherwise comparable groups, differentiated on the basis of whether the loss of income as a result of the Depression exceeded or fell short of 35%. The fact that the youngsters in one sample were eight years older than those in the other permitted a comparison of the effects of the Depression on children who were adolescents when their families became economically deprived versus those who were still young children.

The results for the two groups presented a dramatic contrast. Paradoxically, for youngsters who were teenagers during the Depression years, the family's economic deprivation appeared to have a salutary effect on their subsequent development. They did better in school, were more likely to go to college, had happier marriages, exhibited more successful work careers, and, in general, achieved greater satisfaction in life, both by their own and by societal standards, than nondeprived children of the same SES. These favorable outcomes were more pronounced for adolescents from middle-class backgrounds but were evident among their lower-class counterparts as well. Elder hypothesized that the loss of economic security forced the family to mobilize its own human resources, including those of its teenagers. The youths had to take on new responsibilities to work toward the goal of getting and keeping the family on its feet. This experience provided them with effective training in initiative, responsibility, and cooperation. In the words of the banished duke, "Sweet are the uses of adversity."

Alas, adversity was not so sweet for children who were still preschoolers when their families suffered economic loss. Compared to controls from nondeprived families, these youngsters subsequently did less well in school, showed less stable and successful work histories, and exhibited more emotional and social difficulties, some still apparent in middle adulthood.

The pertinence of Elder's research for the current scene is underscored by two recent Associated Press surveys (Roberts, 1980; White, 1980) of social agencies around the country. These agencies reported a rapid rise in the incidence of family conflict and child abuse directly related to the impact of increasing inflation, energy costs, and, especially, unemployment of the family breadwinner. It would appear that the immediate costs of current economic policies are being paid primarily in prices that are difficult to index—the anguish and pain of young parents and their children, particularly at very young ages, who are living under progressively more stringent economic conditions.

These developments take on added significance in the light of the severe cuts in programs and resources hitherto available to low-income families in the U.S. That major reductions in federal spending are absolutely essential cannot be questioned. The crucial issue is what, or more pointedly, who is being cut. Equally critical is the way in which the remaining funds are being used. What kinds of programs are to be retained, and how will they be reorganized to achieve their maximal impact? The response to this question constitutes our fourth and final preposterous proposal. It argues nothing less than the *reorganization of federal programs now based on a deficit model into new structures that emphasize empowerment, initiative, and self-respect.*

As these words are being written [1985], two new developments are occurring on the national scene that give these issues even graver significance. Family policies of long standing are being disowned, and the programs that they sustain are being dismantled, with little more than cursory examination of the consequences of such decisions for the well-being of the nation's families and children. Even more awesome, however, is the fact that these changes are receiving massive support from the general public. There is a new separatism across the land. The fragmentation and isolation first seen in the world of families is now being manifested in all the institutions and segments of our society. In the public and in the private sector, there is a turning away from concern with the problems of others to a preoccupation with maintaining and maximizing the status and power of particular interest groups. Such privatism threatens the basic social contract on which our American society is based, for we were founded, and have thus far sustained ourselves, on the principle of *e pluribus unum*. What has happened to the *unum*? What is the state of the *union*?

These questions would seem to take us far beyond the domain of children and families. The very fact that this seems to be so points to the heart of the problem. One telling criterion of the worth of a society—a criterion that stands the test of history—is the concern of one generation for the next. As we enter our third century, we Americans, compared to other industrialized societies, appear to be abandoning that criterion. Yet we are a curious country. Not bound by age-old traditions, we tend, in the last analysis, to act more on pragmatic than on ideological grounds. But we do so only at the last possible moment; we make it by the skin of our teeth. By the skin of our teeth we won the revolution that gave birth to our republic; by the skin of our teeth we survived our Civil War; by the skin of our teeth we recovered from the Great Depression; by the skin of our teeth we got out of Vietnam. Today there are grounds for believing that we face an even more ominous challenge to our national vitality, this time once again on our own ground. It would appear that the process of making human beings human is breaking down in American society. To make it work again, we must reweave the unraveling social fabric and revitalize the human bonds essential to sustaining the well-being and development of both present and future generations.

References

Assembly of Behavioral and Social Sciences, Advisory Committee on Child Development. (1976). *Toward a national policy for children and families.* Washington, DC: National Academy of Sciences.

Bane, M. J. (1976). *Here to stay: American families in the twentieth century.* New York: Basic Books.

Bronfenbrenner, U. (1975). Reality and research in the ecology of human development. *Proceedings of the American Philosophical Society, 119,* 439–469.

Bronfenbrenner, U. (1979). *The ecology of human development: Experiments by nature and design.* Cambridge, MA: Harvard University Press.

Bronfenbrenner, U., & Crouter, A. C. (1981). *Work and family through time and space.* Chapter prepared for the National Academy of Sciences Panel on Work, Family, and Community.

Elder, G. H., Jr. (1974). *Children of the Great Depression.* Chicago: University of Chicago Press.

Elder, G. H., Jr. (1979). Historical change in life patterns and personality. In P. Baltes & O. Brim (Eds.), *Life-span development and behavior* (Vol. 2, pp. 117–159). New York: Academic Press.

Elder, G. H., Jr., & Rockwell, R. C. (1979). The life-course approach and human development: An ecological perspective. *International Journal of Behavioral Development, 2,* 1–21.

Gilligan, C. (1977). In a different voice: Women's conception of self and of morality. *Harvard Educational Review, 47,* 196–204.

Harnischfeger, A., & Wiley, D. E. (1975). *Achievement test score decline: Do we need to worry?* St. Louis, MO: CEMREL.

Hetherington, E. M., Cox, M., & Cox, R. (1978). The aftermath of divorce. In J. H. Stevens Jr. & M. Matthews (Eds.), *Mother-child, father-child relations* (pp. 149–176). Washington, DC: National Association for the Education of Young Children.

Hetherington, E. M., Cox, M., & Cox, R. (1979a). The development of children in mother-headed families. In H. Hoffman & D. Reiss (Eds.), *The American family: Dying or developing* (pp. 117–146). New York: Plenum.

Hetherington, E. M., Cox, M., & Cox, R. (1979b). Play and social interaction in children following divorce. *Journal of Social Issues, 35*(4), 26–49.

Kamerman, S. B. (1980). *Parenting in an unresponsive society.* New York: Free Press.

Kamerman, S. B., &. Kahn, A. J. (1978). *Family policy: Government and families in fourteen countries.* New York: Columbia University Press.

Kamerman, S. B., & Kahn, A. J. (1981). *Child care: Family benefits and working parents.* New York: Columbia University Press.

Roberts, S. V. (1980, May 17). Economic squabble sets off family tensions. *New York Times.*

U.S. Bureau of the Census. (1981). *Current populations reports, Series P-20. Marital status and living arrangements, March 1980.* Washington, DC: Government Printing Office.

U.S. Senate, Committee on the Judiciary. (1975). *Our nation's schools—A report card: "A" in school violence and vandalism.* Preliminary report of the Subcommittee to Investigate Juvenile Delinquency. Washington, DC: Government Printing Office.

White, J. S. (1980, October 4). Unemployment scene as another killer disease. Associated Press Dispatch, *Ithaca Journal.*

Wynne, E. (1980). *Looking at schools: Good, bad, and indifferent.* Lexington, MA: Lexington.

Article 18

Strengthening Family Systems

This article is a plea for developmental scientists to engage in experimental interventions aimed at meeting the needs of children. Its theme is caring. Children need the consistent and reliable care of their parents and other adults, but to provide that care parents need the support of employers, schools, and the society as a whole. Just as we are becoming more aware that we have the capacity to destroy the natural environment and must take vigorous steps to preserve it, we must use our growing knowledge of the ecology of human development to protect and strengthen it in the face of threats we have unwittingly created.

The unthinking exercise of massive technological power, and an unquestioning acquiescence to the demands of industrialization, can unleash forces that, if left unbridled, can destroy the human ecosystem. Based in the family unit, but extending far beyond, this ecosystem comprises the social fabric that sustains our capacity to live and work together effectively and to raise our children and youth to become competent and compassionate members of our society.

The heart of our social system is the family. If we are to maintain the health of our society, we must discover the best means of nurturing that heart. What does a family system need to grow and succeed? What do children, our society's future, need within that system to thrive? These

Source: Bronfenbrenner, U. (1988). Strengthening family systems. In E. F. Zigler & M. Frank (Eds.), *The parental leave crisis: Toward a national policy* (pp. 143–160). New Haven, CT: Yale University Press.

questions point to an ecological approach to the study of human development. Forming the foundation for scholarly research over the past decade, this approach seeks to clarify and define what conditions are best suited to our development as individuals and as members of society. In this regard, the ecology of human development has been defined as "the progressive, mutual accommodation between the developing person and the changing properties of the immediate and broader contexts in which the person lives" (Bronfenbrenner, 1979a, p. 21).

Like a set of Russian dolls, the contexts of human development work in a nested fashion, each one expanding beyond but containing the smaller one. Each one also simultaneously influences and is influenced by the others. Thus the context of the family fits into that of the neighborhood; the context of the neighborhood into the larger contexts of city, work, and government; and all contexts into the largest context of culture. Whatever factors affect any larger context will filter down to affect the innermost unit, the family (Bronfenbrenner, 1979b).

The two contexts of work and family represent central activities necessary for human survival. Work serves as a means for transforming our environment. From an evolutionary viewpoint, human beings are remarkable in their capacity to make such transformations. It is primarily parents who show us how environments can be changed and thus prepare us for the world of work. To a greater extent than for any other living creature, the capacity of human offspring to survive and develop depends on care and close association in activity with older members of the species. Without extended parenting, we are unable to perform in the world we have created.

Yet today, particularly in the United States, these two principal contexts for human development, family and work, are often pitted against each other. Given the growing disarray in the lives of families and children, our society needs to move rapidly to reunify these two key spheres of activity. The testimony of this book reveals a dilemma that many working parents feel: all too often a person cannot do a good job in one sphere without making sacrifices in the other. Nowadays, with work frequently an economic necessity for both parents, less by decision than by default, we allow our families and our children to absorb the stress and suffer the consequences.

In this chapter I attempt to delineate the nature of the family ecosystem and its scope; the processes taking place within it; how and why the work-parenting conflict is affecting that structure; and what can be done to retard or even to reverse prevailing trends of the work-family conflict.

Environmental Principles of Development

Because this chapter specifically addresses the issue of children's development in regard to the parenting relationship, my focus is on children's needs: What are the implications of mass societal changes for the development of children? To examine this issue, it is necessary to determine which environmental and social conditions are most crucial for the development of human beings from early childhood on. In all analysis of the available knowledge on this topic, I have found it sobering to discover that the principal conclusions from these data could be summarized in two tentative formulations. Shorn of their technical terminology, the two statements do not sound very earthshaking; but when applied to our present world, they may shake us up nevertheless.

1. In order to develop normally, a child needs the enduring, irrational involvement of one or more adults in care of and in joint activity with that child. In short, *somebody has to be crazy about that kid*. Someone also has to be there, and to be doing something—not alone but *together* with the child. This brings us to the next point, which defines a second environmental condition equally essential if development is to occur.

2. The involvement of one or more adults in joint activity with the child requires public policies and practices that provide opportunity, status, resources, encouragement, stability, example, and, above all, *time* for parenthood, primarily by parents but also by other adults in the child's environment, both *within and outside the home*.

The two formulations epitomize much of what we know about human development, for they identify the two environmental conditions both necessary and desirable for human learning and human development, for enabling us to become human.

The family is at the heart of the first formulation. Of all the settings that help make us human, the family provides the most important developmental conditions: the love and care that a child needs to thrive. A healthy child and future adult is one who has such devoted people actively engaged in its life—those who love it, spend time with it, challenge it, and are interested in what it does and wants to do, in what it accomplishes from day to day. Other settings, such as school, church, or day care, are important to a child's development, but none can replace this basic unit of our social system: *the family is the most humane, the most powerful, and by far the most economical system known for making and keeping human beings human.*

Further, it is the family that determines our capacity to function effectively and to profit from later experience in the other contexts in which human beings live and grow—the school, peer group, higher education, business, community, and our society as a whole. In all those settings, what we learn, as well as what we can contribute, depends on the families we come from and the families in which we now live. This is true from early childhood on, until the day we die.

But the family is not without its vulnerabilities. To a far greater extent than we have previously imagined, the capacity of the family to function effectively, to create and sustain competent and compassionate human beings, depends on the support of other, larger contexts. Either social support (such as a business providing family benefits for its workers) or lack of support filters down to the innermost social unit, the family, and determines the confidence or stress that parents bring to their relations with their child. Even the decreased interaction resulting from the stresses and demands of work can impair the quality and effectiveness of the parent-child bond.

Family Changes and Their Effects

That the family is changing and under great stress seem to be common knowledge—if we are willing to admit it. Today the topic is, once again, in vogue. The mass magazines from *Newsweek* and *Time* to *Woman's Day, Ms.,* and *Esquire* carry feature stories on the subject, every national organization wants an address on this topic at its annual convention, and the major television networks produce documentaries on the family breakup, complete with statistics and case studies. Nowadays, we all know about the rocket rise in single-parent homes (today more than a fifth of the nation's children reside within them), the decline of extended-family households (they are almost gone now, save among blacks and ethnic minorities), and the falling birthrate (except among unwed teenage girls). In short, American families—adults and children sharing a household—are getting smaller.

So far as the development of the young is concerned, one of the most consequential changes is the rise in maternal employment. In this respect, 1978 was a landmark year: for the first time, the majority of American mothers were in the labor force. Since 1970, the increase has been greatest among mothers of children under three, but regardless of the ages of their children, the majority of working mothers are employed full time. Given current economic pressure and aspirations, few have any other choice.

The Phenomenon of Working Mothers

As many more mothers go to work, and fathers do not usually go back into the home, there are fewer adults left in the household to look after the child (Bronfenbrenner & Crouter, 1982). In increasing numbers of families, there is only one parent, usually the breadwinner, and that parent works full time. What is the significance of the conditions for the requirement stipulated in the second statement of "opportunity, status, resources, encouragement, stability, example, and above all time for parenthood"? What does this complex of circumstances imply, in turn, for the earlier statement? To be sure, when parents are working full time, their irrational involvement with the child may not diminish, it may even increase. But what happens to joint activity?

Evidence shows that, in contrast to other modern nations, American society has given little recognition to the demands of parenting and thus has left parents with little time to meet those demands. Frighteningly, in many families, joint activity never begins—the time needed to build foundations is denied them from the start. An overwhelming number of new mothers, both single and married, are expected to return to work within three or four weeks of an infant's birth. Parenting by fathers is given even less time and encouragement. A four-week or two-week leave treats childbirth as a purely physical experience, and the developing parent-infant relationship is ignored. In a recent provocative book, *Working and Caring,* T. Berry Brazelton (1985) delineates four stages necessary to build a relationship of joining interaction and mutual trust. At the end of four weeks, Stage 1 is barely completed. Mothers report that they deal with this loss through denial: denial of the infant's and their own emotional and interactive needs, lest they perform badly at work and lose jobs they cannot afford to lose. The question is not just what happens to time for parenting but what happens to the development of the infant.

With such demands on a parent's time, the infant is in danger of becoming an object, another duty to be taken care of. A typical day for working parents might be as follows: get up, dress for work, change baby, help the children dress, fix breakfast, feed the children, drop off children at day care, go to work, leave work, pick up children, go home, feed the baby, prepare dinner, eat dinner, play if there is time, clean up, put children to bed. To be sure, there is a lot of activity, but not much that can be joint or interactive. Nor are parents given much time for themselves. Furthermore, this schedule may not be one the family is permitted to grow into, establishing interactive patterns first and then adapting them to outside demands. One of the great changes in child care over the last few years is the increasing number of three- and four-week-old infants—even two-week-old infants—in day care centers. Clearly, such conditions imposed by the work-parenting conflict can make it difficult to establish the good foundation of joint activity so necessary to the growth and maturation of the young child.

Although the issue of an infant care leave focuses mainly on the first year of life, the conflict between the demands of work and parenting can continue throughout much of a child's life. In *Parenting in an Unresponsive Society*, Kamerman (1980) analyzes the principal findings of a survey of 200 working mothers in both single- and two-parent families. Two themes that emerge from this study have special relevance to a family leave plan. The first is the severe stress reported by both single parents and two-worker families around the issue of obtaining satisfactory child care. In contemporary American society, providing for such care often requires a delicately orchestrated schedule combining the use of day care centers, babysitters, and shifting parental responsibilities. The strains generated by the task of establishing and maintaining these complex arrangements are documented in both statistical data and case study vignettes. The second theme emerging from the survey relates to the heightened stress experienced by the mother in single-parent households, where all the burdens of work, child rearing, and coordinating child care arrangements fall on her shoulders. In such situations, the desire for parenting and caring may be there, but the "time for parenthood" may be rapidly diminished.

There is a further aspect to this stress that parents may feel. Currently, parents are provided leave time for their own needs—but often not for their children's needs. As a result, putting first things first, parents often use their own leave time not to care for their own health or personal needs but to attend to their children's illnesses or problems. Such a confounding of leave time to meet too many demands or to cover too many contingencies allows parents little time for their own needs, and stress begins to build.

The Changing American Family

Regrettably, as yet too few investigators have taken the next step of examining the impact of familial stress on the behavior and development of children. One review of the research (Bronfenbrenner & Crouter, 1982) gave some evidence that conflict between work and family roles reduces both the quantity and the quality of parent-child interaction and is associated with lower achievement in school, particularly among boys. The studies in this area are weakened, however, by the failure to establish the successive causal links between the objective conditions at work and at home, the degree and nature of stress generated by these conditions, their effect on family functioning, and the resultant impact on the behavior and development of the child. This causal chain is now being delineated in relation to single-parent families (Dornbusch et al., 1985; Hetherington, Cox, & Cox, 1978, 1979; Steinberg, 1987). For example, Hetherington and her colleagues traced the progressive deterioration in mother-child inter-action following divorce and its disruptive carryover effects on the social behavior and academic performance of children in school.

While some working parents may thrive on multiple demands on their time and energy, the opposite also often occurs. In addition, parents who work are often overwhelmed by having too much asked of them by too many people. As we have seen, parents are caught up by social and eco-nomic forces over which they have little control. They do not choose work over parenting; rather, they struggle to survive the conflicts of the two. And circumstantial evidence at least suggests that children are the ones who pay the price.

For these reasons, it is instructive to examine trends in data on children that parallel those that have taken place for families. The most salient statistics are time-series data reflecting the impaired well-being and devel-opment of children as manifested in declining levels of academic perfor-mance and rising rates of child homicide, suicide, teenage pregnancy, drug use, and juvenile delinquency (Assembly of Behavioral and Social Sciences, 1976; Bronfenbrenner, 1986a, 1986b; U.S. Senate Committee on the Judiciary, 1975).

The title of a Senate report published a decade ago still applies to the present scene: *The Nation's Schools—A Report Card: "A" in School Violence and Vandalism* (U.S. Senate Committee on the Judiciary, 1975). Then, as now, the pattern was not restricted to larger cities, slum areas, or particu-lar ethnic groups. As the title implies, school violence is a national phe-nomenon. Every school now has its security budget and often a security force. As Wynne (1980) has documented, the American school has become a breeding ground of alienation, vandalism, and violence.

These trends constitute danger signs for American society. Three additional features are especially disquieting. First, all of the demographic changes are occurring more rapidly among younger families with small children and are increasing in direct proportion to economic deprivation and urbanization, reaching their maximum in low-income families living in the central core of our large cities (Assembly of Behavioral and Social Sciences, 1976; Bronfenbrenner, 1986a, 1986b). Second, the rate of change has not been constant but has accelerated markedly since the mid-1960s.

It was precisely during this same period that the scope and budgets of federally sponsored programs directed at low-income families were expanded. Yet it is clear that this expansion was not adequate to arrest, let alone reverse, the demographic trends reflecting disarray in the lives of families and children. The third and perhaps most telling fact revealed in the data is that the general trend is not limited to the urban poor; it applies to all strata of society. Indeed, in terms of the proportion of working mothers, number of adults in the home, single-parent families, teenage pregnancy, falling achievement scores, or exposure to vandalism and violence in the schools, the experiences of middle-class families today [1987] increasingly resemble those of low-income families of the 1960s. It is this expanding pattern of change that makes the search for new strategies an imperative for those concerned with the well-being and development of children in the 1980s. As a society, America—especially industrial America—needs to recognize that the family represents the most critical unit of society. Without time for and recognition of parenting as the key nurturant force in all of society, we are faced with the potential disintegration of our social fabric.

The Need for a National Infant Care Leave Policy

The Deficit Model

Until recently, the concept of the family has received attention in America in direct relation to the degree of its demise. Repairing a faltering family has been at the base of many public policies and practices, both past and present. I call this approach the *deficit model:* in order to get help, a family has to prove that it has become "inadequate." Yet this very inadequacy is indirectly a product of public attitudes. We in America tend to believe that family integration and growth come naturally and that family responsibility is a private matter—even as we put its members in a position that leaves little support or time for family life. The belief that our families need no national recognition or protection paradoxically leads to more families than ever needing that support.

When a family is finally inadequate enough, it can get some support. The deficit model pervades all arenas, but its distinctive properties are revealed in highest relief in our welfare system. To qualify for help, potential recipients must first prove over and over, with corroborating documentation, that they and their children are in fact the inadequate persons they claim to be. Moreover, our mode of service is categorical: to obtain needed help, potential recipients must first be classified into the types of problems they represent. The only way in which they become whole human beings again is to have enough things wrong. Then they can be defined, and dealt with, as "problem children," or, better still for bureaucratic purposes, as "multiproblem families."

Business and the Infant Care Leave Policy

Alternatives to the deficit model are beginning to emerge in several spheres. The first arises from a dawning national recognition of the need for support for parenting. Currently [1987] before Congress, the proposed Family and Medical Act would require that businesses provide extended time for new parents to spend with their infants before returning to work and also that parents who must attend to time-consuming, family problems—such as a child's illness—be given the time and support to do so. The act is seriously deficient in one area—financial provision during the leave time—but it does recognize the need for both time to parent and job protection during that time.

Businesses are also beginning to address independently the conflict between work and parenting. As documented in a recent review by Kamerman and Kingston (1982), an increasing number of public and private employers are offering their employees fringe benefits designed to be responsive to family needs. Among them are such provisions as maternity leaves, family health plans, on-site day care, part-time jobs, job sharing, sick leave for parents when children are ill, and flextime. The last involves a schedule whereby employees work full time but have some freedom in determining hours of arrival and departure. Nollen and Martin (1978) estimated that 2.5 to 3.5 million workers (6% of the total labor force) are in some variation of flextime. These businesses and corporations recognize that employee contribution and family satisfaction have a direct relationship to each other.

Two problems arise as businesses address the parenting-work conflict without a coherent national policy. The provision of family benefits associated with work has been concentrated primarily in large corporations, whose employees are already in a more favored economic position. By contrast, those most in need of such benefits, such as heads of single-parent households or of large families, are likely to have low-paying jobs or no jobs at all. This circumstance therefore serves to widen the already existing gap between the rich and the poor.

Further, many small and midsize businesses, and even large ones, choose not to address the parent-work conflict because they believe they cannot afford to provide family leaves. Employers may not recognize the increased benefits to themselves and society in general that can accrue if they accept and provide for the duality of work and parenting. What is needed now, however, is not numerous, small, disparate leave policies but an overall, societal awareness of and commitment to the importance of family integrity to society at large. A national policy for an infant care and parenting leave represents a first step in achieving that awareness and needed change in direction.

There is evidence that, in the United States, work-associated family benefits may not by themselves have much impact on the capacity of families to function effectively in their child-rearing role. For example, Bohen and Viveros-Long (1981) obtained measures of family strain and of participation in home activities from employees working in two federal agencies, one of which operated with flexible hours and the other of which did not. Ironically, significant differences favoring flextime were found for only one group of families— those without children. Two explanations were proposed for the absence of effects on families with children: first, that the arrangement did not go far enough to meet the complex scheduling problems experienced by today's parents; second, that child-rearing values were not sufficiently salient to ensure that the flexible time would be used for parental activities.

Thought needs to be given to policies through which families can be supported by all of society—policies fostering attitudes and actions that recognize, maintain, and strengthen families. We need to create social forms that encourage and allow us to help one another; an infant care leave is but one of those forms. The following hypothetical cases address three crucial contexts affecting the well-being and development of children in contemporary society: the school, the family's social networks, and the parents' world of work.

Facing the Future

The last problem in the establishment of a national infant care and family leave policy is perhaps the most important one we face as a nation: it concerns the millions of families who would be unaffected by such a policy because the parents are not employed, come from a background not conducive to employment, and have no future in employment. Until these families are rewoven into the fabric of society, the parenting and family crisis can never truly be resolved. Work and parenting are but two halves of a social whole: parenting is that process of creating mature and productive adults who in turn, through their work and service, contribute to society.

The implications of the foregoing evidence and argument are underscored by recent census figures and research findings. The official U.S. Census report an family income for 1980 documented what it described as "the largest decline in family income in the past World War II period," resulting in the addition of 29.3 million persons below the poverty level, for a total of 13% of the U.S. population (U.S. Bureau of the Census, 1981, p. 1). By 1981, this figure had risen to 31.8 million (U.S. Bureau of the Census, 1982, p. 1). As revealed in the tables accompanying the report, the poverty rates for children were even higher, especially for the very young. Specifically, as of March 1984, more than one fourth (22%) of all children in America up to the age of six were living in families below the poverty line, compared to 13% for the population as a whole and 16% for those under 65. The poverty line is based on the minimum income sufficient to meet the cost of the Department of Agriculture's economy food plan. The index is adjusted to reflect the different consumption requirements of families based on size, composition, and other relevant demographic factors.

The effects of this most recent economic downturn (1986) are already being reflected in research findings. In a longitudinal design, Steinberg, Catalano, and Dooley (1981) studied the effects of inflation on 8,000 families in California. Correlational analyses of data over a 30-month period revealed that increases in child abuse were preceded by periods of high job loss, thus confirming the authors' hypothesis that "undesirable economic change leads to increased child maltreatment" (p. 975). An Associated Press report on this research begins with the lead sentence: "The toll of children battered, maimed, and slain by parents and other relatives is climbing, and experts say the economy—especially unemployment—appears to be a key factor" (Hyman, 1982). Alas, for once the media did not exaggerate the facts.

Such findings give added significance to the growing number of children being cast into poverty in our own time. They also raise questions about the severe cuts that have been put in force affecting programs and resources made available to low-income families and their children in the United States. Even more destructive than these cuts is the implicit philosophy that we hold as a nation toward the economic needs of families. The United States fails to recognize the importance of jobs for the survival of families, not only economically, but—what is even more important—psychologically. By tolerating growing unemployment now, the United States risks creating new generations of unemployable Americans.

There are those who say that that is exactly what we are doing, that Americans have ceased to care about each other. Such critics claim to see the rise of a new separatism across the land, a turning away from a concern with the problems of others to a preoccupation with maintaining and maximizing the status and power of particular groups. To be sure, such phenomena are occurring in some segments of American society, but I do not believe that they constitute the broader and deeper streams and strengths of contemporary America. At this moment, the best of America is conscience-stricken and confused. The country is momentarily immobilized by the conflict between the distinctive values derived from its past and the dissonant realities created by the economic and social changes taking place not only in the United States but around the world. The vacuum created by this temporary inertia leaves the field open to destructive forces that can divide the nation. Once again the Union is threatened, not the political union of the states, but the spiritual union of the basic parts of our pluralistic society—the diverse families, communities, generations, and religious and cultural groups that make the magic of America. The nation was founded, and has thus far been sustained, on the principle of *e pluribus unum*. What has happened to the *unum*? What is the state of the union?

These questions would seem to take us far beyond the domain of child and family policy, yet this fact points to the heart of the problem. One telling criterion of the worth of a society—a criterion that stands the test of history—is *the concern of one generation for the next*. A nation's child and family policy is the measure of that concern. Under these circumstances, what is the responsibility of the developmental researcher concerned with policy issues at a time of national crisis? The answer to that question leads in two directions. Social scientists are subject to an ethical code that prohibits them from exposing children to situations that are injurious to their welfare. Unfortunately, there is no such restriction on the nation as a whole or on its duly empowered leaders and policy makers. The latter are free to run their economic and social experiments without such niceties as prior parental consent or review by qualified professionals. It remains the responsibility of social scientists, however, to monitor these experiments and give early warning of any unintended effects. What will be the consequences of cutting back funds for prenatal care, child nutrition and health, day care, and recreational and vocational programs for school-age children? What will be the consequences of refusing to create a national mandate providing time for essential parenting? In assessing these effects, researchers must use the best scientific methods at their command. There may be difficulties in finding matched control groups, but there should be no problem with sample size. It is the irony and limitation of our science that the greater the harm done to children, the more we stand to learn about the environmental conditions that are essential for the human condition. It therefore becomes our professional obligation to employ the most advanced research designs at our disposal in order to forestall the tragic opportunity of significantly expanding our knowledge about the limits of the human conditions for developing healthy human beings.

The responsibilities of the researcher extend beyond pure investigation, especially in a time of national crisis. Scientists in our field must be willing to draw on their knowledge and imagination in order to contribute to the design of social inventions: policies and strategies that can help to sustain and enhance our most precious human resources—the nation's children.

References

Assembly of Behavioral and Social Sciences, Advisory Committee on Child Development. (1976). *Toward a national policy for children and families.* Washington, DC: National Academy of Sciences.

Bohen, H. H., & Viveros-Long, A. (1981). *Balancing jobs and family life.* Philadelphia: Temple University Press.

Brazelton, T. B. (1985). *Working and caring.* Boston: Addison-Wesley.

Bronfenbrenner, U. (1979a). Beyond the deficit model in child and family policy. *Teachers College Record, 81*(1), 95–104.

Bronfenbrenner, U. (1979b). *The ecology of human development: Experiments by nature and design.* Cambridge, MA: Harvard University Press.

Bronfenbrenner, U. (1986a). Alienation and the four worlds of childhood. *Phi Delta Kappan, 67,* 430–436.

Bronfenbrenner, U. (1986b). The war on poverty: Won or lost? America's children in poverty: 1959–1985. *Newsletter of the Division of Child, Youth, and Family Services, 9,* 2–3.

Bronfenbrenner, U., & Crouter, A. C. (1982). Work and family through time and space. In S. B. Kamerman & P. Kingston (Eds.), *Families that work: Children in a changing world* (pp. 39–83). Washington, DC: National Academy Press.

Dornbusch, S. M., Carismith, J. M., Bushwall, S. J., Ritter, P. L., Leiderman, H., Hastorf, A. H., & Gross, R. T. (1985). Single parents, extended households, and the control of adolescence. *Child Development 56,* 326–341.

Hetherington, E. M., Cox, M., & Cox, R. (1978). *Mother-child, father-child relations.* Washington, DC: National Association of the Education of Young Children.

Hetherington, E. M., Cox. M., & Cox, R. (1979). Play and social interaction in children following divorce. *Journal of Social Issues, 35*(4), 26–49.

Hyman, J. (1982). Economy blamed for increase in child abuse. Associated Press.

Kamerman, S. B. (1980). *Parenting in an unresponsive society.* New York: Free Press.

Kamerman, S. B., & Kingston, P. (Eds.). (1982). *Families that work: Children in a changing world.* Washington, DC: National Academy Press.

Nollen, S.D., & Martin, V. (1978). *Alternative work schedules.* New York: AMICOM.

Steinberg, L. D. (1987). Single parents, step parents, and the susceptibility of adolescents to antisocial peer pressure. *Child Development, 58,* 269–275.

Steinberg, L. D., Catalano, R., & Dooley, D. (1981). Economic antecedents for child abuse and neglect. *Child Development, 52,* 975–985.

U.S. Bureau of the Census. (1981). *Money income and poverty status of families and persons in the United States* (Current Population Reports, Series P-60, No. 127). Washington, DC: Government Printing Office.

U.S. Bureau of the Census. (1982). *Money income and poverty status of families and persons in the United States* (Current Population Reports, Series P-60, No. 134). Washington, DC: Government Printing Office.

U.S. Senate Committee on the Judiciary. (1975). *Our nation's schools—A report card: "A" in school violence and vandalism.* Washington, DC: Government Printing Office.

Wynne, E. (1980). *Looking at schools: Good, bad, and indifferent.* Lexington, MA: Heath Lexington.

Article 19

Child Care in the Anglo-Saxon Mode

The shared Anglo-Saxon heritage of the United States, the United Kingdom, and Canada, mixed and matched by other ethnic traditions in all three countries, contributes to distinctive approaches to child care that differ from those found in other countries. National child care policies are examined in this article in relation to the status of children and families, other types of family support systems, family structure, and economic resources. The cross-national comparison yields some proposals for new directions in U.S. child care policies.

Family Support Systems

When one compares the English-speaking countries with other modern nations from this perspective, the results are hardly encouraging. Canada's *Report of the Task Force on Child Care* (Cooke, 1986) concluded that the United States, Canada, and the United Kingdom all rate in the bottom third of the countries studied with respect to coverage of child care. The same pattern reappears with respect to other types of family support. For example, the average legislated maternity leave in the Scandinavian countries is 34 weeks, in the Eastern European countries is 23 weeks, and

Source: Bronfenbrenner, U. (1992). Child care in the Anglo-Saxon mode. In M. E. Lamb, K. J. Sternberg, C. P. Hwang, & A. G. Broberg (Eds.), *Child care in context* (pp. 281–291). Hillsdale, NJ: Lawrence Erlbaum.

in Western Europe and Canada is 16 to 17 weeks. By contrast, the United Kingdom offers only 6 weeks, and in the United States there are no statutory requirements (Towson, 1985).

On a broader front, the comparative lack of family support systems in the United States is so extreme as to make it unique among modern nations. The extent of this uniqueness is well reflected in the following passages from a recent assessment of the status of social policies and practices relating to children in Europe and the United States.

Almost all European countries—including Belgium, Denmark, France, Italy, and West Germany—provide free (or low-fee) and optional, public or privately financed preschool or child care programs for children about age 3 (or younger) to school age. The United Kingdom does not have such a system; Canada is currently debating a substantial expansion. All the countries mentioned thus far, and many others including Japan, but not the United States, provide health insurance or health services for children and their families. All have somewhat comparable social insurance systems. . . . The U.S. unemployment insurance system compares unfavorably in both replacement rates and duration, thus adding poverty and low-income problems affecting families with children.

All the countries, again including Japan, but not the United States, also provide statutory short-term disability or sickness benefits through their social insurance system.

In contrast to the United States, almost all industrial countries provide a public, universal, child benefit—a child or family allowance—either as a direct cash benefit or a refundable tax credit, based on the presence and number of children in a family. Typically, such allowances are equal to about 5 percent to 10 percent of average gross wages for each child. (Kamerman & Kahn, 1988, pp. 363–364)

Family Structure

The need for family supports, including child care, clearly depends on the structure of the family and the circumstances under which it lives. In 1990, the U.S. Bureau of the Census published its first international comparison of the status of families and children (Hobbs & Lippman, 1990). Among the principal findings highlighted in the report are several that emphasize even further the need for quality child care programs.

The proportion of U.S. children living in single-parent families grew 2.5 times between 1960 and 1986. Nearly 1 in 4 now lives with only one parent.

More children, by far, both in number and percent, live in single-parent families in the United States than in other countries compared. The percentage has also increased substantially since 1960 in every country studied, but the gap between the United States and other developed countries has widened. (p. 7)

Unfortunately, the report cited specific percentages for only five countries. A more extended comparison, however, revealed that divorce rates are highest in the English-speaking world (Figure 19.1).

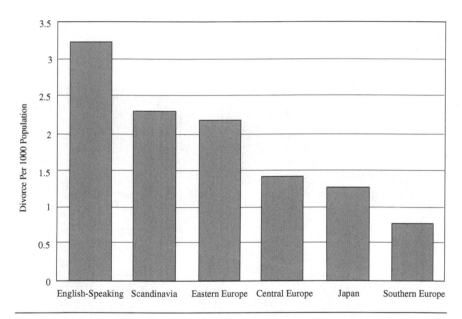

Figure 19.1   Six worlds of divorce. (Source: Demographic Yearbook New York, United Nations, 1991.)

It is instructive to examine the changes in divorce rates in English-speaking societies on which the graph in Figure 19.1 is based. The results reveal a marked increase in divorce rates beginning in the second half of the 1960s, with the United States by far showing the steepest rise. The trend reached maximum at the end of the 1970s and has since shown a slight downward trend.

There is another characteristic of families and children from English-speaking countries that distinguishes them from their counterparts, at least in Western Europe: only the Eastern bloc has a higher rate of teenage pregnancies and births. When comparing the levels in the five English-speaking

Child Care in the Anglo-Saxon Mode

nations (the United States, New Zealand, England, Australia, and Canada), the four largest countries in Western Europe (Italy, Sweden, France, and West Germany), and Japan, a familiar pattern is revealed. The highest levels are seen in the English-speaking countries, the second highest in the Western European, and the lowest in Japan (United Nations, 1988, 1989, 1990).

Economic Resources

Finally, the United States and other English-speaking countries take the lead among developed nations in one other respect even more consequential for the well-being of both families and children. Once again the finding is highlighted in the recently published international comparison by the U.S. Bureau of the Census of the status of children and families in developing societies: *"The U.S. has more poverty than other industrialized societies"* (Hobbs & Lippman, 1990). The findings are based on an analysis carried out by Smeeding, Torrey, and Rein (1988). The results are summarized graphically in Figure 19.2. Once again, the data are consistent with the general trend, among economically developed nations, for children and families in English-speaking countries to experience greater environmental stress, with the pattern being most pronounced in the United States.

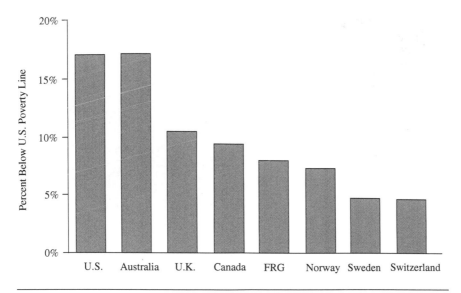

Figure 19.2   Poverty among children in eight developed societies. (Source: Adapted from Smeeding, Torrey, & Rein, 1988, p. 96.)

The situation of U.S. children in poverty has an additional distinctive feature, shown in Figure 19.3. Over the last three decades, children and the elderly living in poverty have reversed positions. During this period, the proportion of adults over 65 in poverty has fallen dramatically from almost 25% to less than 12%. By contrast, the proportion of the children in poverty rose markedly from the early 1970s to the early 1980s, with a slight recovery, followed by a high plateau in the late 1980s. By 1992 almost a quarter of all children under six lived in families below the poverty line. Over 60% of these families were female-headed households with no husband present, and 40% of that group in turn were in the labor force, so the product of these two percentages, equaling 25%, provides a conservative estimate of the need for day care among poor children of single-parent mothers—a total of 1.3 million, compared to only 0.2 million in the middle 1970s, which is almost a sevenfold increase.

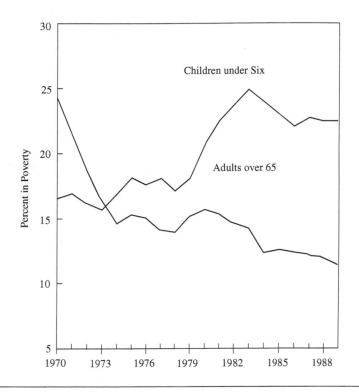

Figure 19.3   Young and old in poverty (1979-1989). Children under 6 and adults 65 and over.

Possible Sources of the
Anglo-Saxon Family Syndrome

Families with young children in English-speaking countries live under conditions of greater environmental stress than their counterparts in other developed societies. What accounts for the pattern of greater vulnerability for the nations in this common language group? Insofar as I can determine from a search of the literature, the communality has not previously been recognized explicitly. What has not escaped attention, however, is the comparatively low priority accorded to children and families in the United States as compared with other developed countries.

Why "not for children?" A common answer given in the United States is: "Children don't vote." But they do not vote in any other country either. A key to the riddle is found in the account of that remarkable early French observer of the American scene, Alexis de Tocqueville (1961). After visiting the United States in the 1830s, he identified the emphasis on individualism as the hallmark of U.S. society. As many scholars have noted since that time, this orientation continues to pervade U.S. life and social institutions.

Why should emphasis in the United States on individualism allow for policies and programs in support of the elderly but not of the young? Kamerman and Kahn (1988) suggest an answer:

> American society has found symbols and values different from social solidarity and family policy around which to construct its unity. . . . This country has chosen individualism as a central value. It has sustained its complex, multicultural and multireligious diversity, and avoided value confrontations by separating church from state and keeping national government out of the family, unless it can define a particular family as dangerous or endangered. (p. 375)

Over the years, in published articles, public statements, and congressional testimony, I have expressed similar views, ending with a somewhat pessimistic prophecy: "Things have to get worse before they get better" (Bronfenbrenner, 1973, p. 137). That is also what has been coming true in 1992. Indeed there are grounds for believing that families and children are becoming an endangered species. There are indications that the growing disarray in the lives of many U.S. families is affecting the development of both competence and character in their children (Bronfenbrenner, 1986).

What will it take to turn this trend around? For that to happen, it will require the development and implementation of policies based on a broader set of considerations than those that have guided our actions thus far. At the same time, if the policies are to be effective, they must rest on values that are consistent with who we are and what we wish to be as a nation.

Future Contexts for Child Care

What might such values be in the United States? Once again, Tocqueville (1961) provides us with a clue. In his perceptive account, *individualism* was but the first of two orientations distinguishing the then newly established U.S. social order. The second was a propensity—as he perceived it, almost a passion—for *volunteerism*, especially in the form of grassroots initiative and cooperation. This orientation has special significance for U.S. child care policy, and it was explicitly drawn upon in the design of Head Start. Parents and relatives, as well as members of the local community, were encouraged to take an active role in the direction and implementation of the program and did so on a fairly large scale (Zigler & Valentine, 1979). In my judgment, this is one of the principal reasons not only for the demonstrated effectiveness of this program but also for its initial and continuing widespread acceptance across diverse social and political strata of U.S. society. The program represents an implementation of what I have proposed as a general guiding principle for the design of child and family policies and programs in the United States: "The need is to create formal systems of challenge and support that generate and strengthen informal systems of challenge and support, that in turn reduce the need for the formal systems" (Bronfenbrenner & Weiss, 1983, p. 405).

Finally, since then, a third salient U.S. value has come to play an increasingly prominent role across many segments of the United States: this is the emphasis on *economic success* and the rewards that it brings in power and material possessions. Paradoxically, it is this growing orientation that has generated new concern for the state of the nation's families. Specifically, an emerging interest in child and family policy springs from the growing recognition and apprehension on the part of the nation's business leaders with respect to two rapidly escalating economic problems. The first relates to the quality and dependability of the available workforce in an age of increasing economic competition, both domestically and internationally. The second is the increasing and enormous cost of providing for, or—alternatively and more frequently, neglecting—the growing segments in the national population of *so-called* "uneducables" and "unemployables." Witness the following excerpts from a recent, three-column article in the *New York Times* (Pear, 1990):

> The United States Chamber of Commerce does not normally lobby for poor children. Nor does the National Association of Manufacturers usually advocate expansion of government programs. But these two business groups joined doctors, hospitals, health insurers and advocates for children in a successful campaign to persuade Congress to expand Medicaid to cover all poor children through the age of 18.
>
> An Administration official said, with a mixture of admiration and dismay, that the coalition was "an unbeatable political combination."
>
> Karen B. Brigham, manager of health care policy for the Chamber of Commerce, said: "Poor children are not a natural constituency of ours. But it is important to the business community to have a healthy, productive work force. . . . Early preventive care for children will reduce the incidence of chronic disabling conditions among workers in later years." (p. 24)

To be sure, statements by other coalition members reveal that motivations are mixed. Thus, a lobbyist for the National Association of Manufacturers, representing 13,500 companies, commented that "hospitals have been shifting costs from people who cannot pay their bills to the people who do pay. Most of those paying patients have private health insurance provided by employers, who thus shoulder an extra burden." And the president of an association representing commercial insurance companies acknowledged that "his group instigated the coalition partly out of concern that the persistence of large numbers of uninsured people might lead to a clamor for national health insurance."

These are not isolated cases. On the very next day, President George Bush signed the compromise bill on the federal deficit, which included massive cuts for many government programs but, because of pressure from similar coalitions, had incorporated major provisions of the Act for Better Child Care.

Conclusions

In my commentary I have sought to show that, like human development itself, the course of child care policy and practice is shaped in substantial degree by its broader context in time and place. The data presented in this chapter indicate that, for the past few decades, these contexts have been deteriorating in the English-speaking countries. There are signs, however, that in the United States, where children are at greatest risk—at long last "the times, they are a-changing."

References

Bronfenbrenner, U. (1973, September 25). Testimony before the U.S. Senate's Committee on Labor and Public Welfare. First session on examination of the influence that government policies have on American families (128–173). Washington, DC: Government Printing Office.

Bronfenbrenner, U. (1986, Fall). A generation in jeopardy: America's hidden family policy. Testimony presented at a hearing of the Senate Committee on Rules and Administration, July 23, 1986. *Newsletter of the Division of Developmental Psychology of the American Psychological Association*, pp. 47 54.

Bronfenbrenner, U., & Weiss, H. (1983). Beyond policies without people: An ecological perspective on child and family policy. In E. F. Zigler, S. L. Kagan, & L. Klugman (Eds.), *Children, families, and government* (pp. 393–414) New York: Cambridge University Press.

Cooke, K. (1986). *Report of the Task Force on Child Care*. Ottawa, Ministry for the Status of Women.

Hofferth, S., & Lippman, L. (1990). *Children's well being: An international comparison*. Washington, DC: U.S. Bureau of the Census.

Kamerman, S. B., & Kahn, A. J. (1988). Social policy and children in the United States and Europe. In J. L. Palmer, T. Smeeding, & B. B. Torrey (Eds.), *The vulnerable* (pp. 351–380). Washington, DC: Urban Institute Press.

Pehl, P. (1990, November 4). Deficit or no deficit, unlikely allies bring about expansion in Medicaid. *New York Times*, p. 24.

Smeeding, T. Torrey, B. B., & Rein, M. (1988). Patterns of income and poverty: economic status of children and the elderly in eight countries. In J. L. Palmer, T. Smeeding, & B. B. Torrey (Eds.), *The vulnerable* (pp. 89–119) Washington, DC: Urban Institute Press.

Torqueville, A. de (1961). *Democracy In America*. New York. Schocken.

Townson, M. (1985). *Paid parental leaves. An international comparison*. Ottawa Force or Child Care.

United Nations. (1980 91), *Demographic yearbook*. New York: United Nations.

Zigler, E., & Valentine, J. (Eds.). (1979). *Project Head Start: A legacy of the War on Poverty*. New York: Free Press.

Afterword

Stephen F. Hamilton and Stephen J. Ceci

The articles in this volume portray the unfolding over seven decades of a conception of human development, guidance on research designs to enable scholars to understand how it occurs, and implications for policy makers and practitioners of what we know for what we should do to make human beings human. The conception is humanistic and optimistic. It emphasizes the human capacity to grow and adapt to many different circumstances and to continue developing, and the person's ability to shape her or his own development. But it is not a naïve conception. How could it be when its author is steeped in Russian literature and was a refugee as a child from that country's tortured revolution? The threats Bronfenbrenner identifies to the realization of human developmental potential spring from society's neglect, its failure to attend to the ways in which economic and social change undermine families and thereby constrain development. His calls for attention to deteriorating conditions are always coupled with recommendations for ways to improve those conditions.

Bronfenbrenner's guidance about research has had such a powerful impact that the observation he made in the late 1970s is now, thankfully, no longer true. He wrote, "Much of developmental psychology, as it now exists, is *the science of the strange behavior of children in strange situations with strange adults for the briefest possible periods of time*" (Bronfenbrenner, 1979, pp. 18–19, emphasis in original). Growing use of the term *developmental science* recognizes that human development is no longer the provenance only of developmental psychology but also of several other disciplines. Researchers' embrace of ordinary behavior in natural settings as it continues and changes over time is testimony to the profound influence he has had on the study of human development. His advice to study the process not only in laboratories but also in the natural settings where people live their lives has been taken by enough gifted researchers that we now know far more than we did 30 years ago about development in families, day care programs, schools, youth organizations, and many other contexts. Indeed, the formulation of the bioecological model was motivated by his observation that researchers became so captivated with studying contexts that they were neglecting development.

The evolution of the ecology of human development perspective into the bioecological model recognizes the centrality of the person in the process of developing within a variety of interacting contexts over time. This theoretical formulation enabled Bronfenbrenner to reinterpret research that had been done in the past, to pose hypotheses for exploration in new research, and to reveal the forces that promote or undermine human development. When we understand, we can act. If we know how to make human beings human, we are obligated to do our best to do so. Bronfenbrenner's recommendations about that have been numerous and varied over the years. They were instrumental in the design of Head Start. He has frequently testified before congressional committees and spoken with leaders of government and industry. His approach is now embodied in a wide range of policies and practices.

Several themes persist across the years and the specific issues. Most central is that children must be nurtured and educated to be able to maintain and strengthen their society. In *Two Worlds of Childhood* (see Article 15 of this book), he proposes that societies be judged according to "the concern of one generation for the next." Closely linked to this theme is the family's critical function as "the best way to make human beings human."

This insight about the central role of the family being true, the challenge for policy makers and practitioners is to support and complement the family, especially families that are less capable of carrying out this function well, whether because they have too little income or too little time. His observation that every adult who is responsible for the care of a child needs another adult to rely on for encouragement and assistance typifies his deceptively simple wisdom.

In sum, the compelling and exciting stream of ideas presented in this volume constitutes certain evidence of the enormous intellectual and sound societal contributions of Urie Bronfenbrenner's bioecological theory. Urie Bronfenbrenner is the principal architect of the ecology of human development and of the bioecological theory of human development. He may have learned from Lewin and others, but he took their ideas in new directions far beyond previous scholars' conceptions. His vision was of the importance of the ecology of human development perspective was farsighted because of his own stature. This volume testifies to the range and depth, and the science and the humanity, of its author.

Author Index

Subject Index

Fisher, R. A., 72
Fisichelle, V. R., 31
Franz, J. G., 23
Freeman, F. S., 42

Gage, N. L., 243
Galilean research paradigm, 109
Galton, F., 74
Garabino, J., 32
Genetic factor, role in psychological
    development, 32–33
Gewirtz, H. B., 29–30, 35
Gewirtz, J. L., 29–30, 35
G.I. Bill, 196
Goodenough, F., 29
Gottlieb, G., xii
Great Depression study, 84–85, 89,
    120, 147–148, 256–257

Handbook of Child Psychology, xi, xxii,
    42, 60–61, 132, 287
Head Start, 196, 208, 280, 284
Henri, V., 20
Heredity/environment, contribution
    to development
    bioecological model, 177–178
        proposition concerning proximal
            process, 178–181
        proximal *vs.* physiopsychological
            process, 177
    how/not how much question,
        174–175
    illustrative research
        design/hypothesis, of
        proximal processes
        development potential in
            advantaged/stable *vs.*
            impoverished/disorganized
            environment, 181
        experimental levels effect on
            actualized genetic potential,
            182–183
        genetic potential buffering for
            dysfunction in
            disadvantaged/disorganized
            environment, 181–182
        h2 level according to process
            level, 180–181

h2 value associated extreme
    process level, 181
low/normal birth weight child
    development by SES,
    179 (fig)–180
overview of, 178–180
overview of, 175–177
Heritability, definition of, 176
Heritability coefficient (h2), 238–241
    See also Heredity/environment,
        contribution to development
Hetherington, E., 249–251, 266
High-/low-education family study,
    153–155, 156–157
Holzinger, J., 238
Honzik, M. P., 237, 238
Human development
    definition of, 187
    definition of ecology of, 95, 261
    See also Psychological study, of
        human development
Human development research
    future perspective for
    child fantasy world, 56–57
    conception of ecological
        environment in, 50–51
    definition of development in, 50
    difference in settings among
        cultures, 51
    ecological orientation of, 51–53
    theory of environmental
        interconnections, 55
    See also Bioecological theory;
        Ecological systems theory

Individualism, in United States, 279–280
Infant, evolution of research on, 61–62
Infant mortality, 211
Inflation effect on family study, 270
Integrative research, *vs.* piecemeal,
    variable-oriented research, 18–20
Intelligence
    measuring, 20
    See also Intelligence, cause of
        invariance in
Intelligence, cause of invariance
    in fraternal twins reared apart
        study, 241

About the Author

Urie Bronfenbrenner is the Jacob Gould Schurman Professor Emeritus of Human Development and Psychology at Cornell University. His career-long devotion to theory and research in the domains of children and families has earned him international recognition. He is widely regarded as one of the leading scholars in developmental psychology, child rearing, and the interdisciplinary domain of his own creation—the ecology of human development. His widely published contributions have won him honors and distinguished awards both at home and abroad. He holds six honorary degrees, including three from European universities: the University of Gothenburg, Sweden; the University of Münster, Germany; and the Technische Universität of Berlin. The 1996 award from the American Psychological Association, henceforth to be given annually in his name, is for the "Lifetime Contribution to Developmental Psychology in the service of Science and Society." In 1994, in recognition of Urie Bronfenbrenner's scholarship and leadership in linking basic research to social policy, the Bronfenbrenner Life Course Center was established at Cornell University.

About the Foreword and Afterword Authors

Richard M. Lerner is the Bergstrom Chair in Applied Developmental Science and the Director of the Institute for Applied Research in Youth Development in the Eliot-Pearson Department of Child Development at Tufts University. A developmental psychologist, Lerner received a Ph.D. from the City University of New York. Lerner is author or editor of 55 books and more than 400 scholarly articles and chapters. He edited Volume 1, Theoretical Models of Human Development, for the fifth edition of the *Handbook of Child Psychology*, which contained one of Professor Bronbenbrenner's major presentations of his bioecological model. He is editing the sixth edition of the *Handbook* as well, which again will have a chapter by Professor Bronfenbrenner about his theory.

Stephen J. Ceci, Ph.D., holds a lifetime endowed chair in developmental psychology at Cornell University. He is the author of approximately 300 articles, books, and chapters. He has given invited addresses at major universities around the world and has been named keynote speaker at numerous international scientific psychology meetings. Ceci's honors and scientific awards include a Senior Fulbright-Hayes fellowship, a National Institute of Health Research Career Scientist Award, the American Academy of Forensic Psychology's highest honor, the Lifetime Distinguished Contribution Award, the American Psychological Association's 2002 Lifetime Distinguished Contribution Award for Science and Society, and the Society for Research in Child Development's 2003 Award for Distinguished Contributions to Public Policy for Children. Ceci has received the IBM Supercomputing Prize, three Senior Mensa Foundation Research Prizes, and the Arthur Rickter Award. He currently serves on seven editorial boards; the Advisory Board of the National Science Foundation's Social, Behavioral, and Economic Science Directorate; the

National Academy of Science's Board on Cognitive, Sensory, and Behavioral Sciences; and the Canadian Institute for Advanced Research's Human Development Program. Ceci is the founder and co-editor of the American Psychological Society journal *Psychological Science in the Public Interest*, which is partnered with *Scientific American*. He currently serves on the White House Task Force on Federal Research Priorities for Children. He is a fellow of seven divisions of the American Psychological Association, the American Psychological Society, and a fellow of the American Association for the Advancement of Science (AAAS). In 2003 Ceci was the recipient of the American Psychological Association's highest award, its Distinguished Scientific Contribution for the Application of Psychology.

Stephen F. Hamilton is Professor of Human Development at Cornell University, Co-Director of the Family Life Development Center, and Associate Provost for Outreach. His research in adolescent development and education investigates the interaction of school, community, and work during the transition to adulthood. As a Fulbright Senior Research Fellow, he spent a year studying Germany's apprenticeship system. The book that resulted, *Apprenticeship for Adulthood: Preparing Youth for the Future*, helped guide the School-to-Work Opportunities Act of 1994, as did the youth apprenticeship demonstration project that he and Mary Agnes Hamilton directed (*Learning Well at Work: Choices for Quality*). Together they have since studied how adults mentor youth at work and co-authored a chapter on "Contexts for Mentoring" in the forthcoming *Handbook of Adolescent Psychology*. Another co-authored chapter, "School, Work, and Emerging Adulthood," will appear in a book on emerging adulthood. They are co-editors of *The Handbook of Youth Development: Coming of Age in American Communities*.